THE HUMAN WILL IN JUDAISM
The Mishnah's Philosophy of Intention

Program in Judaic Studies
Brown University
BROWN JUDAIC STUDIES
Edited by
Jacob Neusner,
Wendell S. Dietrich, Ernest S. Frerichs,
Calvin Goldscheider, Alan Zuckerman

Project Editors (Project)

David Blumenthal, Emory University (Approaches to Medieval Judaism)
William Brinner (Studies in Judaism and Islam)
Ernest S. Frerichs, Brown University (Dissertations and Monographs)
Lenn Evan Goodman, University of Hawaii (Studies in Medieval Judaism) (Studies in
Judaism and Islam)
William Scott Green, University of Rochester (Approaches to Ancient Judaism)
Ivan Marcus, Jewish Theological Seminary of America
(Texts and Studies in Medieval Judaism)
Marc L. Raphael, Ohio State University (Approaches to Judaism in Modern Times)
Norbert Samuelson, Temple University (Jewish Philosophy)
Jonathan Z. Smith, University of Chicago (Studia Philonica)

Number 103
THE HUMAN WILL IN JUDAISM:
The Mishnah's Philosophy of Intention
by
Howard Eilberg-Schwartz

THE HUMAN WILL IN JUDAISM
The Mishnah's Philosophy of Intention

by
Howard Eilberg–Schwartz

Scholars Press
Atlanta, Georgia

THE HUMAN WILL IN JUDAISM
The Mishnah's Philosophy of Intention

© 1986
Brown University

BM
497.8
.E35
1986

Library of Congress Cataloging in Publication Data

Eilberg-Schwartz, Howard, 1956-
    The human will in Judaism.

    (Brown Judaic studies ; no. 103)
    Bibliography: p.
    Includes index.
    1. Mishnah--Theology. 2. Intention--Religious
aspects--Judaism. I. Title. II. Series.
BM497.8.E35   1986   296.3'2   85-24968
ISBN 0-89130-938-1

Printed in the United States of America
on acid-free paper

For my parents,

Leon and Joan Schwartz

Table of Contents

Part Two
The Function of Plans in the Mishnaic System

Preface

In our everyday lives, we are constantly taking account of one another's intentions. When a person does something that offends or hurts us, we generally take account of that person's intention. Typically, we hold a person responsible for what he or she did intentionally, while we usually forgive a person for accidental occurrences. The idea of intention, therefore, is intimately linked to our judgments about what does and does not constitute responsible behavior.

The concept of intention is also critical to Judaism, especially as it took shape in late antiquity (100-600 C.E.). Intention plays a prominent role in the law and theology of Judaism, as reflected in the central documents of the rabbinic canon, namely, the Mishnah, the Tosefta, the Talmud of the Land of Israel, and the Talmud of Babylonia. Understanding how intention functions in these documents is critical to grasping the nature of Judaism represented in these sources. Just as our conception of intention is connected to more general notions of responsibility, so the idea of intention in these documents is integrally related to the sages' conception of human responsibility as well as their understanding of the divine-human relationship.

Specifically, this study examines the role of intention in the Mishnah, a handbook of rules written ca. 200 C. E., by a group of sages living in the Land of Israel. This document presents a complete system of thought on what it means to live a life in accordance with the divine will. We turn to the Mishnah in particular because it is the founding document of the rabbinic canon, namely, the books which together testify to Rabbinic Judaism. The Mishnah serves as the point of departure for several other rabbinic works, including the Tosefta, the Sifra, the Talmud of the Land of Israel, and the Talmud of Babylonia. In providing the foundation for the rabbinic canon, the Mishnah gave shape, in important respects, to the Judaism which developed during the period in question.

The fundamental premise of this system of Judaism is that intention constitutes the human counterpart to the divine will. In the view of these sages, the capacity to formulate intentions is what makes human beings like God. The sages therefore ascribe to human intention powers which in their judgment are analogous to God's. This study seeks to show, through a careful examination of the Mishnah's rules, how this basic idea informs the mishnaic system as a whole.

Acknowledgments

It is with deep appreciation that I thank my teachers and colleagues who supported me during my years of graduate education in general and the writing of this book in particular. First and foremost, I wish to thank Professor Jacob Neusner for his encouragement and help during my graduate work. The merits of this book are to a great extent the product of the ongoing conversation we have had about the project at hand. He devoted a great deal of time and energy to reading and commenting upon every line of this work and his insights are reflected throughout. In addition, his conception of education played a profound role in shaping my own development as a teacher and scholar. I thank him for the innumerable ways he contributed to my education and career.

Special thanks also go to Professor Wendell Dietrich, whose seminars on 19th century Jewish and Christian religious thought played a substantial role in shaping my own conception of this book and of religious studies in general.

Many friends and colleagues also read and commented upon this work during various stages of its preparation. Professor Paul Lauritzen (John Carroll University) was kind enough to discuss with me a variety of issues in analytic philosophy which were relevant to the problem of intention. Professors Roger Brooks (University of Notre Dame), Martin Jaffee (University of Virginia), Louis Newman (Carleton College), and Paul Flesher all made important contributions to the formulation and conception of this work. I thank each of them for the support and encouragement they gave me during the process of bringing this project to fruition. Without their concern and friendship, this project would not have been possible. I also wish to thank Professor Judith Romney Wegner (Williams College) who devoted a great deal of her time to improving the style of this book. My graduate work was made possible by the financial support of Brown University, including a University Fellowship (1982), and two Teaching Fellowships (1983-84).

This book has undergone a number of substantial revisions since its acceptance as a Ph. D. dissertation. I wish to thank the following people who urged me to rethink aspects of the original work and thus helped me move beyond my initial formulation of the problem and its solution. In particular, I wish to thank Professors Marvin Fox (Brandeis University), William Scott Green (The University of Rochester), Luke Johnson (Indiana University), Martin Jaffee (University of Virginia), and Louis Newman (Carleton College). Each of these people read the work with great care and made numerous important suggestions as to how it might be improved, both conceptually and stylistically.

Many of their comments have been incorporated in the final version of this book. In addition, Chapter Three reflects the insights of my colleagues in Religious Studies at Indiana University, who devoted a colloquim to discussing this aspect of my work.

I wish to acknowledge a debt to my teachers from the Jewish Theological Seminary of America and Duke University who contributed in important ways to my education. My close friend, Rabbi Alan Londy, also played a formative role, by pointing me in the right direction many years ago. Special thanks also go to a number of friends who were there when it counted: Rob and Laura Cable, Lisa deFilippis, Rabbi Alan Flam, Judy Semenoff, and Rosanne Zeidenweber. I also wish to thank Joshua Bell at Verbatim Word Processing for help in preparing this book for publication. The publication of this book was made possible by the Max Richter Foundation.

This entire project would have been inconceivable without the help of my wife, Amy Eilberg. Her nurturance and support sustained me through the ups and downs of graduate education. Without her perpetual concern and encouragement, this book would not have come to fruition. Many of her insights are reflected in the pages of this work, for she has read and listened to it in all of the various stages of its preparation. I thank her for the many sacrifices she made to make my success possible, and for overlooking the numerous ways my work has interfered in our joint lives together. She has been at one and the same time a soul mate, a friend, and a colleague.

Finally, I wish to thank my parents Leon and Joan Schwartz, to whom this book is dedicated. They have supported me in every conceivable way during the many years of my education. It is they who gave me the wisdom to value my mind, the directedness to pursue my ambitions, and the sensitivity to value understanding. They have gone beyond the call of duty in providing financial support for the many years of my education. I thank them from the bottom of my heart for their boundless generosity and concern.

Howard Eilberg-Schwartz

September 22, 1985
Departments of Religious Studies, Near Eastern Languages and Cultures
Indiana University
Bloomington, Indiana

Introduction

Defining the Problem

This study examines how the idea of intention functions in the system of the Mishnah. By intention, I refer to two separate but closely related concepts.[1] First, this term designates the capacity of human beings to formulate plans. That is to say, we can speak about a person formulating an intention to act in a particular way at some future time. For example, we say that a person intends to take a trip. When the term intention bears this meaning, it denotes the answer a person would give to the question, "What do you plan to do?" Second, the term intention also designates the purpose with which a person acts. We say, for example, that a person performs a given action with a specific intention. In this case, the word intention refers to the answer a person would give to the question, "Why did you do that?"[2] Obviously, the two meanings of intention are closely related to one another. Both rest on the more basic assumption that people are purposive beings who formulate goals and execute actions which are designed to achieve those goals.

The concept of intention plays a critical role in the mishnaic system.[3] The importance of intention is evident from the fact that this concept appears with great frequency in all six divisions of mishnaic law, namely, laws of agriculture, laws of festivals, laws of women, civil law, laws of holy things, and laws of purity. The even distribution of the concept throughout the Mishnah's law indicates that intention is an idea which draws the interest of the Mishnah's framers regardless of the general topic they are discussing. Intention, therefore, is a concept which is central to the Mishnah's message.

As this study seeks to show, intention is important because it is intimately connected to the Mishnah's theological concerns, including the concept of God and the nature of the divine-human relationship. In exploring the role of intention in the Mishnah, therefore, we expose the fundamental theological conceptions of its framers. In addition, we shall see that the concept of intention plays a prominent role in the Mishnah's reformulation of the biblical heritage. On the one hand, the authors of the Mishnah are preoccupied with the same range of issues that intrigued the writers of the priestly strand of Scripture (P), such as issues of purity, sacrifices, and classification. On the other hand, the Mishnah substantially revises the priestly world view. It turns out that the concept of intention serves as the point of departure for the Mishnah's critique of the priestly conception of reality. For example, the Mishnah reworks the priestly system of purity by making human intention an important factor in determining whether something can or cannot absorb impurity. This idea is foreign to the biblical authors and constitutes a mishnaic innovation.

This study, then, takes as its point of departure the statements which the Mishnah makes about intention. But the larger goal is to use intention as a key for understanding the character of the mishnaic system and its relationship to prior forms of Judaism. By determining where intention is an important conception in the Mishnah, and by discovering why this concept surfaces in certain laws within the Mishnah and not in others, we grasp the philosophical and theological premises which underlie the system as a whole. At the same time, the study of intention will indicate how the Mishnah reworks and thereby critiques conceptions embedded in the priestly strand of Scripture. Describing and interpreting the Mishnah's reformation of Scripture constitutes one of the central tasks of this study.

Three specific questions provide the focus of our inquiry. First, we wish to know how intention functions. In other words, what role does intention play in those rules in which the concept of intention makes its appearance? Second, we want to determine when and why the Mishnah appeals to intention. As we shall see, in some rules the Mishnah takes account of a person's intention, whereas in other rules it treats intention as irrelevant. We wish to know, therefore, the factors that determine when the Mishnah will consider intention an important topic. Third, we need to examine the larger theological and philosophical assumptions which serve as the foundation for the Mishnah's theory of intention. Only by understanding how the framers of the Mishnah conceive of the divine-human relationship can we grasp when and why they consider intention important. In what follows, we take up each of these questions in more detail.

The Function of Intention in the Mishnah

Intention plays two separate roles in the Mishnah, one quite familiar to us, and the other completely alien to our way of thinking. First, intention serves a function in the Mishnah which corresponds to the role that it plays in our everyday lives. We often appeal to a person's intention when deciding whether to hold that person responsible for what occurred. Generally, we consider a person responsible for anything he or she does intentionally. By contrast, we typically do not blame a person for what happens inadvertently.

The Mishnah also takes account of a person's intention in evaluating human actions. To determine whether a given act violates divine law, the Mishnah appeals to the intention with which that person acted. Suppose, for example, that a merchant mixes produce of two different qualities with the intention of deceiving his customers as to the true value of the merchandise. In this case, the action constitutes a transgression because the merchant intends to cheat another person. By contrast, if he combines produce of different grades simply because he needs to accumulate enough for a bulk sale, the act does not fall into the category of a violation because he had no intention of committing fraud (M. B.M. 4:12).

Just as the Mishnah's framers appeal to intention to determine whether a given act falls under the rubric of a transgression, they also appeal to an actor's intention to determine whether the act in question discharges a religious duty. For example, mishnaic law requires Israelites to recite a prayer called the *Shema*. Now if an Israelite recites the words of this prayer for the express purpose of praying, he has discharged his obligation. But if he recites the words of the prayer for some other purpose, for example, in order to learn the prayer by heart, he does not receive credit for having fulfilled his duty. Since he did not intend to pray to God, the recitation of the prayer does not discharge his obligation (M. Ber. 2:1). So in the Mishnah, as in our daily lives, intention serves as a criterion for evaluating human action.

Intention plays a second role in the Mishnah, which finds no precise equivalent in our frame of reference. According to the Mishnah, the mere formulation of an intention has the effect of classifying objects. That is, when an Israelite forms the intention to use an object for a specific purpose, that object falls into one of the categories which the framers of the Mishnah consider important. To understand this rather strange idea, it is essential to know several facts which the sages take for granted.

The Mishnah devotes a great deal of attention to placing objects into categories. We shall see, for example, that distinguishing between "useful" and "useless" things and between "food" and "waste" is a central preoccupation of the Mishnah's framers. Adopting the perspective of Leviticus, the sages of the Mishnah believe that God has divided the various objects in the world into different categories and specified a set of laws to govern each category of object. For example, in the mishnaic system, all useful objects can contract impurity and therefore must be protected from contamination, while useless objects cannot become contaminated under any conditions. Consequently, once an object falls into a given classification it becomes subject to a given class of rules. In the sages' judgment, moreover, the failure to observe those rules governing a given category of object results in an infraction of divine law. In the Mishnah, therefore, an Israelite can carry out the divine will only by determining the classification of each household object and by observing the rules which govern that category of thing.

How are issues of classification related to intention? In the Mishnah, intention has a kind of "magical" power which determines the classification of various objects. When a person formulates an intention to use an object in a particular way, that object falls into the category designated by his intention. For example, if he intends to eat a given substance, that substance immediately falls under the rubric of food, and thereby becomes subject to the the mishnaic rules governing food. But if instead of planning to eat a substance, he intends to discard it, that substance is then classified as waste, and hence becomes subject to a different set of laws. Intention therefore has the power to alter the basic properties of an object by changing the category into which that object falls. One of the central problems of this study is to explain why intention plays this rather unusual role of classifying objects.

On the surface, it would seem that the two roles of intention just described are unrelated to one another. In one case, intention serves as a criterion for evaluating actions, while in the other, intention functions to classify objects. However, as this study will show, the two roles of intention in the Mishnah are intimately connected to each other. Both rest on similar theological notions about the character of God and the nature of the divine-human relationship.

When and Why Intention Matters in the Mishnah

In investigating the role of intention in the Mishnah, we need to determine when intention matters in the Mishnah and why it is important in those contexts and not in others. The first task, therefore, is purely descriptive. We begin by noting that the concept of intention appears in certain kinds of cases rather than others. This leads to the central interpretive problem, namely, isolating the factors that determine why intention appears in one context but not in another. In carrying out this exercise, we need to work at two different levels of generalization. At the most general level, we wish to know when and why intention figures more prominently in some areas of mishnaic law than in others. For example, the category of intention is generally irrelevant in tort cases, namely, situations where an individual has caused harm to a person or property. When determining liability for damages or injury, the sages ignore the actor's intention. The offender must pay compensation to the victim, even if the injury or damage occurred by accident. By contrast, intention plays a central role in cases involving the cult or religious law. In this context, the intention with which a person performs an act determines the severity of the penalty. For example, one who intentionally writes during the day of rest incurs the divine penalty of a premature death.[4] But one who unintentionally writes during the Sabbath day incurs only the minor penalty of a sin-offering (M. Shab. 12:5).[5] Here, in a case involving religious law, the actor's intention determines the severity of the transgression. The critical problem, therefore, is to discover why intention plays a prominent role in cultic and religious law, and no role at all in torts.

We need to carry out the same exercise at a less general level as well. We want to determine why *within* a given area of law intention plays a role in some cases but not in others. The following two rules illustrate this problem. Both rules take up the case of an Israelite who combines grain of different qualities. Here, the problem is to determine whether the act of combining the produce constitutes a transgression of the law. If the individual's purpose in mixing the grain is to deceive the customers as to the true value of the produce, the act constitutes a violation. If his goal is merely to accumulate enough for a bulk sale, the act does not fall under the rubric of a violation. For the present purposes, the important point is to note that the sages appeal to the actor's intention in only one of these two cases:

I.   A.   A merchant [who sells produce in bulk amount] may buy [grain] from five [different] threshing floors and put [it] into a single storehouse [even though the grain is of different qualities].

     B.   [And he may buy wine] from five [different] wine presses and put [the wine] into a single vat [even though the various types of wine are of different qualities].

     C.   [He may do so] provided that he does not *intend* to mix [the produce for fraudulent purposes. That is to say, if he mixes the grain so as to accumulate enough for a bulk sale, his action does not constitute a transgression. But if his purpose in combining the produce is to deceive his customers as to the true value of the merchandise, his act constitutes a violation.]

                                                        M. B.M. 4:12

II. A.   [By contrast, a householder who sells produce] may not mix produce [from one field] with produce [from another field] even if [both types of produce] are recently [picked, and presumably of the same quality].

                                                        M. B.M. 4:11

The two cases at hand are nearly identical. Both discuss whether a person who mixes produce of different qualities is guilty of committing fraud. Yet, only in the case of the merchant does the Mishnah appeal to intention. If the merchant intends to commit fraud, his act transgresses the law (I B). But if he simply intended to accumulate enough produce for a bulk sale, the act of combining the grain or fruit does not constitute a violation (I A-B). However, in the case of a householder, intention is irrelevant. No matter what he intended, the sages consider the householder guilty of having transgressed (II A). These cases illustrate the larger problem we wish to address in this study, namely, determining when and why intention matters in a given case.

Law and Theology in the Mishnah

In seeking to understand the role of intention, we need to explore the underlying theological and philosophical assumptions which inform the mishnaic system. This study, therefore, draws attention to the integral relationship between law and theology in the system of the Mishnah. I will argue that the sages' conception of God and their understanding of the divine-human relationship inform what they say about intention. Consider, for example, the fact that intention matters in cases involving religious law but not in torts. We can understand why intention is important in the one context and not the other only by appealing to the sages' theological conceptions. As I will argue in Chapter One, the sages of the Mishnah believe that the responsibility of human beings to each other differs from their responsibility towards God. Consequently, the sages distinguish tort cases, where the injured party is another human being, from cases involving the transgression of religious law, where the offense is committed against God.

In looking for the connections between the Mishnah's theory of intention, on the one hand, and its theology, on the other, we are attempting to reach beneath the sages' formulation of their rules to the underlying assumptions of their thought. This is true in two different respects. First, the sages themselves do not explicitly link their statements about intention to either their views of God or the divine-human relationship. In searching for the links between mishnaic theology and law, therefore, we look for connections to which the framers themselves did not explicitly call attention.

Second, the sages do not present their theological views in a systematic fashion. To be sure, the Mishnah contains a variety of statements about God and the responsibility of humanity to God. But the sages do not systematize these statements into sustained essays on various aspects of theology, and consequently, their theological presumptions remain largely implicit in their statements. An important part of this study, therefore, is to use the mishnaic statements on intention to uncover the underlying theological assumptions that inform the Mishnah as a whole.

This search for the interplay between law and theology distinguishes the present study of intention from other studies of the same topic.[6] While others have examined the concept of intention in rabbinic literature, they generally have approached the topic strictly as a problem in jurisprudence. In other words, they have treated the Mishnah exclusively as a legal system without paying attention to the theological and philosophical ideas which inform the sages' conception of intention.[7] In this study, by contrast, we treat the Mishnah not only as a legal document, but also as a religious system which takes as its point of departure certain ideas about what it means to live a life in accordance with the divine will. Consequently, this study seeks to explain when and why intention matters in the Mishnah by appealing to the theological conceptions upon which the system of the Mishnah rests.

Intention as a Philosophical Problem

In using the concept of intention as a means of exploring the underlying ideas of the mishnaic system, our study also dovetails with certain developments in contemporary philosophy. During the past thirty years, intention has become an important topic in analytic philosophy, particularly in philosophical psychology.[8] There are a variety of reasons why contemporary philosophers have taken an interest in intention, most of which need not concern us in the present context.[9] Nonetheless, certain conclusions reached by these philosophers are relevant for this study. Some thinkers, beginning with Strawson, claim that intention and other concepts related to human action (e.g. goals, motives, desires) constitute the most basic concepts in which we carry on our thinking.[10] According to this account, the aim of philosophy is to identify, classify, and find the interconnections between the categories and concepts we use in thinking about the world. In so doing, we arrive at an understanding of the basic intellectual equipment which governs our thinking. According to Strawson, we achieve this goal by understanding how the concepts related to human action (i.e., concepts such as intention, motives, desires) work in ordinary language. Some philosophers refer to this type of analysis as "descriptive metaphysics," because by describing how our concepts work in ordinary language, one arrives at the metaphysical assumptions which inform our everyday life.

In one respect, the study at hand constitutes an exercise in descriptive metaphysics. By understanding how intention works in the Mishnah, we seek to expose the fundamental categories which the framers of the Mishnah use in thinking about their world. In another respect, however, this study rejects some of Strawson's assumptions. Strawson and his followers regard intention as a basic category of the human mind, and thus conceive of intention as a category that operates independently of a given cultural or religious tradition.[11] By contrast, we treat intention as an idea which is shaped by other conceptions which people hold. We attempt to show that the way intention operates in the Mishnah depends upon the particular world view and theological assumptions of the group which formulated this system.

Method of Inquiry

To investigate the Mishnah's concept of intention, we trace through the mishnaic system two Hebrew terms which designate the concept of intention, namely, the terms *kavvanah* and *mahshabah*.[12] The term *kavvanah* (and its related verbal forms) generally refers to the intention with which a person performs an action.[13] To provide an example in the sages' own language, "An Israelite may break a jar on the Sabbath day provided that he does not intend (*ykwwn*) to use the bottom half of the jar for a pot (M. Shab. 22:3)." Here, the word *ykwwn* (a verbal form of *kawwanah*) refers to the intention with which the Israelite breaks the jar. By contrast, the word *mahshabah* (and its related verbal forms) refers to the intention an individual formulates before he or she actually begins to act.[14] Thus if a man is planning to use an object, the framers say that "he *hsb* (planned) to put it to use" (M. Oh. 13:1).

The two types of intention designated by the words *kavvanah* and *mahshabah* play different roles in the Mishnah. The Mishnah appeals to a person's *kavvanah* (i.e., the intention that accompanies an action) in order to determine whether one's action constitutes a transgression or fulfillment of divine law. *Mahshabah* (i.e., plan), by contrast, serves to determine the classification of an object in a person's possession. When an Israelite formulates a plan to use an object for a particular purpose, he in effect places that object into a given category.

For two reasons, our study of intention proceeds inductively through an analysis of the Hebrew terms for intention. First, the sages themselves do not present a theory of intention in abstract form. Although the sages frequently invoke the concept of intention, they rarely rise above the details of their rules to formulate abstract propositions about when and why intention matters. Consequently, we must proceed inductively by contrasting those cases in which the sages appeal to intention with similar cases in which intention is irrelevant. By isolating the differences between these two sets of cases, we discover the factors that determine why intention appears in one context and not another.

There is a second equally important reason why we focus on the Hebrew words which designate intention. In general, the way people use words tells us a great deal about the concepts which those words denote. This is because understanding a concept by definition involves knowing when and why that concept can be used in certain contexts and not in others. We can elucidate the Mishnah's concept of intention, therefore, by determining why the Mishnah uses the terms for intention when it does.

In tracing the Hebrew terms for intention through the Mishnah, we by no means exhaust all the cases in which the sages invoke the concept of intention. In many passages the framers take up the problem of intention without specifically using the terms which denote or even suggest that concept. This is true in the following case, for example, in which the sages discuss the Scriptural prohibition against cultivating the land during the Sabbatical year (M. Sheb. 3:6). According to Scripture, every seventh year Israelites must allow their land to lie fallow as a sign that the land belongs to God (Lev. 25:1-7). In the rule at hand, the sages want to know whether clearing stones from a field during the Sabbatical year transgresses the law against preparing the land for cultivation. In mishnaic law, if an Israelite clears the stones of his field for the purpose of cultivating the land, he has committed a transgression. But if he collects stones from the field in order to build something, he has not violated the law, because he did not intend to prepare the land for growing crops. In turning to the rule itself, we note that the word for intention does not appear in the Mishnah's rule but only in the bracketed language which I have supplied to clarify the meaning of this passage:

A. [As regards] a wall consisting of ten stones, [each of which is so large that it can] be carried only by two men--
B. these [stones] may be removed [from the field during the Sabbatical year. The fact that they remove large stones indicates that their intention is to use the stones for the purpose of construction. Consequently, this act does not violate the law against cultivating the field during the Sabbatical year.]
C. [The preceding rule applies only if] the height of the wall is ten handbreadths [or more].
D. Less than this, [that is, if the wall is less than ten handbreaths high],
E. he may chisel [stones from the wall]

F.   but he may level [the wall] only until it is one handbreadth from ground
     level, [but not raze it. This indicates that he does not intend to use the
     land under the wall for cultivation, for if he did, he would remove the
     entire wall.]

M. Sheb. 3:6[15]

We see here that the sages sometimes invoke the concept of intention even
when they do not use the words that denote that idea. Consequently, our study of
the Hebrew terms which designate intention provides only a representative
sample of the cases in which the Mishnah discusses that topic. Additional
studies will be necessary to determine whether the results of this investigation
apply to all the mishnaic rules involving intention.

Having now spelled out the questions this study asks and the methods
adopted to answer those questions, let me conclude with a broad outline of how
this study unfolds. The investigation falls into two parts. Part I examines rules
that treat intention as a criterion for evaluating human action. That is to say, in
these rules, the sages appeal to an actor's intention to determine whether his or
her action constitutes a violation or fulfillment of divine law. I have further
subdivided these rules into two chapters. Chapter One takes up cases in which a
person's action misfires. In other words, the actor sets out to do one thing but
accidentally does something else. The issue here is whether the actor is
responsible for what occurred. Chapter Two takes up cases in which the actor
does precisely what he or she intended. At issue in these rules is the purpose of
the action. Here, the sages want to know *why* the individual performed the act in
question. The answer to this question, as we shall see, affects the legal outcome.
If the act in question was performed for a purpose which the law prohibits, the
actor has transgressed the law. But if the same act was performed for some other
purpose, it does not represent a violation of the law.

Part II of our study examines the role of plans in the system of the
Mishnah. As previously discussed, in the Mishnah a person's plan has the power
to classify objects and thus essentially change the properties of those objects.
When a person intends to use an object for a specific purpose, he or she *ipso
facto* places that object into a particular category. Thus, if a man intends to eat a
given substance, that substance falls into the category of food and becomes
subject to the mishnaic rules governing food. The cases in which intention
serves this function fall into two groups. Chapter Three examines the role of
plans in the Mishnah's system of purity. Here, we see how an Israelite's
intention has the power to determine whether a given object belongs to the class
of things that absorb cultic impurity. In Chapter Four, we turn to cases in which
a priest's intention defines the status of a sacrificial animal. Depending upon
how the priest intends to use the animal in question, it either falls under the
rubric of a properly slaughtered animal or an improperly slaughtered one.
Finally, the concluding chapter draws together the various strands of our
argument, looking for the underlying ideas that emerge from each part of the

Mishnah's system. In this context, I attempt to account for the Mishnah's theory of intention by relating what we find to the social characteristics of the group that produced this document.

With the larger picture in hand, let me explain the strategy of argument within each chapter. In what follows, I present rules of the Mishnah relevant to the problem of intention. In addition to translating these passages, I add in brackets extra language which is designed to clarify the meaning of the rules under discussion. Many of the passages we shall examine take up obscure points of law. Consequently, to facilitate understanding those rules, I provide a brief introduction to each passage, explaining the legal issues involved and the facts pertinent to that case. Immediately following the translation of each law, I discuss its implications for the present study of intention.

It is important to realize that no single tractate of the Mishnah is devoted exclusively to the issue of intention.[16] Rather, as I said before, the idea of intention surfaces in the sages' discussions of other topics. For this reason, the Mishnah's principles of organization cannot dictate the logic of our argument. Instead, four specific issues will frame the discussion of those rules involving intention. We begin each chapter by examining rules which illustrate the role that that particular type of intention plays in the Mishnah. Second, we take up cases which enable us to determine why intention plays that role. Third, because Scripture provides the foundation for many mishnaic ideas, we ask how the Mishnah's conception of intention relates to Scripture's. Consequently, we need to determine which aspects of the Mishnah's theory of intention derive from Scripture, and which are innovations. Finally, we examine rules which illustrate why intention plays a more important role in certain contexts than others within the mishnaic system.

The four issues just enumerated define the program of inquiry in two respects. They serve as the larger structure which frames our discussion of the Mishnah's rules. In addition, they also provide an angle of vision from which to view individual cases. That is, these questions tell us what to look for and what to ignore when we read specific mishnaic rules. In sum, this study seeks to move from case to context to concept, from detail to principle, and from philology to theology.

Part One

AN ACTOR'S INTENTION IN THE SYSTEM
OF THE MISHNAH

Chapter One

When an Action Misfires:
Effect on Liability and Reward

A person's action sometimes misfires, producing an unintended result. This presents an interesting philosophical problem. On the one hand, the person did not act with the intention of producing the result that actually ensued. But, on the other hand, the action did cause those results. Should the lack of intention absolve the actor from responsibility? In this chapter, we examine how the Mishnah deals with this problem.

In theory, the Mishnah, like other legal or religious systems, will fall somewhere between two extremes on a spectrum. At one end of the spectrum are teleological systems which evaluate what a person does by reference to the purpose, or *telos* of his or her action.[1] In such a system, the actor's intention plays a paramount role in determining liability. For example, if a woman falls off a roof and injures someone, she incurs no penalty. Since she had no intention of causing injury, she cannot be held responsible. At the other extreme of this spectrum fall systems which espouse a theory of strict liability. In such a theory, intention plays no role whatsoever, hence the term "strict," meaning that the person incurs liability for all the action's consequences, whether intended or not.[2] By this theory of responsibility, the woman who falls off a roof would be held liable for whatever injury she caused, even though she had no intention of causing anyone harm.

This hypothetical spectrum provides a useful tool for analysing the mishnaic system. The problem at hand is to determine where on this spectrum the system of the Mishnah falls. Does it fall closer to teleological systems or to systems which favor strict liability? To answer this question, we examine those mishnaic rules employing the Hebrew word *kavvanah,* which we defined in the introduction as meaning an actor's intention. Approximately half of the cases that employ this word involve the problem of the unintended result. We begin our study with these cases, asking whether the lack of intention serves to exempt an actor from liability.

Examination of these rules discloses a striking fact. Intention plays a critical role in cases that involve cultic and religious law, but it has no relevance at all in civil cases involving physical injury to people or damage to property.[3] In cultic and religious law, an actor's intention plays a decisive role in determining the punishment. Adopting the scheme put forward in Leviticus (Lev. 4:2,13, 22, 27), the Mishnah's framers impose a more severe penalty for an intentional transgression than for an unintentional one. When a person intentionally transgresses a religious or cultic law, he or she incurs the divine punishment of a premature death.[4] But if an actor unintentionally violates a cultic or religious law, the Mishnah invokes a less severe penalty: the actor is merely required to bring a sin-offering to the Temple to expiate the sin.[5] The actor's intention thus serves to differentiate an egregious offense from a minor one. We see, therefore, that in cultic and religious law, the Mishnah's theory approximates what we have defined as a teleological point of view. In evaluating actions, the framers take account of the *telos* of that action. However, since the Mishnah imposes a penalty, albeit a minor one, for an unintentional sin, its theory clearly is not purely teleological. If it were, unintended acts would incur no liability at all.

By contrast, in torts, the Mishnah propounds a theory of strict liability.[6] In this context, intention is totally irrelevant to the legal outcome. Even when an Israelite inadvertently causes damage or injury, full restitution must be made to the injured party. The critical question for this study is to determine why in cases involving torts the Mishnah disregards the actor's intention, while in laws pertaining to the cultic or religious domain intention is of paramount importance.

The answer emerges when we understand how, from the perspective of the mishnaic system, tort cases differ from cases involving the cultic or religious domain. It turns out that these cases differ from one another in one critical respect. In torts, the injured party is always a human being. But in the case of cultic and religious law, the offense is committed against God. This difference proves crucial for determining the assignment of liability. When a human being suffers physical injury or damage, he or she sustains a loss that can be assessed purely in monetary terms. Moreover, the injured party, being a human being, cares only about receiving compensation for the loss. To the victim, the actor's intention is of little import. However, most transgressions of religious or cultic law constitute an offense against God's authority, not an injury to God's person or property.[7] In the Mishnah's view, what matters to God is not what the actor did so much as the intention with which he or she did it. An intentional transgression signifies a blatant repudiation of God's hegemony, whereas an unintentional violation results from a momentary lapse, not a deliberate rejection of divine rule. In the divine-human relationship, therefore, the actor's intention provides the standard by which God measures the seriousness of an offense against divine authority.

Linguistic evidence internal to the Mishnah lends support to this dichotomy we have drawn between offenses against God and those against human beings. To begin with, the Mishnah explicitly states that some sins are against human beings, whereas others are committed against God (M. Yom. 8:9). Moreover, the Mishnah generally employs a different moral vocabulary in describing the two types of offenses. Offenses against God are called "transgressions" or "sins" (*cbyrh, psc, h't*), while offenses against human beings are referred to as "damages" (*nzykyn*).[8] Finally, the Mishnah assigns different penalties for the two types of offenses. Sins against God either invoke the divine punishment of a premature death or the minor penalty of a sin-offering. For offenses against fellow human beings, by contrast, the Mishnah generally requires compensation alone. While these distinctions are not hard and fast in the Mishnah, they indicate that the sages distinguished between two types of offenses. In what follows, we see how the theory outlined above actually emerges from the Mishnah's rules.

Strict Liability in Torts

In determining responsibility for damage or bodily injury, the Mishnah completely disregards an actor's intention. Even if the harm caused was unintended, the Mishnah requires the actor to make restitution. The Mishnah expresses this principle indirectly, by contrasting the laws governing the damage caused by animals with the laws governing damage caused by human beings. To understand the following passage, therefore, we must first consider the mishnaic rules for damages caused by animals.

If an ox tramples someone's property, the owner of the animal must compensate the injured party (Ex. 21:35-37). The amount of the compensation, however, depends on whether the animal has caused damage in the past. If the ox has been known to gore, the owner must make full restitution to the injured party, because he has had prior warning that his animal may cause damage, if not restrained. But if the animal had not caused damage on prior occasions, the owner need pay only half the damages. He had no reason to suspect that the ox would gore. In the passage at hand, the Mishnah explicitly equates a human being with an ox which has been known to gore. Translating this into more abstract language, the Mishnah is saying that a person is expected to take precautions against causing damage, just as one would control a dangerous animal. If one nonetheless causes damage, full restitution must be made to the injured party:

A. Human beings are always treated as an ox which has previously been known to gore [that is, when humans cause damage they must make full restitution as in the case of an ox which has caused damage on previous occasions],

B. whether [the damage is caused] unintentionally or intentionally,

C. whether [the actor causes the damage] when awake or asleep.

                                        M. B.Q. 2:6

In this rule, the Mishnah states a general principle about the role of intention in torts, namely that an actor's intention plays no role whatsoever in assigning liability. A person must make full restitution, even for damage caused inadvertently. For example, even if one causes damage while sleeping, which by definition is unintentional, the injured party must still be compensated (C). In tort cases, therefore, the Mishnah espouses what we have defined as a theory of strict liability.

We now turn to rules which illustrate how the general principle described above actually works itself out in specific situations. These cases show that regardless of intention, the actor is held responsible for any damage that is directly or indirectly caused by his or her action.

I.   A.   [If] a person left a pitcher in the public domain,
     B.   and another [person] came [along], tripped over it, and broke it--
     C.   he is exempt [from compensating the owner for the broken vessel].
     D.   But if he was injured by it,
     E.   the owner of the pitcher is liable [to compensate the victim] for his injury.

                                                          M. B.Q. 3:1[9]

II. A.   [If] a person spilled water in the public domain,
     B.   and another person was injured [by slipping] in it--
     C.   [the person who spilled the water] is liable [to pay] for his injury.
     D.   [If] a person hides thorns or glass [in the public domain],
     E.   [or if a person] constructs [on the edge of his property] a fence from [branches containing] thorns,
     F.   [or if a person's fence] fell into the public domain,
     G.   and other persons are injured by them [that is, the glass, thorns, or fence]--
     H.   the [owner] is liable [to pay] for the victims' injuries.

                                                          M. B.Q. 3:2

In all of these examples, the actor unintentionally inflicts damage or injury on another party. Consistent with the principle stated above-- that intention does not affect liability-- the Mishnah holds the actor liable. For example, even though the Israelite at hand did not leave the pitcher in the road with the intention of harming someone, the injured party must receive compensation (I E). Why does the Mishnah invoke a theory of strict liability? First, and most obviously, the Israelite in question should have anticipated that the action would produce a mishap. A reasonable person, for instance, knows that someone is likely to trip over anything left in the middle of the road. Since the results stem from the actor's negligence, the Mishnah holds the actor personally responsible, even though he or she did not intend to produce damage or injury.

There is a second, equally important, reason why the Mishnah imposes liability. Whenever a person suffers a monetary loss as a result of someone else's action, the framers believe the victim is entitled to compensation. As it turns out, this explanation accounts for several otherwise inexplicable rules. For example, in the following cases the actor unintentionally does harm. But here the consequences of the act could not possibly have been foreseen or prevented.

Consequently, the Israelite cannot be charged with negligence. But despite the absence of negligence, the actor is still held responsible.

I. A. [Concerning] two potters who were walking in single file,
   B. and the first potter tripped and fell,
   C. and the second potter tripped over the first potter--
   D. the first potter is liable for the injuries to the second potter.

M. B.Q. 3:4

II A. [Concerning] a person who fell off a roof,
   B. and injured someone else...
   C. he is liable for the injury [he inflicts on another party].

M. B.Q. 8:1

Here, the sages obviously do not consider the actor negligent. Neither the potter nor the individual who fell off the roof could have anticipated stumbling or falling. The imposition of liability, therefore, has nothing to do with any fault of the actor.[10] The Mishnah's single overriding concern is that an injured party receive compensation for damage. Neither the actor's intention nor the facts of the case affect liability. It strikes us as unfair that a person should be penalized for something which was done unintentionally and which also could not have been anticipated. However, from the Mishnah's standpoint a greater injustice is done if the victim does not receive compensation. The Mishnah, therefore, considers the interests of the injured party to be decisive in determining the legal outcome. These cases, therefore, unequivocally demonstrate the Mishnah's espousal of a theory of strict liability in tort cases.

Only one sage disagrees with the theory thus far presented. In the case to follow, Judah considers the actor's intention relevant in fixing liability. Yet, even though Judah invokes the criterion of intention, we shall see that he does so in a limited way.

A. If a [person's] pitcher [which was full of water] broke in a public domain,
B. and someone slipped in the water, or was injured by its shards,
C. [the owner of the vessel] is liable [to compensate the victim for his injuries].
D. Rabbi Judah says, "If he intended [to break the jar][11] he is liable [for the ensuing injuries].
E. But if he did not intend [to break the jar] he is not liable."

M. B.Q. 3:1

At first sight, it would appear that Judah totally dispenses with a theory of strict liability, because he takes account of the actor's intention. But close inspection reveals that in reality Judah accepts a modified theory of strict liability. Although he takes account of whether the actor intended to break the jar, he ignores another aspect of his intention, namely, the actor's purpose in breaking the jar. Did the actor break the jar in order to harm someone, or merely because he wanted to remove something stuck inside?[12] Since Judah ignores this aspect of the actor's intention, he does not depart entirely from a theory of strict liability.

Having shown that intention plays almost no role in tort cases, we need to consider why this is so. I suggested earlier that the Mishnah ignores an actor's intention when the damage or injury is quantifiable. When the harm can be measured solely in pecuniary terms, there is no need to appeal to intention. The actor is simply expected to pay compensation. If this theory is correct, we should find that in civil cases in which a person sustains a loss which is not capable of quantification, the Mishnah dispenses entirely with strict liability. In these cases, therefore, we should expect the actor's intention to play a role in fixing responsibility.

Let us put our theory to the test. Suppose someone shames or humiliates another person. Shame or humiliation generally involve a social disgrace that cannot be assessed solely in monetary terms.[13] On our theory, the actor's intention should prove crucial in cases such as this. And so it does. In the rules that follow, the Mishnah imposes liability only if the actor intentionally inflicted the indignity. But if this was inadvertent, the actor incurs no penalty.

I.   A.   One who strikes his fellow is liable to pay him....for any indignity inflicted...
     B.   [However, if] a sleeping person shamed [another] person,
     C.   he is exempt [from paying him for the indignity].
     D.   [Likewise, if] a person fell off the roof causing both injury and humiliation --
     E.   [the one who fell] is liable for the injury, but exempt [from paying the victim] for the indignity,
     F.   as it is written, "[If two men get into a fight with each other, and the wife of one comes up to save her husband from his antagonist] and puts out her hand and seizes him by his genitals, [you shall cut off her hand (Deut. 25:11)]."
     G.   [This scriptural statement implies that] one is liable for causing shame only when one does so intentionally.

                                        M. B.Q. 8:1

II. A.   Even though one pays the injured party [money for the shame that he caused him],[14]
     B.   he is not forgiven until he begs [forgiveness] from the victim, [because money alone cannot adequately compensate a person for humiliation].

                                        M. B.Q. 8:7

These cases demonstrate the integral connection between the role of intention and the nature of the offense committed. Only in cases involving physical injury or damages does the Mishnah advocate a theory of strict liability. This is why the man who injures someone by falling off the roof is held liable.

But he is not responsible for causing someone embarrassment or shame (I D-G). Similarly, a sleeping man is liable for producing damage (M. B.Q. 2:6), but not for causing humiliation (I B-C).

There is an obvious difference between cases involving physical injury or damage and those involving shame or humiliation. When a person suffers humiliation, the loss is not measurable solely in pecuniary terms (III). Consequently, the sages must rely on another criterion for determining responsibility. The criterion they adopt is the actor's intention. This is what serves as a yardstick for measuring an offense against a person's position or standing in a community.[15] A deliberate act of humiliation blatantly violates a person's human dignity and injures his or her reputation in the community. An unintended act, by contrast, may cause embarrassment, but not actual insult. A person, for example, suffers much greater humiliation if someone intentionally spits in his face than if this happens by accident.

On the surface, one type of case would seem to contradict the thesis that the Mishnah espouses a theory of strict liability in rules involving physical injury. I refer to cases involving homicide. Homicide cases clearly resemble torts in that physical injury is done to another human being. This might lead us to expect that in such cases intention would be irrelevant. It turns out, however, that the perpetrator's intention determines the severity of the punishment.

I. A. If an Israelite intended to strike an adult,
    B. and there was not sufficient force behind his blow to kill the adult
    C. [and the man dodged, with the result that] the blow struck a child
    D. and there was sufficient force behind the blow to kill the child,
    E. and the child died,
    F. the actor is exempt [from the death penalty].
                                                    M. San. 9:2

II. A. If a man intends to strike his fellow
    B. [but the person dodges, with the result that] he strikes a [pregnant] woman
    C. and causes her to miscarry,
    D. he must pay the value of the aborted fetus.
    E. How does one reckon the value of a fetus?
    F. One determines how much the woman was worth before she miscarried
    G. and [substracts from that sum] the amount of her worth after she aborted [the fetus. The difference between the two figures will be the worth of the child. This entire procedure takes for granted the sale of slaves on an open market. One can assess a woman's value by determining the price she would receive if she were sold as a slave].
                                                    M. B.Q. 5:4

Several reasons account for the importance of intention in homicide cases. At the simplest level, the Mishnah is adopting the position of Scripture, which unequivocally states that the intention of the actor is decisive in homicide cases (Ex. 21:12-14, Num. 35:9-25). Second, in the system of the Mishnah, a human life is invaluable; nothing can replace it. The Mishnah compares the murder of a human being to the destruction of the world (M. San. 4:5). Unlike tort cases, therefore, the "injury" is not measurable in pecuniary terms. Consequently, the Mishnah resorts to the actor's intention just as it did in cases involving humiliation, where the injury also was not quantifiable.

Third, evidence internal to the Mishnah tells us that its framers conceived of murder as an offense against God. In Part II of this study, we shall see that the Mishnah adopts the biblical view that humans are created in God's image. Consequently, the murder of a human being by definition constitutes a rejection of God's authority and therefore invokes the penalty of death by beheading, precisely the same penalty imposed for apostasy (M. San. 9:1). As we shall see below, in the religious and cultic law, intention plays a crucial role in determining whether an act constitutes an offense against God. Since homicide cases potentially constitute a rejection of divine rule, the actor's intention plays a decisive role in determining the severity of the punishment.

This interpretation gains support from the second case quoted above (II). This situation is parallel to the first case, with one important difference. Here, when the man misses the person he intended to strike, he causes a woman to miscarry. In this case intention plays no role in fixing liability. Even though the actor did not intend to hit the woman, he must pay for the value of the damage. Now this case more closely resembles a tort case than a violation of religious law. To begin with, the Mishnah does not conceive of a fetus as a full human being,[16] and therefore, the death of a fetus does not constitute a rejection of God. Moreover, when a miscarriage occurs, it is possible to decide the seriousness of the offense by measuring the financial loss which has been sustained (II E-G). Since the damage is quantifiable, the Mishnah considers intention to be irrelevant.

The Importance of Intention in Cultic and Religious Law

The fact that the role of intention depends on the nature of the offense enables us to understand the importance of intention in cultic and religious law, to which we now turn. Transgressions of cultic and religious law more closely resemble cases of humiliation than cases involving physical injury or damage. In cases involving cultic or religious law, the victim of the offense is not a human being, but God. Since God cannot suffer bodily injury, the Mishnah abandons the theory of strict liability in cases of cultic transgression.[17] To be sure, transgressions of cultic and religious law may constitute a challenge to God's authority. In this respect, they are analogous to cases involving humiliation, for here God's honor is at stake. The importance of intention in cultic and religious law, therefore, accords fully with our argument concerning cases of humiliation. Just as intention measures the seriousness of an offense against a person's reputation, it likewise provides a criterion by which to judge a transgression against divine law. An intentional violation indicates that the actor blatantly denies God's sovereignty; the sinner here justly receives the severe penalty of a premature death.[18] By contrast, when a person accidentally violates the divine law, God's authority has not been challenged, and therefore the actor incurs only a relatively minor penalty of a sin-offering.

I.   A. Concerning these [transgressions listed below],

      B. the intentional transgression invokes the divine penalty of a premature death,

      C. but the unintentional transgression invokes the [penalty of] a sin-offering.

M. Ker. 1:2

II A. [The following] thirty-six [transgressions] listed in Scripture invoke the divine punishment of premature death [if performed intentionally, as specified at I A]:

      B. one who has intercourse with his mother, his father's wife, his daughter-in-law (Lev. 18:6-7),

      C. a man who commits sodomy with another man, or who commits bestiality, and a woman who commits bestiality (Lev. 18:22-23),

      D. one who [on separate occasions] has intercourse with a woman and her daughter, or with another man's wife, one who has intercourse with his sister, with his paternal aunt, with his maternal aunt, with his wife's sister, with his brother's wife, with his father's brother's wife, and with a menstruating woman (Lev. 18:17-20),

      E. one who blasphemes [God's name] (Num. 18:30), one who commits idolatry, one who sacrifices his children to [the god] Molech (Lev. 18:21), one who practices necromancy (Lev. 20:6),

      F. one who profanes the Sabbath (Ex. 31:14), one who eats holy things while in a state of cultic impurity (Lev. 22:3), one who enters the Temple while in a state of cultic impurity (Lev. 15:31), one who eats fat of an animal (Lev. 7:25-26), or its blood, or eats parts of a sacrifice after the time specified for its consumption (Lev. 7:18, 19:8), or eats from something which falls into the category of refuse,[19] or one who slaughters or burns a sacrifice outside the Temple court (Lev. 17:9),

      G. and one who eats leavening on the festival of Passover (Ex. 12:15), and one who eats or labors on the Day of Atonement (Lev. 23:30),

      H. and one who makes [for personal use] a mixture of oil [similar to that used in the Temple], and one who makes [for personal use] a mixture of spices [similar to that used in the Temple], and one who annoints himself with the sacred annointing oil [for the high priest],

      I. and [one also incurs premature death for the failure to perform the following] religious obligations: [the obligation to carry out] the Passover sacrifice (Num. 9:13), and [the obligation to perform] the circumcision [of one's son (Gen. 17:30)].

M. Ker. 1:1

Intention matters in these cases because they all involve a transgression of divine law. Most obviously, the violation of Temple procedure (F), the misappropriation of Temple goods for secular use (H), and the transgression of festival laws (F, G) constitute offenses against God's jurisdiction. In addition, the Mishnah, following Leviticus, treats sexual violations such as incest and bestiality as offenses against God (B-D). As I said above, intention plays a prominent role in transgressions of divine law, because it serves as the criterion for distinguishing a blatant repudiation of God's sovereignty from a momentary lapse. One who intentionally transgresses does so in the knowledge that the act is forbidden.[20] Since in such a case, the actor does not feel compelled to live according to God's law, he or she incurs the divine punishment of a premature death. An unintentional transgression, which stems from mere inadvertence or error, does not signify a repudiation of divine will. For an unintentional violation, therefore, the Mishnah imposes only the minor penalty of a sin-offering.

The same conception emerges even more clearly from the Mishnah's discussion of another type of religious transgression, namely, when a person misappropriates goods which are designated for Temple use. In this case a non-priest eats heave-offering, a part of the crop which Israelite farmers are commanded to set aside for priestly consumption in the Temple. This constitutes a violation of divine law because the Israelite has put to personal use what belongs to God. This case is of interest to our argument for two reasons. First, it closely parallels the tort cases we previously discussed. In those cases, damage was done to another person's property. Here, the Mishnah speaks about a person doing damage to divine property. This rule, therefore, provides an important illustration of the mishnaic view that violations of religious law differ from similar cases in the civil realm. Second, this case also makes explicit the notion that an offense against God is not capable of quantification.

I.   A.   [An Israelite] who unintentionally *(swgg)* eats heave-offering
     B.   pays back the principal and an additional fifth [of its value].
     C.   The same [rule applies to] one who [unintentionally] eats [produce in the status of heave-offering], to one who [unintentionally] drinks [liquids in the status of heave-offering], and to one who [unintentionally] anoints [him or herself with oil in the status of heave-offering].
                                                        M. Ter. 6:1

II. A.   [A non-priest] who intentionally *(mzyd)* eats heave-offering
     B.   pays back the principal, but does not pay the [added] fifth.
                                                        M. Ter. 7:1

III. A.   [Non-priests who eat] heave-offering and first fruits
     B.   are liable to the [divine punishment] of death [if the act was intentional], or to the fine of the added fifth [if it was unintentional].
                                                        M. Bik. 2:1 (M. Hal. 1:9)

In one respect, the Mishnah's ruling here corresponds to its treatment of torts. As in tort cases, the Mishnah requires the actor to pay for any damage which was caused, whether or not it was produced intentionally. Consequently, the offender must in all cases recompense the Temple for having misappropriated the heave-offering.

However, there is a fundamental difference between this case and the law of torts. In torts, compensation alone suffices, whereas here, the actor is subject to an additional punishment of either a fine or the death penalty, depending upon his or her intention. This is because in religious and cultic law, the Mishnah is also interested in determining whether the act constitutes a challenge to divine authority. As we have learned to expect, the answer to this question depends on the actor's intention. If the non-priest unintentionally eats heave-offering, he or she must pay an additional fifth of the heave-offering's value as a fine. But an Israelite who does so intentionally is *not* required to pay the penalty of the added fifth, because this person is subject to the divine punishment of death (I B, II, III). This case proves, therefore, that intention serves as a criterion for measuring the severity of the offense to divine authority. When a person unwittingly violates a law, there is no significant repudiation of divine will involved. Hence, such a violation is only subject to the minor penalty of a fine. But a mere monetary fine cannot atone for the sin of intentionally violating divine law, for this constitutes an affront to divine authority, which cannot be compensated.

We now understand why intention predominates in religious and cultic law and plays virtually no role in civil law. The Mishnah appeals to intention to determine the severity of any offense which is not capable of quantification. Religious offenses are generally not measurable in pecuniary terms, because a person cannot do bodily damage to God. Moreover, even when a specified amount of damage is done to divine property, the sages still want to know whether the act constitutes a rejection of divine authority. In all religious and cultic transgressions there is an aspect of the offense which is not subject to quantification. Consequently, in this area of law, the actor's intention must play a prominent role. In civil law, by contrast, the majority of cases involve simple damages or injury, which do not constitute an affront to the victim's human dignity or status. In this area of law, therefore, the damage is almost always entirely quantifiable. Only in rare cases, such as those involving humiliation, do the sages need to rely on human intention.

The Mishnah does not limit the role of intention to cases involving transgressions of religious law. The actor's intention is also critical in determining whether his or her action satisfies a religious obligation. For example, an Israelite discharges a religious duty only by deliberately performing the requisite act. If the act is performed unintentionally, the actor's obligation is not fulfilled.

The following example illustrates this function of intention. It involves people who want to fulfill their obligation to give certain gifts to the Temple, or who want to take a religious vow of abstinence. For the present purposes, the nature of these obligations need not concern us. What is important is that the deliberate or inadvertent character of the act's performance determines the legal outcome.

A. [If] a person intends to say, "[This grain will be dedicated to the Temple as] heave-offering,"
B. but [accidentally] said, "tithe"--
C. [And if a person intends to say, "This grain will be dedicated as] tithe,"
D. but [accidentally] said, "heave-offering"--
E. [and if a person intends to say, "This animal will be dedicated to the Temple as a] burnt-offering,"
F. but [accidentally] said, "offering of well-being,"--
G. [And if a person intends to say, "This animal will be an] offering of well-being,"
H. but [accidentally] said, "a burnt-offering,"--
I. [And if a person intends to say], "I [vow to God that I] will not enter this house,"
J. but [accidentally] said, "that house"--
K. [And if a person intends to vow to God that] "I [will forgo benefit] from this person,"
L. but he [accidentally] says "that person"--
M. [in all of these cases] he said nothing [i.e., his words produce no legal consequences],
N. unless his words and his intention correspond.

M. Ter. 3:8

In this case, intention plays a critical role in determining whether the person's words produce legal consequences. Normally, if a person states aloud that he dedicates a pile of grain as a particular agricultural gift to the Temple, or that an animal will serve as a particular sacrifice, those objects immediately assume a consecrated status. But here, since the actor did not say what he intended, his words produce no legal consequences. Neither the grain nor the animal falls into the specified category. In the case at hand, therefore, intention performs the same role as in cases involving transgressions. There, a judgment that the actor had repudiated God's authority depended upon the actor's intention. Here, the sages take account of intention to determine whether the act constitutes an affirmation of God's authority. If a person inadvertently performs an act that would normally fulfill a religious obligation, the act obviously does not signify an attempt to carry out God's will. It occurred merely through happenstance. For this reason, the actor has not discharged the religious duty in question.

Human Intention and Divine Will

The fact that intention plays such a crucial role in religious law points to one of the basic theological assumptions of the mishnaic system: intention is the human counterpart to the divine will. From the standpoint of the Mishnah, being made in God's image means having the capacity to act like God by thinking, planning, and formulating intentions. This point will emerge more clearly in the second part of this study, where I show that the Mishnah ascribes to human intention powers which are analogous to the ones that the biblical story of creation ascribes to the divine will. This correlation between divine will and human intention helps account for the importance of intention in religious and cultic law. By intentionally violating a law, a person in effect has set the human will against God's, because the Mishnah conceives of the laws as an embodiment of divine will. Consequently, the intentional violation of divine law indicates the actor's failure to recognize the limitation of human will. This person, therefore, justifiably incurs the penalty of a premature death, so that further rejection of divine will becomes impossible. When people follow God's law, however, they affirm the resemblance between themselves and God, bending their will to divine will.

The following case comes closer than any in the mishnaic system to explicitly correlating human intention and divine will. Here, the sages interpret an intentional action as an attempt to evade the divine will. The case at hand concerns a person afflicted with a skin-disease. In levitical law, if a white spot appears on a person's skin, he or she becomes cultically unclean and must be sequestered until the spot disappears. At that time, the person must undergo an elaborate rite of purification (Lev. 14). In the law at hand, the Mishnah takes up cases in which the diseased skin does not disappear spontaneously, but is cut off, whether intentionally or accidentally. Does the removal of the diseased skin render the person clean, as would its natural disappearance? The answer depends upon whether the Israelite intentionally cut away that skin.

A. [Concerning] a person upon whom a white spot of skin appeared,
B. and [that piece of skin] was cut off [when he bumped into a sharp object],
C. [the man immediately] becomes clean.
D. [But] if he cut off [the spot of skin] intentionally--
E. Rabbi Eliezer says, "[He only becomes clean once] he suffers a new bout of skin disease, and recovers from it. [Since he cut off the diseased skin, one cannot determine when the disease has run its course. Consequently, the person must wait until he suffers a new bout of disease and it disappears. Only at that point, can he be certain that the original disease has passed]."
F. Sages say, "[He becomes clean only if] his entire skin becomes white. [In mishnaic law, when a person's entire skin turns white, this is a sign that the disease has run its course (cf. M. Neg. 8:1). In sages' view, therefore, since the person cannot determine when the initial bout of the disease has ended, he only becomes clean when his entire skin turns white.]"
G. [However] if the white spot appeared on the corona [of a baby boy's penis, the father] may circumcise [the child, even though he

intentionally cuts off the diseased spot. In this case, the cutting away of the diseased skin renders the child clean.]

M. Neg. 7:5

When a person intentionally cuts off a spot of diseased skin, this constitutes an explicit attempt to circumvent God's law. By taking matters into his own hands, the actor has attempted to restore himself to a clean state. Consequently, Eliezer and the sages both subject the offender to a harsh penalty. He must wait an interminable period of time before he is considered clean. It is important to realize, however, that an intentional removal of diseased skin does not always signify a rejection of divine law. For example, although the father intentionally cuts off the diseased skin of his son in order to perform the rite of circumcision, this does not constitute a renunciation of God's law (G). On the contrary, by performing the act of circumcision, the father carries out the ultimate affirmation of God's sovereignty, for the act of circumcision signifies the man's readiness to subject his son to God's covenant. Under these exceptional circumstances, therefore, the intentional removal of the diseased skin constitutes acceptance rather than rejection of divine law. In consequence, the child is immediately restored to a clean state.

The accidental removal of diseased skin, by contrast, does not represent a spurning of divine law. When the diseased skin is cut off inadvertently, the person obviously was not trying to evade the law. Indeed, it would appear from this case that the Mishnah's framers actually regard the accidental loss of the diseased skin as resulting from divine intervention.[21] Though the person's diseased skin is normally removed through natural healing, God sometimes does so by causing an accident. Since the sages regard the unintentional results as stemming from divine will, the loss of the diseased skin in that case restores the individual to a clean state. The Mishnah explicitly equates unintentional results with divine intervention in the following passage involving an Israelite who is reciting aloud a special prayer called The Prayer:

A. If one who recites The Prayer made a mistake,
B. it is a bad omen for him.
C. If he [made a mistake while functioning as] the agent of the community [that is, he recites The Prayer aloud on the behalf of his fellows],
D. it is a bad omen for the community, because an agent is equivalent to the principal [who appointed him, in this case his fellow worshippers].
E. [The following] was said of Rabbi Hanina son of Dosa:
F. When he was praying on behalf of the sick,
G. he would say, "This one will live and this one will die."
H. They said to him, "How do you know that?"
I. He said to them, "If my [recitation of] The Prayer is fluent, I know that [the sick person] has been accepted [by God].
J. "If not, I know that he has been rejected [by God]."

M. Ber. 5:5

Here, as in the previous rule, the Mishnah treats an unintentional occurrence as a divine action. A slip of the tongue is regarded in this case as a sign of divine disfavor, the assumption being that God caused the person to make a mistake. The story about Hanina makes a similar point. Hanina knows from the way he recites a prayer whether the person on whose behalf he is praying will live or die. If he recites the words haltingly, it is a sign that God will take the person's life. Again, the presumption is that God takes an active role in determining the fluidity of one's prayers.

While the Mishnah often attributes unintentional results to divine intervention, in some exceptional cases it does not. It sometimes claims that the unintended results stem not from an act of God but from the actor's negligence. If, for example, it turns out that an Israelite failed to take reasonable precautions to prevent a transgression, the Mishnah treats the unintentional violation as a repudiation of divine authority. Had the actor really cared about complying with God's law, he or she would have taken measures to avert the violation. This point emerges from a complicated rule involving the prohibition against working on the Sabbath.

The Mishnah's framers regard carrying objects to be an act of labor and hence forbid that act on the day of rest. However, they do permit circumvention of this law by a legal fiction: by placing the object inside one's garment, a person may transport it without incurring liability. The individual thereby treats the object as an article of clothing, which is, in effect, worn rather than carried. However, in order to make this legal fiction work, the actor must prevent the object from sliding from one side of the body to the other. If it moves about, the sages no longer consider it part of one's attire and the person is held liable for carrying it. In the case at hand, a person carries an object inside his or her garment, with every intention of keeping it in place. Nonetheless, the object accidentally swings around the body. As we shall see, if that occurrence could have been anticipated, the Israelite incurs liability.

A. [Concerning] a person who [carries an object such as a key inside his garment and] intends to carry [it] in front of him [i.e., inside the front of his garment]--

B. but it swings around behind him,

C. he is exempt [from any liability].[22]

D. But [concerning a person who intends to carry it] behind him--

E. and it swings around in front of him,

F. he is liable for [violating the law].

G. Nonetheless, the sages made [the following qualification]:

H. [Concerning] the woman who attaches [an object] to her underskirt,

I. whether she attached it in front of her or behind her, [if it swings around to the other side],

J. she is liable [for violating the law].

K. [This is] because [underskirts] usually swing around the body [and therefore, she should have anticipated this occurrence].

M. Shab. 10:4

In all of these cases, the movement of the object was unintended. Yet, in two of these cases, the Mishnah holds the actor liable (D-F, G-K). Here, the movement of the object resulted not from an act of God but from the actor's negligence. Both the man and woman should have been able to foresee and prevent the movement of the object. Consequently, the sages consider them responsible even though they had no intention of producing those results. The question naturally arises as to how the sages decide whether a particular unintended result signifies a rejection of divine rule. After all, in the previous case, the Mishnah ascribed an unintended result to divine intervention, whereas here, it ascribes it to human negligence.

The sages distinguish human negligence from divine action by taking account of the normal conduct of the typical Israelite. If in the circumstances in question the average person could have anticipated and prevented the consequences, the actor should have been able to avert the transgression. Consequently he or she is liable for violating God's law, despite the lack of intention to produce those consequences. But if the typical person could not have foreseen or averted the results, the actor at hand could not have been expected to prevent the transgression. Consequently, in this case the sages classify the occurrence as an act of God.

A similar concern dominates the Mishnah's discussion of food purity (Tractate Makhshirin). In this context, the Mishnah seeks to distinguish phenomena caused by human beings from those resulting from divine acts or natural processes. To understand why this issue arises, we need to familiarize ourselves with the Mishnah's conception of food impurity. Following Leviticus, the sages of the Mishnah maintain that food, under certain specified conditions, can become contaminated by sources of impurity, such as a dead reptile, or a corpse (Lev. 11:29-38). Leviticus further prescribes that food absorbs impurity only if "water is put" on it (Lev. 11:38). The Mishnah interprets the expression "if water is put" to mean that food can absorb impurity only if a human being is responsible for moistening the food, that is, the water must be willfully or intentionally put on the food; it cannot merely fall on the food by accident. Therefore, if the moistening of the food is the result of a divine act, as for example when it rains, the food cannot become contaminated, because in this case, a person has not moistened it.

Translating this into more abstract language, the Mishnah is distinguishing between human causes, on the one hand, and natural occurrences or divine acts, on the other. In Part II of this study, I will explain why human beings have the power to make things absorb impurity. In the present context, suffice it to say that in the Mishnah's view, God has turned over to humans the role of determining what can and cannot become contaminated. Consequently, if a person causes his or her food to be moistened, it can subsequently become contaminated. But if God causes the food to become wet, it cannot absorb impurity. Several examples will show how the Mishnah seeks to distinguish results produced by divine and human causes.

I. A. [If] a householder wet down [the floors of] his house and [subsequently] put wheat in the house, and the wheat grew damp--
    B. if [it grew damp] on account of the water [which he sprinkled], [the wheat] falls under the category of something upon which "water is put" [and therefore it is capable of absorbing impurity].
    C. But if the wheat grew damp on account of the [sweat from the] stone [walls], the [wheat] does not fall under the rubric of something upon which "water is put" [and so is not capable of absorbing impurity].
    D. If a householder washed his clothes in a trough and [subsequently] put wheat in it, and the wheat grew damp--
    E. if [it grew damp] on account of the water [he put in the trough], [the wheat] falls under the category of something upon which "water is put" [and therefore is capable of absorbing impurity].
    F. But if the trough sweated on its own,[23] [the wheat] does not fall under the rubric of something upon which "water is put" [and therefore it cannot absorb impurity].

M. Makh. 3:4

II. A. The sweat from [the stone walls] of houses, from cisterns, trenches, or caves
    B. is clean [that is, if it moistens food it does not make the food susceptible to impurity].
    C. Human sweat is clean.
    D. [If] a person drank unclean water and sweated--
    E. his sweat is [nonetheless] clean.
    F. If he dipped in water which had been drawn [from a well or stream] and he [subsequently] sweated--
    G. his sweat is unclean [that is, if it moistens food, that food is capable of absorbing impurity].
    H. If [after getting out of the water] he dried himself, and he subsequently sweated--
    I. his sweat is clean.

M. Makh. 2:1

In these rules, the Mishnah distinguishes between two types of cases: 1) instances in which the householder directly caused the moistening of his produce, and 2) situations in which the produce became wet as a result of natural or divine causes. For example, if the produce soaks up water which the Israelite brought into the house, the produce can subsequently absorb impurity. Here, the wetting of the produce was the result of human action alone. But if the moisture originated from the sweating of the stones in the heat (I, II A), the causes were natural (or divine), and hence the moisture has no effect on the food's status.

The same distinction is at work in the second case concerning human sweat (II C-I). Perspiration is normally something over which a person has no control, and hence, if sweat falls on food substances, it has no effect on the food.[24] By the same token, the sweat produced after drinking has no power to alter the status of food, because the sweat is not a direct result of a person having taken a drink. Indeed, the person would have sweated whether he or she took the drink or not.[25] When a person takes a dip, however, the sages believe the water that subsequently appears on his body was absorbed during his swim, and is not actual sweat.[26] Consequently, that liquid is attributed to human causes, and so has no power to alter the status of food. In these examples, therefore, the Mishnah consistently attempts to distinguish results caused by human beings from those stemming from divine action.

In many instances, however, a combination of factors contributes to the moistening of food, as in the case of a householder who leaves produce on the roof of his house, with the result that it is moistened by the dew. Here an ambiguity arises, because both human and divine (or natural) causes play a role. Turning to this case, we see that the Mishnah deals with the ambiguity once again by resorting to the actor's intention:

I.   A.   [If] a householder takes his produce to the roof because of insect infestation, [that is, he wishes to dry them in the sun so that the insects will leave the fruit],[27]
      B.   and dew falls upon the produce--
      C.   [the dew] does not fall under the rubric of "if water is put."
      D.   If he intended (ntkwwn) for this [to happen, that is, he took produce to the roof with the intention of having the dew moisten it]--
      E.   [the dew which falls on it] falls under the rubric of "if water is put." [Since he intended for the produce to become moistened, the dew makes the produce capable of absorbing impurity.]

                                                            M. Makh. 6:1

In determining whether to ascribe the results principally to the householder's action or to God's act of causing the dew to fall, the Mishnah takes account of the actor's intention. If his intention was to save the fruit from infestation, the wetting of the produce was incidental to the action. In fact, he took the food to the roof with precisely the opposite intention, namely, to dry it in the sun. For this reason, the framers treat the moistening of the produce as principally a divine act. Since human causes were not the primary cause of the results, the liquid does not make the food susceptible to impurity (A-C). If, on the other hand, the householder intended to moisten the produce, he has taken advantage of a well-known divine act for his own purposes. Although strictly speaking he was not the sole cause of the results, what he did was tantamount to wetting down the produce himself. For this reason, the Mishnah attributes the results to human causes, with the result that the food can absorb impurity.

In summary, the Mishnah appeals to intention to determine whether to ascribe an occurrence to the actor at hand or to other causes. This is the same reason that an actor's intention plays such an important role in cases involving transgressions of the law. When a person intentionally performs an act which violates the law, he or she is the sole cause of the action. The actor has in effect set human will against divine will, and therefore incurs the severe penalty of a premature death. But if what happens was inadvertent, the actor is not the only cause of the results. Other factors must have interfered in the execution of the act. Since human will was not at cross purposes with God's, this person incurs only the minor penalty of a sin-offering. Throughout our discussion, we have assumed that it is obvious whether an act constitutes an intentional violation. In fact, the sages consider distinguishing intentional from unintentional acts to be an extremely subtle problem. We now direct our attention to this intriguing issue.

Distinguishing Intentional From Unintentional Acts

The need to distinguish intentional from unintentional actions raises an important question. What constitutes "acting intentionally"? Obviously, when a person does precisely what was intended, we say he or she has acted intentionally. Conversely, when the intended and resulting actions are totally dissimilar, we say the person has done something unintentionally. In some cases, however, a person's action can be intentional in one respect but unintentional in another. Take, for example, a man who intends to throw a stone into the street, but accidentally throws it through a neighbor's window. In one respect, the resulting act was unintentional, for he did not mean to cause damage. In another respect, however, the resulting action was intentional: the man performed the very type of act he had in mind. He intended to *throw* the stone and in fact *threw* the stone. How similar must the intended and resulting actions be to warrant calling the act "intentional" as opposed to "unintended"? This is an important question, because, as previously discussed, in cultic and religious law, the Mishnah invokes legal consequences only if that action was intentional.

The following cases taken together permit us to see how the Mishnah deals with this difficult question. These cases are drawn from a variety of legal contexts in the mishnaic system. All of them, however, employ an identical Hebrew formula: they speak about "a person who intends x but [accidentally] does y (*kwwn l...w ^csh 't...*)." The fact that the same linguistic formula appears in all of these cases demonstrates that, although they appear in different legal contexts, they all address the same theoretical issue, namely, defining an intentional action. Consequently, in examining these cases together as a unit, we may deduce the Mishnah's definition of an intentional action.

Examination of these rules will show that in determining whether a given act is intentional, the sages compare it to the act that the person had intended to perform. They say the person has acted intentionally only if the intended action and resulting action[28] are identical in four respects:

First, the intended and resulting actions must fall into the same category. For example, if the actor intended to *throw* a stone, did he in fact *throw* a stone?

Second, the intended and resulting actions must invoke the same legal consequences. That is, had the actor done what he intended, would the act have produced legal consequences identical to the legal consequences of the act he in fact performed? For example, suppose on the Sabbath day a person intends to carry a piece of fruit, but accidentally carries a stone. Here, both the intended act (carrying fruit) and the resulting action (carrying a stone) entail the same legal effects. Carrying fruit and carrying a stone both violate the injunction against laboring on the day of rest. In other cases, the intended and resulting actions invoke different legal consequences, as in the case of an Israelite who intends to kill an animal but accidentally kills a fellow Israelite. In this instance, the intended action (killing an animal) if actually performed would produce a less severe penalty than the resulting action (killing a person). We shall see that the Mishnah only labels as intentional an act which involves the same legal consequences as the intended action.

Third, the Mishnah takes account of whether the intended and resulting actions involve the same type of object. If he intended to break a window, did he in fact break a *window* or did he break something else?

Fourth, when relevant, the framers consider whether the intended action would have produced the physical results which in fact obtained. For example, consider the case of a man who intends to strike a person in the stomach, but accidentally strikes the victim's head and kills him. To determine whether the actor incurs liability in this case, the sages would want to know whether the victim would have died had the actor done what he intended, namely, striking the victim in the stomach. If the intended act would have produced the same physical results which in fact obtained, then the actor is liable for those results. The Mishnah, then, defines an action as intentional only if it corresponds to the intended act in the four respects just listed. If, however, the intended and resulting actions differ from one another in any of these respects, the Mishnah treats what the actor did as unintentional and imposes a less severe penalty.

The Mishnah's four criteria form a strict definition of intentional action. It is "strict" because even the slightest deviation from the original intention deprives the act of all legal consequences. We shall see in fact that the Mishnah sometimes labels as unintentional an act that we would normally call intentional. Consider the following scenario: A man tries to kill another man by striking him in the stomach. The blow, however, lacks sufficient force to kill the victim if it were to strike the intended spot. However, at the last moment the victim dodges and the blow strikes him on the heart and kills him. In Anglo-

American law, the perpetrator would be guilty of murder. Since he intended to kill someone, and in fact accomplished that very result, he would incur liability for murder. The Mishnah, by contrast, does not classify such a case as murder, because the intended act, namely striking the victim in the stomach, would not have produced the results that actually ensued. Even though the actor intended to kill the victim, he is not guilty of murder.

Why do Mishnah's sages define an intentional act so narrowly? By doing so, they insure that an act invokes no legal consequences unless it stems solely from an exercise of the human will. When the intended and resulting actions differ on any of the four criteria mentioned above, the Mishnah assumes that other factors must have intervened in the person's execution of the act.[29] Otherwise, the person would have succeeded in doing exactly what he or she intended. Since in that case the act does not wholly stem from an exercise of human will, the framers strip it of its normal legal consequences.

It is important to realize that the Mishnah does not explicitly provide a definition of an intentional action. The four criteria mentioned above emerge from an analysis of the following cases in which the sages take up this problem. I have ordered these cases so that the intended and resulting actions under discussion become progressively more similar to one another. In the first set of rules, the intended and resulting actions are similar in only one of the respects mentioned above. In the next set of rules, they are identical in two respects, until we finally reach those pericopae in which the intended and resulting actions are identical in all respects. In each of these rules, the framers consider whether the intended and resulting actions resemble one another sufficiently to warrant calling the resulting action intentional. If so, they impose the legal consequences applicable to an intentional act of that particular kind. If not, they either deprive the act of all legal effect or merely impose the minor penalty of a sin-offering.

Intended and Resulting Actions: Belonging to the Same Category of Act

We start with the simplest of the cases adduced by the Mishnah, in which the intended and resulting actions are similar in the first respect mentioned above: both fall into the same category of action. By this I mean that the same verb can be used to describe both what the actor intends and what he does. For example, in the case of an Israelite who intended to write one letter of the alphabet and accidentally wrote a different letter, both the intended and resulting acts can be described by the same verb. The actor intended to write and in fact wrote. To formulate this abstractly, we can say that the actor intended x but did x', where x and x' fall into the same category of action. When the intended and resulting actions belong to the same category, the Mishnah says they have a single name (sm 'hd).[30] As we shall see from the rules to follow, this similarity by itself is not sufficient to make the actor liable for the consequences of the resulting act.

The case at hand, for example, involves a person who inadvertently violates the prohibition against performing creative acts on the Sabbath day. Among other things, the Mishnah regards as a creative act the writing of two letters of the Hebrew alphabet in juxtaposition. This is because in Hebrew the juxtaposition of two letters generally conveys a meaningful idea.[31] By contrast, the Mishnah does not consider the sketching of a single Hebrew character to be a creative act, for no single letter standing alone can convey a meaningful idea. In the rule at hand, a person intends to draw a single letter, but inadvertently writes two. The sages discuss whether he or she is liable for breaking the Sabbath law.

A. [A person who] intended to write [the Hebrew letter] *het*,
B. but [accidentally] wrote two [Hebrew letter] *zayins*,
C. is exempt [from the divine punishment of a premature death].

                                                        M. Shab. 12:5

Let me first explain this case with reference to the English alphabet. Consider a woman who intends to draw the letter H. In the process of drawing this letter, she accidentally produces two letter I's, for the two uprights of the H look like I's.[32] The sages discuss whether this constitutes an intentional violation of the prohibition against writing. In one critical respect, the woman did what she intended to do, for both the intended and resulting actions fall into the same category of act, namely, writing letters. But in the Mishnah, this similarity does not suffice to classify the act as intentional, because the intended and resulting actions obviously differ in another respect. What the actor intended, namely writing a single letter, was fully within the bounds of the law. But what in fact occurred, the drawing of two letters, constitutes a violation. For this reason, the sages regard the transgression as unintentional, and hence, the actor is not subject to divine punishment for an intentional transgression.

The following case makes essentially the same point in a different context:

A. [Concerning a person who] intended *(ntkwwn)* to kill an animal but [by accident] killed a human being [i.e., an Israelite],
B. [and concerning a person who intended to kill] a gentile and [by accident] killed an Israelite,
C. [and concerning a person who intended to kill] a non-viable [human] fetus, [and by accident] killed a viable fetus,
D. [in all of these cases he is] exempt [from the death penalty].

                                                        M. San. 9:2

In these examples, as in the previous case, the intended and resulting actions are similar in one important respect: they constitute essentially the same act, namely, killing. But once again, this similarity by itself does not warrant labeling the act as intentional. From the Mishnah's viewpoint, the difference between the intended and resulting actions outweighs the similarity. Mishnaic law does not regard as a transgression of divine law the killing of an animal, a non-viable fetus, or even a gentile. For reasons which lie outside the framework of the present inquiry, only the murder of an Israelite invokes divine punishment. In the case at hand, therefore, what the actor set out to do did not constitute a transgression of divine law, whereas the actual result does constitute a violation. For this reason, the Mishnah treats the resulting action as unintentional and exempts the actor from the death penalty, the punishment for intentional transgressions of this sort.

In the two cases just considered, the Mishnah exempts the actor because no legal consequences would have occurred had the actor done what he or she intended. In what follows, by contrast, had the person done what was intended, the act would have produced legal consequences which would be similar to those of the act performed. In this case, therefore, the intended and resulting actions resemble one another more closely than in the previous examples. Now they not only fall in the same category, but they also produce similar legal effects. The Mishnah considers whether or not this closer correspondence puts the act into the category of an intentional act.

The case at hand involves Israelites who intend to dedicate a specific type of offering to the Temple. Through a slip of the tongue, however, the Israelite does not say precisely what he had intended. The sages discuss whether the Israelites' words produce the normal legal consequences, namely, consecrating the item in question.

A. [Concerning] the person who intends to say, "[This grain will be] heave-offering,"
B. but [accidentally] said "tithe"--
C. [And concerning a person who intends to say, "This grain will be] tithe,"
D. but [accidentally] said, "heave-offering"--
E. [And concerning a person who intends to say, "This animal will be a] burnt-offering,"
F. but [accidentally] said, "an offering of well-being"--
G. [And concerning a person who intends to say "This animal will be an] offering of well-being,"
H. but [accidentally] said, "a burnt-offering"--
I. [in all of these cases] he said nothing [i.e., his words produce no legal consequences],
J. unless his words and his intention correspond.

M. Ter. 3:8

Here, the intended and resulting acts are more similar to one another than in the previous examples. First, both fall into the same category of action, namely, dedicating an object to the Temple. But in addition, the actor intended an act which if actually performed would have produced legal consequences. Had the householder uttered the words he had intended, the produce would have become consecrated. However, the intended and resulting acts entail different, though comparable, legal effects. The actor intends to consecrate the grain as one type of offering, but mentions a different type of offering. This slight difference suffices, in the sages' view, to exclude the act from the category of intentional acts. For this reason, the act fails to produce any legal consequences at all.

Intended and Resulting Actions: Invoking the Same Legal Consequences

We now turn our attention to cases which satisfy two of the four conditions set out above. Not only do the intended and resulting actions belong to a single category, but they both invoke the same legal consequences. In what follows, the Mishnah asks whether this similarity is sufficient to warrant labelling the action intentional.

The case at hand involves the law against performing acts of labor on the Sabbath day. The Mishnah holds that gathering produce from the field, like all agricultural tasks, falls into the category of labor, and hence is forbidden on the day of rest. Here, a person intends to gather one type of fruit but accidentally gathers another type of fruit.[33] In this case, the intended and resulting actions fall into precisely the same category of transgression. Gathering fruit violates the Sabbath law, regardless of the type of fruit involved. Does this similarity between the intended and resulting actions suffice in the sages' view to classify the transgression as intentional?

A. Said Rabbi Judah, "Even [in a case] where a person intended to gather figs [on the Sabbath day], but [accidentally] gathered grapes [on that day]

B. "and [in a case where he intended to gather] grapes but [accidentally] gathered figs--

C. "and [in a case where he intended to gather] black-stemmed figs,[34] but [accidentally] gathered white-stemmed figs--

D. "and [in a case where he intended to gather] white-stemmed figs, but [accidentally] gathered black-stemmed figs--

E. "Rabbi Eliezer declares the actor liable [for bringing] a sin-offering [to the Temple to expiate him from his unintentional sin].[35]

F. "Rabbi Joshua exempts [him from even the requirement of bringing a sin-offering]."

G. [Commenting upon Joshua's position] said Rabbi Judah, "I am astonished that Rabbi Joshua [would actually] exempt [this person from bringing a sin-offering],

H. "for if that is [the correct ruling] why does Scripture say [the following concerning the sin-offering: 'If any person from among the populace unwittingly incurs guilt by doing any of the things which by the Lord's commandment ought not to be done, and finds himself culpable--once] the sin of which he is guilty [is brought to his knowledge, he shall bring a female goat without blemish as his offering for the sin of which he is guilty (Lev. 4:22-24, 27-30).]

I.   "[Now, the words 'the sin of which he is guilty'] exclude [from the requirement of bringing a sin-offering] a person who is engaged[36] [in a task that is permitted, and accidentally does something forbidden. For this person is not guilty at all. But it does not mean to exclude from the requirement of bringing a sin-offering the case of a person who, from the outset, intends to do something forbidden and by accident does something else that is equally forbidden. He is guilty. Therefore, in the case at hand the individual must bring a sin-offering.]"

M. Ker. 4:3

To understand how this rule contributes to a definition of intentional action, we must review the types of punishments the Mishnah imposes for transgressions of the Sabbath law. We recall that one who intentionally transgresses a law incurs the divine punishment of a premature death, while an unintentional violation incurs only the minor penalty of a sin-offering (M. Ker. 1:1-2). With this distinction in mind, we turn to the case at hand. When on the Sabbath day a person intends to gather one type of fruit but accidentally gathers a different type, is this an intentional or an unintentional transgression? It is clear that the authorities mentioned here do not treat the act as an intentional transgression, for if they did they would impose the divine punishment of a premature death. In their view, since the actor accidentally collected a different species (A-B) or sub-species (C-D) of fruit, the act does not constitute an intentional violation.

This case is a beautiful illustration of the sages' narrow definition of an intentional act. After all, the actor set out to do a forbidden act and ends up doing a similar act that is equally forbidden. In such a case, we would normally say that the person has performed an intentional transgression. The Mishnah, however, does not invoke the penalty for an intentional transgression. This strict definition, as previously discussed, insures that a person incurs liability for divine punishment only when the act stems wholly from an exercise of the human will. If the intended and resulting actions differ, no matter how negligible that difference, the sages assume that other factors intervened in the performance of that action, and the person cannot be held responsible for what occurred.

Since in this case the sages do not regard the act as an intentional transgression, we might reasonably expect them to classify it as an unintentional transgression and impose the appropriate penalty, namely, a sin-offering. Surprisingly, the sages argue this point. Although their dispute does not directly involve the defintion of an intentional act, it is relevant to our more general discussion, for the question of whether this act constitutes an unintentional transgression arises precisely because the sages have defined an intentional act so narrowly.

Eliezer reasons that since the act at hand does not fall into the category of an intentional transgression, it must by definition constitute an unintentional one. Therefore, he imposes a sin-offering on the actor (E). But Joshua demurs. He believes it absurd to classify this act as unintentional. After all, from the very outset, the actor intended to do a forbidden act, and did in fact perform one. In Joshua's view, therefore, this act cannot constitute an unintentional sin, and hence the actor need not bring a sin-offering (F). Joshua's postion obviously leads to a logical inconsistency. On the one hand, the actor does not incur liability for an intentional transgression. Yet, on the other hand, he does not incur liability for an unintended transgression either. For Joshua, then, this violation falls neither into the category of an intentional or an unintentional violation. It falls, so to speak, between the cracks. This inconsistency in Joshua's position leads Judah to propose yet a third solution (G-I).[37]

Judah subdivides unintentional acts into two distinct classes. First, there are cases in which the actor sets out to do something that falls within the bounds of the law, but the act he in fact performs constitutes a violation. We have already discussed examples of this type (M. Shab. 12:5, San. 9:2). Second, there are cases like the one under discussion, in which the actor intended to perform a forbidden act. Basing himself on an interpretation of Scripture, Judah argues that only the latter category falls under the rubric of an unintentional violation.

Closer inspection shows that even Judah's position poses certain difficulties. According to Judah, if a person sets out to perform a permitted act but accidentally does a forbidden one, no penalty is incurred, not even a sin-offering. But this view would seem to contradict Scripture itself. According to Leviticus, for example, if a person intends to eat a permitted food and accidentally eats a forbidden food, a sin offering must be brought to the Temple (Lev. 4:1). This complicated dispute throws into sharp relief the lengths to which the framers will go to retain their strict definition of an intentional act. By refusing to classify the case at hand as an intentional transgression, they force themselves into positions that are logically inconsistent or directly in contradiction of Scripture.

In the rule just discussed, the actor did what he or she intended in all respects except one. The person intended an act that involved one type of object, but the act performed involved a different type of object. For this reason, the Mishnah did not label the action intentional, and hence the actor incurred no liability.

Precisely the same point emerges from the following case, which takes up an issue in the system of cultic purity. Here, the sages discuss an Israelite who wants to purify those household vessels that have become cultically unclean through corpse-uncleanness (Num. 19:11, 14-15). The purification of such objects requires a special rite in which the person mixes the ashes of a red-heifer with water. Hyssop is then dipped into this solution and sprinkled over the contaminated objects. In the case at hand, the Israelite intends to sprinkle one type of object but accidentally sprinkles another type.

A.   [If a person] intended (*ntkwwn*) to sprinkle [the solution] on an object which can absorb impurity,

B. but [accidentally] sprinkled an object which cannot absorb impurity--
C. if there is on the hyssop [sufficient liquid to repeat the sprinkling] he may not repeat [the sprinkling with that solution.[38] That is, he may not use what is remaining on the hyssop to sprinkle an object which does require purification. Since the solution came in contact with the wrong type of object, the solution is invalidated, including even the solution remaining on the hyssop.]
D. [If a person intended to sprinkle] an object which cannot absorb impurity,
E. but [accidentally] sprinkled an object which can absorb impurity [that object nonetheless remains in an impure state.]
F. [But] if there is on the hyssop [sufficient liquid to repeat the sprinkling] he may repeat [the act of sprinkling. Since the solution came in contact with the correct type of object, the solution remains valid. Consequently, he can use what remains on the hyssop to sprinkle other objects.]
G. [The Mishnah now provides examples of the two cases listed above: If a person intended to sprinkle] a human being, [an object which can absorb impurity],
H. but [accidentally] sprinkled an animal, [an object which cannot absorb impurity]--
I. if there is on the hyssop [sufficient liquid to repeat the sprinkling] he may not repeat [the act of sprinkling, for the reason specified at C above].
J. [If a person intended to sprinkle] an animal, [an object which cannot absorb impurity],
K. but [accidentally] sprinkled a human being, [an object which can absorb impurity, the person remains impure].
L. [But] if there is on the hyssop [sufficient liquid to repeat the sprinkling] he may repeat [the act of sprinkling, for the reason supplied at F above].

M. Par. 12:3

This case parallels the previous example, in which an Israelite intended to pick one type of fruit but accidentally picked another type. Here an Israelite intends to sprinkle solution on one type of object but accidentally sprinkles another type. As in the previous case, the misfiring of the action deprives the act of its legal consequences: the sprinkling of the solution has no power to purify the object upon which it landed. Even if it landed on an object which requires purification, that object remains unclean (D-E, J-K).[39]

Intended and Resulting Actions: Involving the Same Type of Object

In the previous examples, the act performed invoked no legal consequences because the intended and resulting acts involved different types of objects. But what happens if a person intends the action to involve one type of object, but accidentally performs an act which involves objects of the same type but in a different location? Does this action fall into the category of intentional or unintentional action? The rule at hand examines this problem. It involves a person who places several items requiring purification in a circle around him. He intends to sprinkle the purifying solution over the objects directly in front of him. But as he swings the hyssop stalk, the solution falls on the objects behind him or off to one side. The question is whether those objects become clean.

A. [If a person] intended to sprinkle [the purifying solution on objects] that are in front of him,

B. but he [accidentally] sprinkled it [on objects that were] behind him--

C. and [if a person intended to sprinkle the solution on objects that were] behind him,

D. but he [accidentally sprinkled objects that were] in front of him--

E. his act of sprinkling is invalid. [Hence, the solution does not purify the vessels on which it landed.]

F. [However, if a person intended to sprinkle vessels directly] in front of him,

G. but [accidentally] sprinkled [vessels] on the diagonal,

H. his act of sprinkling is valid, [with the result that those vessels are restored to a pure state].

M. Par. 12:2

Here, the act intended and the act performed are identical according to three of the four criteria the Mishnah considers important. First, the man performed the category of act he intended to perform, that is, sprinkling. Second, the intended action and the action performed produce the same legal consequences, namely, purification of objects. Furthermore, both actions are essentially identical with respect to the Mishnah's third criterion, namely, the object involved. The actor intended to sprinkle vessels requiring purification and in fact sprinkled such vessels. At the same time, the intended and resulting acts are not absolutely identical, because the actor did not sprinkle precisely the vessels he intended to sprinkle.

In determining whether this difference suffices to exclude the action from the category of an intentional act, the Mishnah invokes a new criterion which is applicable only to the rule at hand, namely, the location of the objects. Picture an imaginary line that extends in either direction from the actor's side. This line divides the area in front of the actor from the area behind him. If an Israelite intends to sprinkle vessels on one side of the line, but sprinkles vessels on the other side, the Mishnah labels the act as unintended. Consequently, the act of sprinkling does not purify the objects in question. But if the person sprinkles vessels on the same side of the line as he intended, the action is considered to be intentional, even if the actor did not sprinkle precisely those vessels he had in mind. In this case, therefore, the solution restores the objects to a clean state (F-H).

The sages invoke the criterion of location for an obvious reason. In so doing, they can determine whether the action stemmed wholly from an exercise of human will, or whether other factors intervened in its performance. When a person sprinkles vessels on the opposite side of the line from those that he intended to sprinkle, something must have interfered with his performance. Since he alone did not bring about the results, his act produces no legal effects. If, however, he sprinkles objects slightly off to one side, the sages assume that no extraneous factors intervened. While some liquid did fall off to one side, this is an inevitable consequence of his act. Although in this case the resulting action does not perfectly correspond to the intended action, we may say that the action stems entirely from an exercise of human will. This being so, the solution effectively purifies the objects upon which it lands.

Intended and Resulting Actions: Producing the Same Physical Results

When relevant, the Mishnah compares the intended and resulting actions with respect to a fourth criterion, namely, the physical results involved. It imposes liability for an intentional transgression only if the intended act would have produced the same physical consequences which actually ensued. But if the actor intended an act which would have produced different physical effects, the Mishnah exempts him or her from the penalty for an intentional violation. This point emerges from a set of cases which, from the standpoint of this inquiry, represent the conceptual climax of the Mishnah's discussion.

The Mishnah systematically examines a series of cases in which the intended and resulting actions are identical with respect to all the variables previously considered. These cases involve a person who intends to kill a particular individual by striking him on a specific part of the body. But just as the actor delivers the punch, the victim dodges. As a result, the blow lands on another part of the victim's body and kills him. The framers discuss whether in such cases the actor is liable for the death penalty, the punishment normally invoked for murder.

I. A. [Concerning a person who] intended to strike another person in the gut [with the aim of killing him],[40]
   B. and there was not sufficient force behind the blow to kill the man [had the actor in fact struck him] in the gut
   C. [but the victim dodged, with the result that] the blow struck the victim's heart,
   D. and there was sufficient force behind the blow to kill [the average person] by striking him above the heart,
   E. and the victim died,
   F. the actor is exempt [from the death penalty].

II. A. [Concerning a person who] intended to strike [the victim] above his heart [with the aim of killing him],
   B. and there was enough force behind the blow to kill him [had the blow landed] above the heart,

D. but [the victim dodged with the result that] the blow struck him in the gut,

E. and there was not sufficient force behind [the blow] to kill [the average person] by hitting him in the gut,

F. but the victim died [anyway]--

G. the actor is exempt [from the death penalty].

III. A. [Concerning a person who] intended to strike the adult [standing nearby, with the aim of killing him],

B. and there was not sufficent force behind [the blow] to kill the [average] adult,

C. but [the victim dodged with the result that] the blow struck the child [standing nearby],

D. and there was sufficient force to kill the [average] child,

E. and the child died--

F. [the actor is] exempt [from the death penalty].

IV. A. [Concerning a person who] intended to strike a child, [with the aim of killing him]

B. and there was sufficient force to kill [the average] child,

C. but [the child dodged with the result that] the blow struck an adult,

D. and there was not sufficient force behind the blow to kill the [average] adult,

E. but [the adult] died [anyway]--

F. [the actor] is exempt [from the death penalty].

V. A. But [concerning a person who] intended to strike a person in the gut,

B. and there was sufficient force behind [the blow] to kill [the average person] in the gut,

C. but [the victim dodged with the result that] the blow struck his heart, [and there was enough force behind the blow to kill the average person by striking him above the heart],

D. and the victim died --

E. [the actor] is liable [for the death penalty].

VI. A. [Concerning a person who] intended to strike an adult,

B. and there was enough force behind his blow to kill [the average] adult,

C. but [the victim dodged, with the result that] the blow struck a child, [and there was sufficient force to kill a child]

D. and the child died,

E. [the actor] is liable [for the death penalty].

F. R. Simeon says, "Even in the case of a person who intended to kill this person and [accidentally] killed that person, he is exempt [from the death penalty]."

M. San. 9:2

In these cases, the intended and resulting acts are virtually identical. First, both fall into the same category of action: the actor intended to strike a person and in fact struck a person. Second, the intended act and the act performed invoke the same legal consequences, because murdering a person, whether by striking him in the stomach or heart, invokes the death penalty. Third, both involve precisely the same kind of object (i.e., human beings) and, sometimes, indeed, the same person. To be sure, the blow landed in the wrong place. But that was due not to the misfiring of the action but to the unpredictable movements of the victim.

Although the actor did what he or she intended, the Mishnah does not necessarily impose liability for an intentional transgression. Before labelling the act intentional, the sages consider whether the blow would have produced the desired results had it landed where the actor intended. That is, the Mishnah imposes the penalty for murder only if the blow would have killed the victim had it struck him in the intended spot (I,III, V,VI).

This demonstrates once more how narrowly the Mishnah defines the category of an intentional act. In the mishnaic system, a person can intend to murder another person, and actually cause his or her death, but nonetheless not incur the death penalty! As I previously explained, the sages believe that a person should incur liability only for an act that stems wholly from an exercise of human will. When the act does not correspond perfectly to the actor's intention, the sages assume that other factors must have intervened in the performance of that action. Since the results cannot be attributed exclusively to the actor's will, the sages therefore do not impose the penalty for an intentional transgression.

The Mishnah also invokes a second criterion in determining whether the actor at hand incurs the death penalty. It asks whether the blow was the sole cause of death. If such a blow normally would not kill the average person, the sages assume that other factors, such as the victim's weak constitution, must have contributed to his or her demise (II, IV). This consideration obviously does not contribute to the Mishnah's definition of an intentional action. However, it does confirm the basic thesis at hand, namely, that the Mishnah's overriding interest is in determining whether the results in a given case can be ascribed *entirely* to the person's action.

Intended and Resulting Actions: A Perfect Correspondence

We have focused thus far on cases in which a person's action misfired in one respect or another. In all of these cases, if the actor had been questioned, he or she would have said that the action had gone awry. We now turn our attention to a different type of case. Here, the actor does precisely what he or she intended. At the same time, however, the action produces unintended consequences. For example, suppose a man cuts down a tree for firewood. Now in performing this act, certain consequences may occur which the man did not specifically intend to bring about, for example, he may have destroyed a bird's nest. In this case, were the Israelite questioned, he would insist that he had done what he intended, namely, cutting down a tree. But destroying the bird's nest was unintended because it did not fall within the scope of his initial intention.

Situations like this one raise an interesting problem for the mishnaic system. On the one hand, the actor is the sole cause of the results; other factors obviously did not interfere with the performance of his action. On the other hand, the consequences which occurred were not something the individual intended to accomplish. As we shall now see, the Mishnah imposes legal consequences only for those unintended results which necessarily accompany an action. Since they are intrinsically related to the intended act, they are treated as if they were intended results. By contrast, unintended results which were not inevitable invoke no legal consequences.

The distinction just outlined emerges from the Mishnah's discussion of food purity, a problem we have explored in another connection. As we recall, in mishnaic law water sometimes has the effect of making food substances capable of absorbing impurity. If a person intentionally uses liquid for any purpose, that liquid makes any food on which it falls capable of becoming contaminated. Water which serves no useful purpose cannot make food susceptible of contamination. In the case at hand, the Mishnah discusses a householder who takes a horse to the river to let it drink. After leaving the river, the water from the horse's snout and hooves falls on produce which is nearby. Does this water have the power to make the food susceptible to impurity?

A.   [Concerning] one who leads his animal [to the river] to drink--
B.   the water that clings to its snout is included in [the category] "if water is put." [That is, the water is included in the category of water intentionally put on the horse's snout. Hence, it has the power to make food susceptible to impurity.]
C.   [But the water that clings to] its legs is not included in [the category] "if water is put."
D.   But if [in taking the horse to the river] he intended to wash its legs,
E.   even the water that clings to its legs is included in [the category] "if water is put."

M. Makh. 3:8

Only the water on the animal's snout can make food susceptible to impurity; the water on its hooves cannot. This is because the wetting of the horse's snout is a necessary consequence of letting it drink. Therefore the householder's intention to let the horse drink by definition includes the intention of getting its snout wet. Since wetting the horse's hooves is not an inevitable consequence of letting it drink, this result is not treated as though it were intended. Hence, the water on the horse's hooves cannot affect the status of food. On the other hand, if from the outset the householder plans to rinse the horse's legs, the water that moistens its hooves has been used intentionally. Consequently, it has the power of making food absorb impurity.

The Mishnah develops a similar distinction in the parallel case of a man who bends over to drink from a stream. In the process of drinking, he gets water on his mouth, lips, and forehead. Subsequently this water falls onto the food he is eating. The Mishnah considers whether this liquid renders the food susceptible of contamination.

A. [Concerning] one who bends over to drink [from a river]--

B. the water that clings to his mouth or upper lip is included in [the category] "if water is put." [That is, this water belongs to the category of water which was intentionally used, and hence it can render food susceptible to impurity.]

C. But [water that falls] on his nose, forehead, or beard, is not included in [the category] "if water is put." [That is, the water on these parts of the face does not belong to the category of water which was used intentionally, and hence, it has no power to make food capable of absorbing impurity].

M. Makh. 4:1

Getting one's lips and moustache wet is an inevitable consequence of drinking from a stream. Consequently, the Mishnah treats water on the mouth and lips as liquid that was intentionally used, and therefore it can make food absorb impurity. But since drinking does not necessarily involve getting one's nose or forehead wet, the Mishnah does not regard water that falls on those parts of the face as though the actor had intentionally used it. For this reason, this liquid can not affect the status of food.

It should now be obvious why the Mishnah makes a distinction between necessary and unnecessary consequences. The sages consider this to be another indication of whether human or divine causes are to blame for what happened. Necessary consequences obviously stem from an exercise of that person's will. Although the person did not specifically intend those results, they are the inevitable outcome of what he or she did intend. But unnecessary consequences signify that something unusual happened; the action produced consequences which it does not normally entail. The sages ascribe these results to other factors, perhaps to divine intervention.

Conclusion

We began this section by asking whether the Mishnah imposes liability for something a person did not intend to do. It turns out that the answer to this question is integrally related to the Mishnah's conception of society, on the one hand, and its conception of the divine-human relationship, on the other. This is why the Mishnah sharply distinguishes between the role of intention in cases involving physical damage or injury to human beings and in cases involving infractions of divine law. In tort cases, an actor's intention does not affect the legal outcome. Even if the injury to another's property was unintended, the

Mishnah requires the actor to pay restitution. Therefore, the sages go so far as to impose liability on a person who injures someone by slipping off a roof (M. B.Q. 8:1) or who causes damage when he or she stumbles and falls (M. B.Q. 3:4). In these cases the actor neither intended to cause harm, nor even to perform the action that caused harm. Nonetheless, mishnaic law holds the Israelite responsible for the results. In religious and cultic law, by contrast, the actor's intention almost always plays a decisive role in determining the legal outcome. When a person's cultic transgression was accidental, the sages invoke only the minor penalty of a sin-offering or a fine. For an intentional transgression, the sinner incurs the divine punishment of a premature death.

From the Mishnah's standpoint, then, the responsibility of human beings to each other differs from their responsibility towards God. In societal relations, the results are the most important thing. Even if the actor was well-intentioned, he or she is held responsible for all adverse effects. In the divine-human relationship matters are precisely reversed. Here, the results per se are less significant than the actor's intention in performing the action. This difference, I have argued, depends on the character of the victim in the particular case. When the victim is a human being, a measurable pecuniary loss is sustained, for which compensation must be paid. It makes no difference whether the actor produced the results intentionally or by accident. In religious and cultic law, however, it is God and not a human being who is the victim. In the sages' view, while a transgression of divine law cannot cause God bodily harm, it does constitute a challenge to God's authority. From the divine standpoint, therefore, the actor's intention becomes paramount, because it indicates whether the act signifies a deliberate repudiation of divine will, or merely a momentary lapse in judgment.

To be sure, there are exceptions in both areas of law. Occasionally, even in societal relations, an Israelite produces harm which is not quantifiable. This is true in homicide cases and in cases involving an Israelite who has shamed or humiliated another. In both of these instances, the damage is not measurable. What determines the severity of the offense in these cases, therefore, is the actor's intention. Similarly, in religious law, there are cases in which an Israelite does quantifiable damage to divine property, for example, by misappropriating Temple offerings. As in tort cases, the offender must replace the damaged property, even if transgression was unintentional.

The fact that intention plays a more important role in religious and cultic transgressions than in civil law reveals a qualitative difference between these two areas of law, as seen by the sages. All religious and cultic transgressions, even seemingly minor ones, potentially constitute a repudiation of divine will. Consequently, intention is always a factor in assessing liablity. In societal relations, by contrast, most acts are not violations of a person's dignity or honor, but merely the result of the normal interaction among people in society. In this area of law, therefore, the actor's intention is rarely relevant.

The centrality of intention in religious and cultic law, as we have seen, generates an intriguing philosophical question: what constitutes acting intentionally? In the sages' view, this is no simple question. In many cases, a person does what he intended in one respect but not in another. How similar, then, must the intended and resulting action be in order to classify what the person did as "intentional?" In their view, a person incurs liability or merits reward only if the action results entirely from an exercise of the will. But if other factors caused the action to misfire, the sages do not hold the actor responsible. The Mishnah never explicitly identifies these "other factors." When the results of an accident are beneficial, the Mishnah apparently ascribes that occurrence to God. On the other hand, when a person's action misfires and produces adverse effects, the sages sometimes ascribe the accident to God's intervention, and sometimes to other extraneous factors. In any case, since the action did not result entirely from an exercise of human will, the Mishnah does not treat the act as intentional.

To determine whether a given action invokes legal consequences, therefore, the framers devise a strategy for sorting out the causes of a person's action. Their strategy, as we have seen, involves comparing the actor's intention to what he or she actually did. If the act differs in any respect from the person's intention, they ascribe the blame to extraneous factors. Hence, in such cases, the action produces no legal consequences. But if the intention and action are identical, the sages conclude that the action stemmed wholly from an exercise of human will.

In turning to the following chapter, we find that once the sages determine that an action results entirely from an exercise of human will, a second important question arises: Why did the person perform that act in the first place? In asking this question, the sages want to determine a second aspect of the actor's intention, namely, the person's purpose in performing the action. As we shall now see, an actor's purpose also plays a crucial role in determining the legal outcome in a given case.

Chapter Two

An Actor's Purpose:
Effect on Liability and Reward

When a person performs an action, the Mishnah takes account of the intention with which the act was performed. That is, what goal or purpose did the person have in mind when carrying out that act? In the mishnaic system, an actor's purpose often has a decisive impact in determining whether a given action invokes liability or merits reward. For example, depending upon the actor's purpose the very same action may or may not constitute a transgression. If one performed the action for a purpose which the law forbids, the action invokes liability. But if the person does the same thing with a licit purpose in mind, no liability is incurred. In some cases, however, the Mishnah totally ignores the actor's purpose. In such cases liability is incurred regardless of why the individual performed the act in question. This raises a crucial question: when and why does the Mishnah appeal to an actor's purpose?

Before exploring this problem, we must first understand how the question of the actor's purpose relates to the general topic of intention. In the previous chapter, we examined cases in which the Mishnah asked whether the actor's intention corresponded to the resulting action. In raising this question, the sages wanted to know whether the actor intentionally performed the act in question. That is, did the person do precisely what was intended or did the action misfire in some respect? In asking about an actor's purpose, however, the sages are interested in a different aspect of intention, namely, the intention with which the person acted.

I am here following Hart, who distinguishes between doing something intentionally and doing an action with a specific intention.[1] To illustrate the difference between these two aspects of intention, consider the case of a woman who breaks a bottle. First, we can ask whether she broke the bottle intentionally. That is, was the breaking of the bottle something she meant to do, or something that occurred by accident? To answer this question, we simply compare the woman's intention to the actual results.

Second, we can also ask about the intention with which she broke the bottle. In posing the latter question, we wish to know *why* she acted as she did. For instance, did she intend to fashion a weapon or did she merely desire to remove something stuck inside the bottle? In the discussion to follow, we will call the intention with which a person does something his or her "purpose."[2] To be sure, the boundary between these two aspects of intention is often extremely fluid. In fact, some thinkers consider this dichotomy to be misleading.[3] Nonetheless, I have retained this distinction because it makes sense of a linguistic distinction which we find in the Mishnah itself.

The Mishnah uses a single term, *kavvanah*, to denote either of the two aspects of intention described above. However, the Mishnah distinguishes the two meanings of *kavvanah* by employing the word in different linguistic formulae. In general, when trying to determine whether a person did something intentionally, the Mishnah uses the formula discussed in the previous chapter: "he intended x but did y." This expression indicates that the action misfired in some respect or other. By contrast, when the Mishnah is speaking about a person's purpose, it generally says, "[Concerning an Israelite] who was doing x-- if he intended to do such-and-such, he is liable. But if he intended to do so-and-so, he is not liable." To cite one example, the Mishnah says, "[Concerning an Israelite] who was reading [the *Shema* prayer] aloud from the Torah [scroll]--if he intended [the recitation of the passages to fulfill his duty to pray], he discharges [his obligation]. If not, he does not discharge [his obligation] (M. Ber. 2:1)." Alternatively, the Mishnah sometimes uses this formula: "An Israelite may do such and such provided that he does not intend to do so and so." For example, the Mishnah says "[On the Sabbath day] a person may break a jar in order to eat the cakes of figs within, provided that he does not intend to produce a container (M. Shab. 22:3)." In both of these examples, the actor obviously performed the act in question intentionally. In the first case, he intended to recite the words of the prayer. In the second example, he intended to break the jar. In these cases, therefore, when the Mishnah refers to the actor's intention, it is referring to the purpose of the act in question. The Mishnah wants to know the Israelite's purpose in reciting the prayer or in breaking the jar. We see, therefore, that the Mishnah distinguishes between the two conceptions of intention by employing the term *kavvanah* in different linguistic formulae. In the present inquiry, we focus on those cases in which the term *kavvanah* designates an actor's purpose.

The Role of an Actor's Purpose in the Mishnaic System

The Mishnah appeals to an actor's purpose to determine whether a given action merits reward or invokes punishment. The rule to follow, for example, illustrates the importance of an actor's purpose in determining whether he has discharged a religious obligation. Mishnaic law requires Israelite men to pray to God, by reciting certain scriptural passages known as the *Shema* (Deut. 6:4-9, 11:13-21, Num. 15:37-41). Men must recite this prayer twice daily, once in the morning and again in the evening. The case at hand involves an Israelite who is reading the Scriptures aloud for the purpose of study. When the time comes to recite the *Shema*, he happens to be reciting the very passages that comprise this prayer.[4] Does this recitation fulfill his duty to pray? The answer, as we shall see, depends upon his purpose in reciting the words of the prayer.

A. [Concerning an Israelite] who was reading aloud [the passages from the Torah scroll that comprise the *Shema* prayer when] the [appropriate] time arrived [for the recitation of the *Shema* prayer]--
B. if he intended (*kwwn lbw*) [his recitation of the passages to fulfill his duty to pray] he has discharged [his obligation].
C. But if he did not [intend the reading of the passages to fulfill his duty to pray, but rather read the passages solely with the intention of studying them] he has not discharged [his obligation, even though he actually recited the words of the prayer].

M. Ber. 2:1

Here, the actor's purpose determines whether the recitation of the scriptural passages fulfills his religious duty to pray. If he recites the passages with the specific intention of discharging his obligation to pray to God,[5] he has fulfilled his duty (B). If he does not have this purpose in mind, he has not discharged his obligation (C). By taking account of the actor's purpose, the Mishnah determines whether the act signifies compliance with divine will. Performing an act with the intention of fulfilling a religious duty indicates the actor's willingness to obey God's law. But if he performs the very same act without specifically intending to fulfill divine law, his act does not constitute an acknowledgment of God's sovereignty. On the contrary, he probably performed that act out of conformity to social pressure or by sheer force of habit.

An actor's purpose also plays a crucial role in determining whether his or her action constitutes a transgression of divine law. The following rule exemplifies this point. The Mishnah discusses the scriptural prohibition against wearing a garment woven from linen and wool (Lev. 19:19, Deut. 22:11). In Scripture, such garments represent a violation of divine law, because the interweaving of animal and vegetable products, such as linen and wool, mixes two categories that God intended to remain separate.[6] The Mishnah takes Scripture literally when it prohibits "wearing" such a garment.[7] In mishnaic law, a transgression occurs only when a person "wears" the garment, that is, when he or she employs it as clothing. If, by contrast, the garment is put on for some other purpose, such as modeling, the act does not constitute a transgression.

A. Clothes salesmen may sell [garments of linen and wool] in the normal manner, [that is, by modeling them on their own person].
B. [This is the case] provided that they do not intend (*mtkwwn*) on a hot day [for the garments to serve as protection] against the sun,

C. and [provided that] on rainy days, [they do not intend the garments to serve as protection] from the rain.

M. Kil. 9:5

In this rule, the actor's purpose determines whether putting on a garment of mixed weave constitutes a transgression of divine law. If one puts on such a garment for the purpose of selling it, this does not constitute a violation of the law, because the actor is "modeling" rather than "wearing" it (A). If, however, the garment is intended to protect the wearer from the elements, it is being employed as clothing and hence violates the injunction against "wearing" a garment of mixed weave (B-C). In this case, the actor's purpose plays a role analogous to its role in the previous law. There, the Mishnah appealed to the man's purpose to decide whether his action signified his compliance with divine will. Here, the actor's purpose determines whether the act constitutes a repudiation of divine will. By having in mind a purpose which the law forbids, one obviously flouts God's authority. But if the very same act is performed with a licit purpose in mind, the actor has not spurned God's sovereignty.

The Two Aspects of Intention: A Comparison

Having discussed the role of an actor's purpose in the Mishnah, we need now relate what we have found to the findings of the previous chapter. Specifically, what is the relationship between the two aspects of intention which the Mishnah defines as important?

As previously discussed, the Mishnah distinguishes between doing something intentionally and doing an act with a specific purpose. Let us recall the difference between these two types of intention by referring to the case just considered. Here, the salesman obviously performed the act intentionally, because the act of donning the garment corresponded in every respect to the intention he had formulated. If he were questioned, he would claim to have done precisely what he intended, because no unanticipated consequences occurred. Having established that the man donned the garment intentionally, we can ask about a second aspect of his intention, namely, his purpose or reason for putting on the clothing. Was it for the sake of modeling or to protect him from the elements?

With this distinction in mind, we see that the two aspects of intention serve different functions in the mishnaic system. In the previous chapter, we found that the Mishnah compares the intended and resulting actions to one another in order to determine the severity of the punishment. When one performs an act intentionally (i.e., when the act and intention correspond in every detail) one incurs the severe penalty of a premature death. But if what happens is unintentional (i.e., the act misfires in some respect), the actor only incurs a minor penalty of a sin-offering or fine.

The laws considered in this chapter show that an actor's purpose serves a different function. It determines whether or not the action constitutes a violation at all. For example, in the case previously discussed, the Israelite's purpose in donning the garment determines whether the act is a transgression. The law permits him to don a garment of mixed weave as long as his purpose is to model the garment. But if his purpose is to wear the clothing for protection, donning the garment constitutes a transgression. The following diagram illustrates the relationship between these aspects of intention:

Performing an Action Intentionally or Not

	A. intended precisely what occurred	B. did not intend what occurred
Purpose in Doing an Action:		
I. licit purpose	no liability	no liability
II. illicit purpose	divine punishment of premature death	sin-offering

This chart shows that an actor's purpose plays the decisive role in determining liability. The Mishnah turns to the actor's purpose to determine whether a religious transgression has occurred. If the purpose is considered legitimate, no penalty is incurred (I A, B). If the law defines the purpose as illicit, the Mishnah always imposes a punishment. However, the severity of the punishment depends on the second aspect of intention, namely whether the actor intentionally did what in fact occurred (II A,B).[8]

With respect to the issue of intention, the Mishnah presents a theory which is the converse of that found in Anglo-American law. In Anglo-American law, an actor can only be convicted of a crime if the act was done intentionally. The severity of the punishment depends on the actor's purpose. In Hart's words,

> In English law and in most other legal systems intention, or something like it, is relevant at two different points. It is relevant first at the stage before conviction when the question is 'Can this man be convicted of this crime?'-even if, in fact, he will not actually be punished. At this stage...it is normally, though not quite always, sufficient, and normally, though not quite always, necessary that the accused did the particular act forbidden by law, and did it intentionally or with something like intention...Intention is also relevant when the stage of conviction is past, and the question is 'how severely is the accused to be punished?' This is the stage of sentencing, as distinguished from conviction. Sometimes the legislature will mark off greater maximum penalty for things done with a certain intention than for the same thing done without that intention.[9]

By Hart's account, Anglo-American law only convicts a person if that person intentionally performed the act in question. But in order to determine the severity of the punishment, Anglo-American law appeals to the intention or purpose with which the action was performed. The fact that mishnaic law differs from English law indicates that the Mishnah's theory of intention is not the only one possible. Rather, it represents a choice among various possibilities. We need to ask, therefore, why the sages adopted this scheme in particular.

It is easy to explain why the severity of the punishment depends on whether the act was done intentionally. The Mishnah inherits this view directly from Scripture. According to Scripture, a less severe punishment is invoked for an unintentional act than for an intentional one (Lev. 4:1-2, 27-28, Ex. 21:12-13, Num. 35:16-27, Deut. 19:4-13). Consequently, this role of intention was predetermined by Scripture. However, in the legal sections of the Pentateuch, and especially the priestly rules of Leviticus, an actor's purpose plays little or no role in determining legal consequences.[10] The levitical rules, among others, espouse a mechanistic view of human action. By this I mean that an action produces legal effects regardless of the actor's purpose. If, for example, a priest follows the proper sacrificial procedure, the act of sacrifice is valid no matter what the purpose in offering it. Likewise, an actor's purpose plays no role in determining whether the action constitutes a violation. A person who puts on a garment made from linen and wool transgresses divine law, irrespective of his or her purpose in donning the garment (Lev. 19:19, Deut. 22:11).[11] We could adduce many other examples to prove that the scriptural laws, which provide the foundation for the mishnaic system, ascribe relatively little importance to an actor's purpose.

The emphasis on an actor's purpose, therefore, constitutes the Mishnah's own distinctive contribution. Consequently, it is significant that the Mishnah gives an actor's purpose the decisive role in determining liability. In effect, this means that the Mishnah's sages want to give intention a much greater role than Scripture allowed. Biblical law limited the role of intention to determining the severity of the punishment. The Mishnah, however, makes the actor's intention a key factor in determining whether or not any violation has occurred at all! By drawing attention to an aspect of intention which was not important in Scriptural law, therefore, the Mishnah found a way to give intention a more dramatic role in determining liability.

The mishnaic emphasis on an actor's purpose reveals one of the basic tendencies of the system as a whole. The Mishnah seeks to reformulate the biblical heritage, especially those biblical conceptions which derive from the priestly writers. The Mishnah clearly owes a substantial intellectual debt to the ideas of the priests. This is evidenced, on the one hand, by the Mishnah's interest in the same range of topics as the priestly writers, namely, the laws of purity, and the Temple cult, and on the other hand, by the Mishnah's preoccupation with issues of classification and taxonomy, both hallmarks of the priestly strand of

Scripture. Nonetheless, the Mishnah critiques the priestly conceptions by making human intention much more important than the priests intended. The stress on intention, moreover, has the effect of relativizing the priestly conceptions. I refer to this as "relativizing" because the Mishnah has a more flexible understanding of the world. For example, in Leviticus, the same kind of act always falls into the same category. It either constitutes a transgression or permitted act. But in the Mishnah, the classification of an act as a transgression depends on the actor's purpose. Consequently, the Mishnah conceives of the possibility that the same movements performed on two different occasions can be a transgression in one case and entirely legitimate in another. In this sense, the Mishnah has a more flexible conception of reality. No action has a fixed status. Whether or not it counts as a violation depends on why the person performed the act in question.

The mishnaic tendency to relativize the priestly rules of Leviticus will also be evident in Part II of this study. Specifically, we shall see that the Mishnah makes the status of various objects dependent upon how people intend to use them. For example, in mishnaic law human intention can have the dramatic effect of determining whether a given object can become contaminated by impurity. The idea that intention can define the status of things also represents a mishnaic innovation and constitutes the same sort of relativizing tendency described above. According to Leviticus, human intention has no role in altering the classification of things, and consequently, the status of objects is fixed and predetermined. In adopting the levitical scheme of classification, however, the Mishnah makes intention a decisive factor in determining the category to which an object belongs. Consequently, the Mishnah allows for the possibility that identical objects can fall into different categories because people have intended to use them for different purpose. By emphasizing the category of intention, therefore, the Mishnah has substantially altered the conceptions embedded in the priestly laws. As we shall now see, however, the Mishnah may well have derived its stress on intention from another strand of biblical thought.

The Emphasis on an Actor's Purpose: The Biblical Antecedents of the Mishnah's Theory

I suggested above that the biblical laws which provide the foundation for the mishnaic system do not place any importance on the purpose of an action. Nonetheless, linguistic evidence suggests that the Mishnah may have been influenced by another stream of thought within biblical literature. The mishnaic word for an actor's purpose, namely, *kavvanah*, derives from two biblical idioms, "to prepare (or direct) one's heart" (*hkyn lb*) or "to be steadfast" (*nkwn lb*), which appear in a variety of biblical sources, such as the Psalms, the prophetic writings, and Chronicles.[12] In particular, we find a striking resemblance between several pericopae in the Mishnah and the following passage from I Sam. 7:3, possibly the work of the Deuteronomist:[13]

And Samuel said to all the House of Israel,
"If you mean to return to the Lord with all your heart,
you must remove the alien gods and the Ashtaroth from your midst
and *direct your heart* (*hkynw lbbkm*) to the Lord
and serve Him alone."

This writer, like other biblical authors, uses the word "heart" to denote what we refer to as the mind, namely, the seat of the intellect.[14] By instructing the people to "direct their heart" to the Lord, this author emphasizes the importance of a person's thoughts, attitudes, and beliefs in the divine-human relationship. Living in accordance with the divine will requires not only disposing of one's idols but focusing one's mind on God.

The Mishnah not only makes a similar point but in fact employs the identical idiom to express its view. In the following pericope, for example, the Mishnah claims that a person does not fulfill the religious obligation of praying to God, unless he or she specifically "directs the heart" towards God.

A. [If an Israelite] was riding on an ass [when the time arrived for saying The Prayer],
B. he must dismount [and turn towards the Temple in Jerusalem while reciting the prayer].
C. But if he cannot dismount [because, for example, he has no one to hold the ass,] he must turn his head about [so that he faces toward the Temple, and then he may recite the prayer].
D. But if he [also] cannot turn his head about [because he must keep his eye on the road], he must [at least] direct his heart (*kwwn lbw*) towards the chamber of the Holy of Holies [i.e., the room in the Temple considered to be God's dwelling place].

M. Ber. 4:5

The resemblance between this case and the passage from I Samuel 7:3 is unmistakable. The Mishnah, as I said, uses the same idiom as the writer of the scriptural passage, namely, "directing the heart (mind)" towards God. Moreover, for the Mishnah's framers, as for the biblical author, an individual's thoughts assume a critical role in the evaluation of his or her commitment to God. Not only must one recite the words of the prayer, but one must focus one's attention on God while doing so. The following case, employing a slightly different idiom, makes this point even more explicit. Here, the Mishnah considers whom God favors more, a person who dedicates an expensive offering or one who donates an inexpensive one. The Mishnah concludes that from the divine standpoint, the person's thoughts matter more than the pecuniary value of the offering.

A. [The fact that Scripture describes both expensive and inexpensive offerings] as a "pleasing odor to God" (Lev. 1:9, 17; 2:2),

B.   indicates that [in God's view] there is no difference between a person who gives [a] more [valuable object] and a person who gives [a] less [valuable one],

C.   provided that the person directs his mind (*ykwwn d*^{c}*tw*) to heaven.

M. Men. 13:11

The Mishnah maintains that God subjects a person's thoughts to close scrutiny. An offering creates "a pleasing odor" to the Lord only if one's mind is directed toward heaven. By implication, if one thinks about something else, the offering would not smell as sweet. These pericopae display both linguistic and conceptual similarities to the scriptural passage quoted above. Of course, on this basis alone, we cannot claim that sages actually derived their emphasis on an actor's purpose from this particular biblical passage. But at the very least, it suggests that the Mishnah carries forward the biblical stream of thought that ascribes importance to the thoughts and intentions of human beings.

The Mishnah, therefore, represents a synthesis of two tendencies within the biblical tradition. On the one hand, the framers of the Mishnah adopt the levitical emphasis on sanctification of human life through adherence to laws of purity and observance of the Temple cult, a system in which proper conduct, not intention, serves as the most important measure of a person's religious commitment. On the other hand, the sages also absorb into their system the biblical tendency that regards human intention as an important dimension in the divine-human relationship. This insight takes us a long way toward understanding the character of the mishnaic document. The Mishnah essentially brings together two streams of thought which, in the biblical writings, were not only unrelated to one another, but were sometimes perceived as being in conflict. The Mishnah's framers, however, do not regard the combination of these elements problematic at all. On the contrary, they actually delight in exploring the issues generated by introducing intention as an important category in cultic law. As we shall now see, one question in particular looms large in Mishnah's discussion: when does the actor's purpose produce legal effects and when does it not?

When and Why an Actor's Purpose Matters

In any given system of rules, an actor's purpose may play a more or less important role. Some systems may appeal to an actor's purpose routinely. Others may consider the actor's purpose relevant only in offences which are particularly heinous. This brings us to the critical question of the present inquiry: under what circumstances does the Mishnah take account of an actor's purpose? An examination of the Mishnah's rules reveals that the Mishnah always takes account of an actor's purpose; but sometimes it appeals to the purpose the actor actually had in mind, whereas at other times it examines the nature of the action and imputes a purpose to the actor. At the very outset, therefore, we must distinguish between two types of purposes. First, we can speak about an actor's subjective intention, that is, how would he or she answer the question, "Why did you do that?" Second, we can speak about the purpose an observer would ascribe to an actor on the basis of observed behavior. That is, if a bystander were to observe the act in question, what would he or she think the actor was trying to accomplish? In many cases, the purpose an actor has in mind differs from the purpose that a bystander would ascribe.

A well-known biblical story illustrates this possibility. Hannah was distraught over not having children, and so in despair, she called on God to help her conceive. Eli, a priest, happened to be observing her and misinterpreted her action.

> As she kept on praying before the Lord, Eli watched her mouth. Now Hannah was praying in her heart; only her lips moved, but her voice could not be heard. So Eli thought she was drunk. Eli said to her, "How long will you make a drunken spectacle of yourself? Sober up!" And Hannah replied, "Oh no, my lord! I am a very unhappy woman. I have drunk no wine or other strong drink, but I have been pouring out my heart to the Lord. Do not take your maidservant for a worthless woman; I have only been speaking all this time out of my great anguish and distress (I Samuel 1:12-16)."

In this case, Hannah's subjective intention differed from the purpose Eli ascribed to her. He thought she was mumbling in a drunken stupor, when in fact she was praying to God. The potential conflict between an actor's subjective intention and the intention imputed to him or her raises an important problem for the Mishnah. What determines the legal outcome, a person's actual purpose or the purpose a bystander would ascribe on the basis of the actor's behavior? The answer, as we shall now see, varies according to circumstance.

It turns out that all the cases in which the Mishnah takes account of an actor's subjective purpose[15] have one thing in common: they involve situations in which the person's action supports alternative interpretations.[16] For example, suppose a person were to break a bottle. From the action alone we would not know whether the individual intends to produce a weapon or merely to remove something stuck inside the bottle. In cases such as this, the Mishnah takes into account the purpose the actor actually had in mind. However, an ambiguity in a person's action does not by itself ensure that the Mishnah will care about what is on the actor's mind. The uncertainty must also involve a problem of determining whether the actor has fulfilled or violated a law. Imagine for a moment that the individual who broke the bottle lived in a society in which the making of weapons was forbidden. If so, the ambiguity involved in breaking a bottle would make it impossible to determine whether the actor had transgressed. If the actor broke the bottle in order to produce a weapon, he obviously disobeyed the law. But if he had a different purpose in mind, breaking the bottle would not constitute a transgression. The Mishnah, then, takes account of an actor's subjective intention 1) when his or her act alone does not reveal a self-evident purpose, and 2) when there is a question of whether the act constitutes a transgression of divine law.

When the purpose of an action appears self-evident, however, the Mishnah pays no attention to the actor's subjective purpose. Consequently, if in Israelite society a particular action normally serves a single purpose, the Mishnah automatically imputes that purpose to anyone who performs that act. For example, the sages claim that in Israelite society, men normally go to synagogue to pray. Consequently, when an individual recites a prayer in a synagogue, the sages reasonably assume he does so for the purposes of prayer. In such a case, the framers automatically credit the Israelite with having fulfilled his duty to pray, even though he may have had some other purpose in mind, for instance, to learn the prayer by heart. This is because the sages take the normal interpretation people assign to a given action more seriously than the subjective interpretation of the actor. In what follows, I will show how the theory set out above is actually implied by the Mishnah's rules.

The Importance of an Actor's Subjective Purpose in Cases Involving Ambiguity

I argued above that the Mishnah takes account of the purpose an actor has in mind only when the action supports alternative interpretations. This point emerges clearly from the following case which involves the injunction to rest on the Sabbath day. Mishnaic law forbids Israelites to perform on the Sabbath day any act of creativity, such as making a pot, writing, or sewing. Conversely, the law permits the performance of destructive acts like tearing or ripping, as long as the act will not ultimately serve a constructive purpose (M. Shab.13:3).[17] For example, an Israelite may not rip the seams of his or her garment in order to resew it, for here, the ripping of the seams constitutes the first step in making the repair. Since the act serves a constructive end, it transgresses the Sabbath law.

In the case at hand, an Israelite breaks the neck of an earthenware jar in order to remove the dried figs which are stuck inside. Is this a transgression of the Sabbath law? The answer, as we shall see, depends upon the purpose the actor had in mind. If the jar was broken solely for the sake of eating the figs, then no transgression was committed. In this case, the breaking of the jar would be purely destructive. If, however, the intention was to remove the figs and then use the jar as a container, the act constitutes a violation.

A. [On the Sabbath day] a person may break a jar in order to eat the cakes of figs within,

B. provided that he does not intend *(sl' ytkwwn)* to produce a container. [In breaking the neck of the jar, the householder inevitably produces a usable bowl from the bottom half of the jar. This constitutes a transgression only if he intended to produce this constructive result. But if he only intended to eat the figs, no violation has occurred.]

M. Shab. 22:3

According to the Mishnah, breaking a jar is an ambiguous action. People either want to gain access to the contents, or they wish to make the pot functional again, by removing what is stuck inside. It is this ambiguity which induces the sages to take account of the actor's subjective purpose. The law at hand, therefore, illustrates two important points. First, it shows that the Mishnah appeals to a person's subjective intention only when the act in question is equivocal. Second, it indicates that a person's action is considered ambiguous when it serves more than one purpose against the background of the norms which are assumed to exist in Israelite society.

The same principles also apply to cases involving the fulfillment of a religious duty. The Mishnah takes account of an actor's subjective purpose when the action supports alternative interpretations. This point emerges from the following rule, which concerns the religious obligations to hear the ram's horn blown on the New Year's Day and to hear the Scroll of Esther read on the Festival of Purim. Normally, Israelites fulfill these obligations by going to the synagogue. In what follows, the Mishnah discusses cases in which an Israelite happens to be passing by the synagogue on Purim or on New Year's Day, when someone is reading the Scroll or blowing the ram's horn. In this situation, the actor's subjective intention plays a decisive role in determining whether or not the religious obligation has been fulfilled.

A. [Concerning] a person who was passing behind a synagogue,
B. or [as regards a person] whose house adjoins the synagogue,
C. and [on the New Year's Day] he heard the sounding of the ram's horn,
D. or [on the Festival of Purim he heard] the reading of the scroll of [Esther],
E. if he intended (*kwwn lbw*) [to fulfill his obligation to hear the blowing the ram's horn, or to hear the reading of the scroll of Esther],
F. he has discharged [his duty].
G. [But] if he did not [intend to fulfill his obligation],
H. he has not discharged [his duty].
I. [This is the case] even though this person heard [the ram's horn, or the reading of the scroll] and that person heard [precisely the same thing],
J. This person [fulfills his obligation because he specifically] intended [to do so and the [other] person [does not fulfill his obligation because he] did not intend [to do so].

M. R.H. 3:7

This rule illustrates how the sages assign importance to an actor's subjective intention when an ambiguity exists in the situation. If an Israelite is walking by a synagogue (A) or living next to one (B) when he hears the ram's horn or the

Scroll, it is unclear whether he intends to fulfill his obligation. Perhaps he has no interest in the sounds emanating from the synagogue, or even finds them a nuisance. The ambiguity in the action induces the Mishnah to lay stress on the purpose the actor has in mind.[18] This rule implies, moreover, that the converse is equally true: when a person performs the requisite religious act in an unambiguous way, - for example, if he hears the blowing of the ram's horn while in the synagogue - the sages would disregard his actual intention. Since under these circumstances the Israelite would appear to be fulfilling his duty, the Mishnah would credit him with having done so.

In the case just discussed, an ambiguity arose because the Israelite performed the requisite religious act in an unusual place.[19] Sometimes, however, an ambiguity arises because an Israelite performs an act in an atypical fashion. This point emerges from a case we have already considered in another context. The Mishnah discusses the obligation of Israelites to recite the *Shema*, a prayer composed of several Scriptural passages. Normally, Israelites recite this prayer by heart. But in the case at hand, a person reads the prayer from a Torah scroll:

A. [Concerning an Israelite] who was reading aloud from the Torah [scroll] [the passages which comprise the *Shema* prayer, when] the [appropriate] time commenced for the recitation [of the *Shema* prayer]--

B. if he intended (*kwwn lbw*) [his recitation of the passages to fulfill his duty to pray] he discharges [his obligation].

C. But if he did not [intend the reading of the passages to fulfill his duty to pray, but rather read them solely with the intention of studying them], he does not discharge [his obligation, even though he actually recited the words of the prayer].

M. Ber. 2:1

Once more the Israelite's action is equivocal. Since he recites the *Shema* prayer from a Torah scroll, it is unclear whether he is merely studying Scripture or whether he is praying. Both interpretations are equally plausible. Since his action does not speak for itself, the actor's subjective intention becomes decisive. Consequently, the Mishnah credits him with having fulfilled his obligation only if he specifically forms the intention of praying.

Sometimes ambiguity arises because in Israelite society a given act serves more than one purpose. This point emerges from the following rule which concerns the obligation to hear the Scroll of Esther read aloud on the festival of Purim. A person may fulfill this obligation either by reading the scroll himself or by hearing someone else read it. But what happens if an Israelite is copying or proofreading the Scroll of Esther, or expounding it to students? Since in each of these cases he actually reads the Scroll, does this reading fulfill his obligation? The answer depends upon the purpose he has in mind.

A.   [Concerning a man who] was copying the scroll, [or] expounding it [to his students], or proofreading it [for scribal errors]--

B.   if he [also] intended (*kwwn lbw*) [to fulfill his obligation to read the scroll], he discharges [that obligation].

C.   But if he did not [have this intention in mind], he does not [discharge his obligation].

M. Meg. 2:2

The ambiguity in the Israelite's action once again explains why his subjective intention is important. Although he actually performs the obligatory act of reading the scroll on the festival, one cannot be certain that he intends to fulfill his religious duty. For here, the very same action also serves another purpose, for example, proofreading. Consequently, the sages do not automatically credit the actor with having fulfilled his religious obligation. Instead, they lay emphasis on the person's actual intention. In order to discharge his duty, therefore, he must specifically intend for the reading of the Scroll to fulfill his religious obligation.

What happens if the action in question is unequivocal? Suppose, for example, when reciting the scroll on Purim, a man was not copying, proofreading, or expounding it. Here, from his action alone, it would appear that his intention was to discharge his religious duty. For why else would he read the scroll on Purim? As we shall now see, the Mishnah claims that as long as a person appears to be fulfilling a religious duty, the actual purpose is irrelevant.

A.   A person who reads [the scroll of Esther] piecemeal or [who] dozes off [while reading the scroll] discharges [his duty to hear the Scroll].

M. Meg. 2:2

This case provides a stunning contrast to the ones previously considered. Here, the Israelite discharges his obligation even though he dozes off! In contrast to the cases cited above, the Mishnah here does not require the Israelite to specifically formulate an intention to fulfill his religious duty. This proves what we have merely inferred from previous laws. When a person appears to be carrying out a religious duty, he need not actually have that purpose in mind. In this case, because the man enters the synagogue on the Festival of Purim and reads from the scroll, one may reasonably assume that he intends to fulfill his religious duty of hearing the Scroll of Esther. Against the background of the norms presumed to exist in Israelite society, no other interpretation is plausible. Although he dozes or lets his mind wander to other matters, he is credited with having fulfilled his religious duty. The Mishnah, therefore, automatically ascribes to an actor the purpose the action appears to serve.

The following familiar rules make essentially the same point, although they do not deal directly with the question of the actor's purpose. Specifically, the

Mishnah discusses whether an Israelite needs to focus his or her attention on God while reciting a set of benedictions known as "The Prayer."

I. A. [Concerning an Israelite] who was riding on an ass [and the time arrived for saying The Prayer],

    B. he must dismount [and turn towards the Temple in Jerusalem while reciting the prayer].

    C. But, if he cannot dismount [because, for example, he is in a hurry], he must turn his head about [so that he faces towards the Temple, and then he may recite the prayer].

    D. But if he [also] cannot turn his head about [because he must keep his eye on the road] he must [at least] focus his attention (*kwwn lbw*) towards the Chamber of the Holy of Holies [i.e., the room in the Temple considered to be God's dwelling place].

                                        M. Ber. 4:5

II. A. [Concerning an Israelite] who was sitting in a boat, in a wagon, or in a raft [all cases in which he dare not stand to face the Temple, lest he capsize or fall off the wagon]--

    B. he must focus his attention (*kwwn lbw*) on the chamber of the Holy of Holies.

                                        M. Ber. 4:6

III. A. One may stand to recite The Prayer only in a respectful manner.

    B. The pious of previous [generations] would wait one hour [before] praying, in order to focus their attention (*kwwnw lbn*) on the Omnipresent.

    C. Even [if] a king would ask [one of these pious men] about his well-being [while the pious man was reciting The Prayer, he] would not answer him.

    D. And even [if] a snake was curled around his ankle [thus threatening his life, the pious man] would not interrupt [his praying].

                                        M. Ber. 5:1

The Mishnah requires an Israelite to concentrate on his or her prayers only when the action is equivocal. This is why a man who remains seated when he says The Prayer must focus his attention on God. Since he is sitting and not standing, it is unclear whether he is praying or merely muttering under his breath (I D, II A-B). In this rule, therefore, focusing one's attention on God serves as a substitute for the physical act of facing the Temple in Jerusalem. By contrast, if a man stands up and faces towards Jerusalem during his prayers, it is obvious that he is praying. Under such circumstances, therefore, the Mishnah does not require the Israelite to focus his attention on God, because his action itself is unequivocal (I A-C). Even if this man let his mind wander to other things, he would still discharge his duty to pray. In the Mishnah's view, therefore, persons who always focus their attention on God when praying go beyond the call of duty. Indeed, only pious men of former generations were actually capable of such supererogatory effort (III B-D).

In sum, the Mishnah takes account of an actor's subjective purpose when the act in question bears more than one plausible interpretation in the context of Israelite society. When the act is unequivocal, however, the sages completely ignore the purpose the actor has in mind. To understand, therefore, when and why the Mishnah discounts an actor's subjective intention, we need to know what makes an action unambiguous.

When Subjective Intention is Irrelevant: The Importance of Social Norms in Evaluating Action

We saw above that the Mishnah treats an action as ambiguous when it bears alternative interpretations in the context of Israelite society. Sometimes, however, an action normally serves only one distinctive purpose. When this is the case, the Mishnah considers the act to be unequivocal. Consequently, it routinely imputes to anyone who performs that act the purpose that it normally serves in Israelite society. Thus if a given action x normally serves purpose y, the Mishnah automatically ascribes purpose y to anyone who does x. We thus find that in the Mishnah, the norms of society provide the definitive interpretation of human action. In allotting reward and punishment, the Mishnah imputes to a person the normal meaning of the act, even though he or she may have had some other purpose in mind.

The fact that the Mishnah takes account of norms in evaluating actions has important implications for the conception of moral conduct in the mishnaic system. In the Mishnah, it is imperative that individuals take account of norms before embarking upon a course of action. Otherwise, the sages might assign to them a purpose that did not actually motivate the act in question. For example, suppose a person performs a given action with an idiosyncratic purpose in mind. The sages will impute to that person the normal meaning of his or her act. As we shall see, this sometimes creates an interesting paradox. In some cases, the sages hold a person liable for transgressing the law even though he or she did not have in mind a purpose which the law forbids.

The theory outlined above emerges from a series of cases concerning Israelites suspected of violating a law. In each case the Mishnah determines whether an Israelite has transgressed by taking account of the normal meaning of the act in question. The first rule involves the mishnaic prohibition against performing routine tasks on the intermediate days of Passover and Tabernacles. These festivals last for seven and eight days respectively; the first and last constituting sacred occasions during which Israelites must cease all their labors (Lev. 23:5-8, 33-34). The intermediate days are regarded as "minor festivals." On these days of lesser sanctity, Israelites may not perform routine work, but may carry out any task that is considered urgent. For example, if a householder is afraid of burglars, he may repair the lock on his door. But if he regards this as a routine task, he may not repair the lock.

In the cases to follow, the sages consider whether various types of activities fall into the category of urgent or routine tasks. As we shall see, if the action in question normally serves a routine purpose, the sages automatically impute that purpose to the actor at hand. Conversely, when the same action may serve either a routine or urgent purpose, the framers appeal to the actual intention of the actor.

I. A. [On the intermediate days of a festival Israelites] may not bring [home repaired] pots from a craftsman's workshop.
    B. [But] if one fears they [will be stolen from the craftsman's workshop during the festival, when the craftsman is not there to guard them],
    C. he may transfer them to another [protected] courtyard [but he may not take them home. If he puts the pots into a guarded courtyard, it is obvious that he is afraid of robbery. Hence his action falls into the category of an urgent task, and is therefore permitted. If, by contrast, he took them home, it would be obvious that he collected them for routine use at home. Hence, taking them home is forbidden on the intermediate days of the festivals.]

M. M.Q. 2:4

II. A. [Concerning the parts of a door such as] the hinge, the socket, the beam, the lock, or the key that were broken [before the festival]--
    B. a [householder] may fix them during the intermediate days of the festival, [if he is afraid of thieves. Since in this case the repair is urgent, it does not constitute a violation of the law.]
    C. [This is the case] provided that he does not intentionally (ykwwn) [postpone] its repair until the festival. [If he purposefully sets aside the work to be done on the festival, then he clearly regards it as routine labor, and not as an emergency. Hence, he is forbidden to do the work.]

M. M.Q. 1:10

III. A. [On the intermediate days of a festival] a person may bring in his produce [from the field] because thieves [might steal it].
     B. And he may remove his flax from the steeping solution so that it does not rot [through excessive soaking. Since both of these tasks are urgent, they do not constitute transgressions.]
     C. [He may perform these acts] provided that he does not intentionally (ykwwn) [postpone] working on it until the festival. [If he purposefully delayed the work, it is obvious he does not regard the tasks as urgent. Hence, they constitute routine work which is forbidden].
     D. But in either case, if he intentionally (kwwn) [delayed] working on them until the festival, [he may not carry out these tasks, even though the flax or produce] may perish [or be stolen. The fact that the person delays the work indicates that he does not regard the task as urgent.]

M. M.Q. 2:3

The first case illustrates how the Mishnah imputes to an actor the normal meaning of his or her action. The Mishnah takes for granted that most householders reclaim their repaired pots because they need to use them. According to societal norms, then, taking home one's pots constitutes a routine task, which violates the law against working on minor festivals. Consequently, the Mishnah holds liable anyone who carries home repaired pottery from the craftsman, even if his or her purpose was to prevent the pottery from being stolen (I A-C). We see, therefore, that when a clearly defined norm exists, the actual intention of the actor is completely irrelevant to the evaluation of his or her action.

Many acts, such as repairing a door (II A-C), gathering the crop (III A, C-D), and removing flax from steeping (III B-D), are ambiguous. Sometimes these tasks comprise the householder's daily routine, whereas at other times they may represent emergency measures, the purpose of which is to avert severe economic loss. As we already know, when an action bears no definitive interpretation, the actor's subjective purpose becomes decisive. In these cases, therefore, if the householder intends the act as routine labor, he has transgressed the law, while if he performs the act with the intention of averting economic loss, he has not transgressed (II C, III C-D).

Above, I claimed that the role of norms in the evaluation of action has important implications for the behavior of individual Israelites. When deciding upon a given course of action, an Israelite must always consider the normal meaning of the intended act. Otherwise, it might turn out that the act he or she performs constitutes a transgression. This point is also made explicit in the first case cited above. According to this rule, a woman who wants to save her pottery from thieves must realize that, no matter what her actual intention, taking it home would constitute routine labor. Consequently, to protect the pots, she must adopt an alternative course of action that is not routine. One option is to put the pots in a guarded courtyard, because people generally do this only as a way of preventing robbery (I B-C). This case, therefore, illustrates the mishnaic assumption that one cannot possibly avoid violating the law unless one familiarizes oneself with the norms operating in Israelite society and takes those into account when planning a course of action.

The Appeal to Norms to Interpret a Votary's Intention

The Mishnah takes account of societal norms not only to define the purpose of an action, but also to determine the meaning of an Israelite's words. When an Israelite makes a statement that requires interpretation, the sages routinely assign to this statement the standard meaning of the words. The speaker's actual intention plays no role at all in the interpretation of his or her language.

The fact that the Mishnah treats language as analogous to action should not surprise us. As we know from earlier discussions, statements, like actions, sometimes produce legal consequences. For example, a person can dedicate an object to the Temple simply by stating aloud that that object constitutes a Temple gift. Having uttered those words, the object in question immediately assumes a consecrated status with the result that the individual can no longer employ it for personal use. Since a person's statements sometimes produce legal effects, it is necessary to arrive at a proper interpretation of his or her words. Just as the purpose of an action determines its legal consequences, so too the meaning of a person's words determines the legal effects of those words.

The Mishnah interprets a person's language by appealing to linguistic norms in Israelite society. When the words bear a standard meaning, the sages totally dismiss the meaning those words have for the speaker at hand. These points emerge clearly from a series of rules governing religious vows. According to the Mishnah, Israelites sometimes vow to God to forego certain pleasures, such as drinking wine or eating a meal at a neighbor's house. When formulating a vow, the votary invokes God's name, which makes the pledge irrevocable. Thus once a vow has left a person's lips, God expects the individual to conduct him or herself accordingly (Num. 30:3). Should the votary subsequently break the vow, divine displeasure is incurred.

In the rules to follow, the Mishnah presents a series of cases in which Israelites have taken vows. In each instance, the sages ponder the scope of the vow in question. That is, from what must the votary abstain? The answer to this question is not always immediately obvious, for in many cases the person has used ambiguous language. For example, suppose a person vows "to be a vegetarian." Must he or she abstain from fish and eggs or only from meat? Examination of the following cases shows that the sages adopt precisely the same procedure for interpreting a vow that they use in determining the purpose of an action. Instead of taking account of the votary's actual intention, the sages consider what the typical Israelite would mean by these words and imputes that meaning to the votary at hand: [20]

I.   A.   One who vows [not to derive benefit] "from seafarers,"
     B.   may [derive benefit] from land-dwellers.
     C.   [But one who vows not to derive benefit] "from land-dwellers,"
     D.   is forbidden [to derive benefit not only from land-dwellers but also] from seafarers, because seafarers fall under the rubric of land-dwellers. [That is, people normally use the expression "land-dweller" as an idiom to refer to human beings in general. Consequently, it includes sailors].

                                                              M. Ned. 3:6

II. A.   One who vows [not to derive benefit] from "anyone who sees the light of day,"
     B.   is forbidden [to derive benefit] even from blind people,
     C.   because he intended [21] [to include not just people who actually see the light of day, but] anyone under the sun [that is, all human beings].

                                                              M. Ned. 3:7

III. A. One who vows [not to derive benefit] "from dark-haired ones,"
   B. is forbidden [to derive benefit even] from bald men and gray-haired men,
   C. but he is permitted [to derive benefit] from women and children [even if they have dark hair].
   D. [This is] because only men are called "dark-haired ones." [That is, the expression "dark-haired" is an idiomatic way of referring to men in general, and does not refer specifically to people with dark hair].

                                                        M. Ned. 3:8

All of these cases emphasize the importance of social norms in determining the meaning of a person's vow. If a person uses an idiomatic expression, the Mishnah assigns the standard connotation of the words to the individual's vow. For example, when a person vows not to derive benefit from "land-dwellers" (I C-D), or not to derive benefit from "anyone who sees the light of day" (II), the votary must forego benefit from all human beings, for in Israelite society, these idioms simply mean people in general. By the same token, when a person vows not to derive benefit from "dark-haired ones," the Mishnah forbids him or her to derive benefit from any male, regardless of hair color (III). This is because the expression "dark-haired ones" functions as an idiom similar to the English expression "tall, dark and handsome." People only use this expression when referring to men. It would be idiosyncratic to use the phrase in reference to a woman or child.

In the mishnaic system, then, if a given expression has a standard meaning, the sages impute that meaning to the votary's words. They simply do not care that the individual may have intended the phrase literally. These rules thus have the same striking implication as the previous examples. When taking a vow, a person must consider the normal meaning of the words he or she decides to use. One must choose expressions that not only convey the intended meaning but that do not normally convey some other meaning. One who fails to take this precaution may be required to abstain from something which he or she did not intend to abjure.

The notion that a person's subjective intention is irrelevant for interpreting his or her words may strike us as rather odd. Upon reflection, however, the Mishnah's theory of how to interpret language bears a remarkable similarity to certain strands of modern literary criticism. Many literary critics claim that once a person puts words on paper, the words assume a meaning independent of the writer's actual intention. In interpreting a literary work, therefore, one need not focus on the author's own meaning. Rather, the critic must bring certain norms of interpretation to bear to disclose the meaning of the document.

The poem is not the critic's own and not the author's (it is detached from the author at birth and goes about the world beyond his power to intend about it or control it). The poem belongs to the public. It is embodied in language, the peculiar possession of the public, and it is about the human being, an object of public knowledge. What is said about the poem is subject to the same scrutiny as any statement in linguistics or in the general science of psychology. [22]

The similarity between this view and that put forward by the Mishnah is obvious. The Mishnah claims that once a vow leaves a person's lips, that person's subjective intention is irrelevant. The vow has, so to speak, entered the public domain. Consequently, linguistic norms are brought to bear in interpreting the vow.

The Mishnah's theory, of course, derives from its own distinctive set of theological assumptions. By emphasizing the importance of norms and the relative unimportance of a person's subjective intention, the Mishnah urges people to view themselves not as individuals, but as integrated units in a larger social system. It is society, not the individual, that determines the meaning of a given statement or a given action. Consequently, people must not act without considering the normal meaning of their behavior. Otherwise, they may be penalized. According to the mishnaic system, therefore, Israelites can live in accordance with God's will only by taking account of social conventions when planning an action or formulating a vow.

The following rule again illustrates the importance of linguistic norms for interpreting the meaning of a person's vow. Here, however, the sages disagree among themselves as to the normal meaning of the vow in question.

A.   One who vows [not to eat] any [creature] "already living,"

B.   is permitted to eat any [creature] that will be born (*hnwldym*)[23] [in the future, because he only means to abjure creatures that at the moment of his vow are already living].

C.   [But one who vows not to eat any creature] "that will be born (*hnwldym*),"

D.   is forbidden [even to eat] any [creature] already living [because the expression "that will be born" is an idiom which refers to living things in general and thus includes creatures that are already alive].

E.   Rabbi Meir [by contrast], permits [the votary at C to eat] even [creatures] already living. [Meir believes people use the expression "that will be born" literally. Therefore, someone who vows to abstain from any creature "that will be born," may eat creatures that are already living].

F.   Sages say, " This person [who vows not to eat any creature "that will be born"] intended (*ntkwwn*) [to abstain] only [from] those [creatures] that will be *born*[24] [i.e., mammals. But he does not intend to abstain from animals that will be *hatched* from eggs, for example, chickens].

M. Ned. 3:9

In the rule at hand, the sages discuss a person who has vowed not to benefit from anything "that will be born." Although each of the authorities cited believes that this vow bears a standard connotation, they disagree about the expression's precise interpretation. This dispute is interesting because it illustrates the various factors the sages consider important in determining what a given vow actually means. The single unnamed authority believes that Israelites normally use this expression as an idiom signifying any living creature (C-D). Thus, in his view one who abjures anything "that will be born" may not eat any living creatures, including those that are already alive.

By contrast, Meir (E) and the sages (F) claim that the expression "that will be born" bears a literal meaning. However, they disagree as to which aspect of the expression takes precedence in determining its meaning. Meir considers the *tense* of the verb to be decisive. In his view, therefore, when a person vows to abstain from animals "that *will be* born," he or she can eat creatures that have been born in the past (E). The sages, on the other hand, believe the *meaning* of the verb to be critical. Consequently, they claim that the votary must abstain from "creatures that are *born*" (i.e. mammals), as opposed to creatures that are *hatched* from eggs (F).

The Mishnah recognizes that sometimes it is impossible to determine the meaning of a person's words by appealing to linguistic norms. This is the case if a person's statement bears two equally plausible interpretations. When social norms provide no definitive interpretation of a statement, the sages appeal to the actual intention the Israelite has in mind. This point emerges from a set of cases concerning a special class of vows. Sometimes, an Israelite vows to treat some household object, such as wine, "as though it were" an object consecrated for God's use. Since mishnaic law forbids one to use consecrated objects, this person has in effect vowed not to use the household object in question.

In the cases to follow, the votary employs a word that has two different meanings. For example, a man vows to treat wine as though it were *herem*. The word *herem* either refers to property consecrated to the Temple or to a fishing net. On the basis of his language alone, therefore, it is unclear whether he has vowed to treat wine like a consecrated or an unconsecrated thing. Predictably, the Mishnah claims that the Israelite's subjective intention resolves the ambiguity.

A. [Concerning] a person who vowed [to treat a particular substance such as wine as though it were] *"herem"* [a Hebrew word that means either a fishing net or property dedicated to the Temple, and hence it is unclear whether he has taken a binding vow],

B. and [subsequently] he said, "[I did not take a binding vow, because] I vowed only [to treat wine] like a fishing net [and not to treat it like property dedicated to the Temple]" --

C. [and concerning a person who vowed, "I will treat this substance as though it were] an offering,"

D. and [subsequently] he said, "[I did not take a binding vow, because] I vowed only [to treat it] like offerings for kings [which have no sanctity. I did not mean to treat it as a consecrated offering to God]" --

E. [and concerning a person who vowed] "Lo, [I will treat] $^c smy$ as a [holy] offering," [and the word $^c smy$ may mean either "myself" or "my bone." Hence, it is unclear whether he vowed to give the monetary value of a bone or himself to the Temple],

F.   and [subsequently] he said, "[I did not take a binding vow, because] I took a vow concerning the bone which I left [at home so that I could refer] to it in taking vows. "[I did not mean to treat "myself" as a holy offering] --

G.   [and concerning a man who vowed] "God forbid (*Konam*) that my wife derive benefit from me,"

H.   and [subsequently] he said, "I only vowed that my former wife, whom I have divorced, [should not derive benefit from me, but I did not vow to forego intercouse with my present wife]"--

I.   in all of these cases (A-H) [the votaries] need not ask [a sage to release them from their vows. God accepts their own self-serving explanations of their vows, and hence they require no dispensation].

J.   "But if they have asked [to be released]--

K.   [then] you must punish them and apply the stringent interpretation to their [vows]," these are the words of Rabbi Meir. [According to Meir, since they asked to be released from their vow, it is obvious that they had intended to take a binding vow, even though they claimed that that was not their intention].

L.   Sages say, "[If they ask to be released do not say that they did not make a binding vow. But] give them another kind of escape hatch [that is, find another rationale for releasing them], and lecture them so that they will not treat vows lightly [in the future].

M. Ned. 2:5

For the purposes of this inquiry, we focus on the underlying point of agreement between Meir and the sages (I). Both authorities maintain that when a person uses ambiguous language, his or her own subjective intention assumes paramount importance. Accordingly, if the votary claims to have vowed to treat wine as a "fishing net," they do not expect this person to abstain from the wine, because the votary claims that he or she had no intention of taking a binding vow. Of course, if an Israelite actually goes to a sage seeking dispensation, it is obvious that, no matter what the person now says, the original intention was to take a real vow. Hence, under these circumstances, Meir and sages regard the vow as binding (K-L).

In the previous rules, linguistic norms played a crucial role in determining the scope of a vow. We now find that they are important also in determining the vow's duration. For example, when a person abjures a benefit "until the harvest," the Mishnah takes into account what the typical Israelite would mean by that expression and imputes that meaning to the votary at hand:

I.   A.   This is the general rule: [as to] any [event that a person mentions in his vow] that [continues for] a definite period of time [for instance, he vows not to eat a certain substance until Passover, which lasts for seven days] --

     B.   if he said, "until [that event] arrives," [the substance] is forbidden until [that event] arrives [but he may eat the substance throughout the duration of the event].

    C.   [But if he said], "until [that event] occurs," [the substance] is forbidden until the conclusion [of that event].

    D.   And [as to] any [event that a person mentions in a vow] that [continues for] an indefinite period of time [for instance, he vows to abstain from a certain substance until the harvest, and the harvest may continue for a period of several weeks]--

    E.   whether he said, "until [the harvest] occurs" or whether he said, "until [the harvest] arrives,"

    F.   [the substance] is forbidden only until [that event] arrives, [but he may eat it throughout the duration of the event.]

M. Ned. 8:3

II. A.   [If a person vows to abstain from a certain food] "until Passover,"

    B.   he is forbidden [to eat it] until [Passover] arrives, [but he may eat it during the duration of the festival in accordance with I B above].

    C.   [If he vows to abstain] "until [Passover] occurs,"

    D.   [he must abstain] until the conclusion [of the festival, in accordance with I C above].

M. Ned. 8:2

The Mishnah ascribes to the votary the standard meaning of his or her words. If, therefore, the words of the vow normally mean "up to and including the duration of an event," the votary must abstain for that entire period, regardless of what was actually intended. But how is the standard meaning of a vow determined? The sages regard two factors as important: the language used and the nature of the event specified. Consider first the importance of the language. Normally when Israelites use the expression "until event x *arrives*," they mean up to but not including the duration of that event (I B, II B). By contrast, when people say "until event x will have *occurred*" they usually mean up to and including the duration of the event (I C, II D). But in addition to the formulation of the vow, the Mishnah also takes account of the nature of the event. One who vows not to drink wine until an event that lasts an indeterminate period of time, such as the harvest, is required to abstain up to but not including the duration of that event (I D-F). The assumption is that most Israelites will not take a vow unless they know its precise duration. Thus, the Mishnah assumes that when the typical person mentions an event of indefinite duration, he or she normally means up to but not including the event.

Two sages, Judah and Yose, introduce a third criterion for determining the standard meaning of a vow. In addition to the language and the character of the event, they also take account of the normal behavior of Israelites during the specified event.

I. A.   Rabbi Judah says, "[If a person says], 'God forbid (*konam*) [25] that I taste wine until Passover occurs,'

B.   "he is forbidden to taste wine only up to the eve of Passover [but not during the rest of the festival],

C.   "because this person intended (*ntkwwn*) only [to abstain] until the time when most people drink wine. [That is, since most people drink wine as part of the first Passover meal, Judah requires the votary to abstain only until that time. Although the votary said, 'until Passover occurs,' which normally means that he intended to abstain throughout the duration of the event, as specified above at M. Ned. 8:2, he need only abstain until the beginning of the festival.]

M. Ned. 8:5

II. A.   "If he said, 'God forbid (*konam*) that I taste meat until the fast day occurs,'

B.   "he is forbidden [to eat meat] only up to [but not including the dinner eaten on] the evening of the fast,

C.   "because this person intended (*ntkwwn*) only [to abstain] until the time when most people eat meat. [Since most people eat meat during the meal prior to a fast, Judah permits the one who took the vow to have meat on that occasion.]"

D.   Rabbi Yose, his son, says, "[If a man says], 'God forbid (*konam*) that I taste garlic until Sabbath occurs,

E.   "he is forbidden [to taste it] up to the eve of the Sabbath [but he may eat it during the Sabbath itself],

F.   "because this person intended (*ntkwwn*) only [to abstain] until the time when most people eat garlic [i.e., use garlic as seasoning. Since garlic is considered a treat, most people use it on the Sabbath. Consequently, Yose permits a person who vows to give up garlic 'until Sabbath occurs,' to eat garlic on the Sabbath.]"

M. Ned. 8:6

In determining the duration of a person's vow, Judah and Yose consider how people normally behave during the event the votary has specified. For example, on the Sabbath most people use garlic in their food (II D-F). Therefore, when an individual vows to abstain from garlic "until the Sabbath," Yose does not expect this person to abstain during the Sabbath itself, for he imputes to the individual the normal intention of eating garlic on the Sabbath.

Closer inspection of this rule also shows that both Judah and Yose ascribe greater importance to some norms than others. In interpreting a person's vow, behavioral norms, such as what people do on particular occasions, take precedence over mere linguistic norms. Consider once again the case of the person who vows to abstain from garlic "until the Sabbath will have occurred." As we previously learned, the Mishnah takes for granted that Israelites normally employ the expression "until event x will have occurred" when they intend to abstain throughout the duration of the specified event (M. Ned. 8:2-3). On the basis of the linguistic norms which are presumed to exist in Israelite society, therefore, we might assume that the votary intends to abstain until the end of the Sabbath. On the other hand, the Mishnah also claims that Israelites almost always use garlic on the Sabbath. According to norms of behavior, we would assume the votary intends to eat garlic on the Sabbath. The two sets of norms, therefore, provide conflicting interpretations of the same vow. The fact that Yose permits the votary to use garlic on the Sabbath day thus indicates that he ascribes greater importance to norms of behavior than to linguistic ones.

The meaning of a vow also depends on a person's state of mind when taking that vow. In the rule to follow, the Mishnah contrasts cases of a man and a woman who employ exactly the same words in taking a vow. But because the woman is inebriated, the sages interpret her vow differently than the man's. Specifically, the cases at hand involve a man and woman who respectively decline a cup of wine by vowing "to abstain from it." On the surface, the language of this vow seems ambiguous. Does the votary mean to abstain only from this particular cup of wine or from wine in general? If the votary has the latter intention in mind, he or she falls into the category of a Nazirite. By scriptural law, a Nazirite must forego not only wine but other grape products as well. In addition, the Nazirite is forbidden to cut his or her hair during the term of the vow (Num. 6:1-8). The Mishnah's framers, as we shall now see, resolve the ambiguity in the vow by considering what a person in that state of mind would normally mean by this vow:

A. [If people] mixed him a cup of wine, and he said, "I [vow] to abstain from it"--

B. he [automatically] becomes a Nazirite.

C. Once there was a woman who was drunk, and they mixed her a cup of wine,

D. and she said, "I [vow] to abstain from it"--

E. The sages ruled that she only intended to say, "This [particular cup of wine] will be [treated] by me as if it were a holy offering." [That is, she only meant to abstain from the particular cup of wine at hand. She did not intend to abstain from wine in general. Hence, she does not become a Nazirite.]

M. Naz. 2:3

In the society presented by the Mishnah, when an Israelite declines a cup of wine and says, "I abstain from it,' he or she normally intends to become a Nazirite. Consequently, in the case at hand, the Mishnah claims the man has taken the Nazirite vow and is expected to obey the appropriate rules. But when an inebriated woman takes precisely the same vow, the sages rule that she did not intend to become a Nazirite. They assume that due to her drunken state she merely used hyperbolic language in refusing the specific glass of wine which was offered.

In neither of these cases, however, does the Mishnah take account of the individual's actual intention. Since in either case the vow bears a normal interpretation, the sages do not care at all about the votary's subjective meaning.

To be sure, here as in previous examples, the votary may not actually have had in mind the intention imputed to him or her. The drunken woman, for example, may actually have intended to take the Nazirite vow. Nonetheless, since the Mishnah always places more importance on the normal meaning of the vow than on the individual's subjective intention, the woman does not become a Nazirite. A drunken person who wants to take the Nazirite vow, therefore, must say so explicitly. Unlike a sober Israelite, an inebriated individual cannot become a Nazirite by innuendo.

To generalize, we have found that the law of vows, perhaps more than any other area of mishnaic law, encourages Israelites to take account of social norms before embarking on a given course of action. In the Mishnah, one who formulates a vow without first considering its standard meaning may end up eating something which should have been renounced, or alternatively, abstaining from something which could have been eaten. In either case, this person has misinterpreted the divine will.

The Variability of Norms Within Israelite Society

The sages believe that some norms describe Israelite behavior in all segments of Israelite society. An idiom, for example, is assumed to be employed by all Israelites, irrespective of occupation or geographic origins. However, the sages do not conceive of Israelite society as entirely homogenous. On the contrary, they recognize and take account of the diversity that exists within it. In the society they imagine, people from different walks of life act differently from one another in important respects. Merchants differ from householders, Galileans from Jerusalemites, and one generation differs from another. Consequently, some norms represent one group of people within Israelite society and not others.

As we shall now see, in evaluating an Israelite's action or statement, the Mishnah makes reference to the particular category of society to which that person belongs. The sages impute to an individual the purpose or meaning a person of the same type would normally have in mind when performing the act or making the statement in question. Consequently, the category of society to which an individual belongs plays a decisive role in determining whether his or her action constitutes a transgression of divine law. In certain cases the very same action may or may not constitute a transgression depending upon the actor's occupation. Likewise, a person's geographic origin plays an important role in the evaluation of his or her vow. The mishnaic system, therefore, encourages Israelites not only to conform to social conventions in general, but also to abide by the specific norms generated by Israelites of their own occupation, geographic origin, and generation.

Norms of Occupational Groups

People in different occupations adhere to different norms. Householders, who head farming establishments, follow one set of norms, merchants another. We shall now see that the Mishnah makes reference to norms of a man's occupational group in interpreting his action. When other people of his occupation perform the act in question for a distinctive purpose, the sages routinely assign that purpose to the actor at hand.

The Mishnah expresses this point in a rule dealing with the laws of fraud. In the mishnaic system, if a man performs any act for the purpose of defrauding his customers, he has violated God's law. [26] Mixing grain of different qualities, for example, constitutes fraud if the purpose of the act is to deceive customers as to the true value of the merchandise. In the rules to follow, the Mishnah considers whether a householder and merchant who combine produce of differing qualities are guilty of fraud. The answer, as we shall now see, depends upon the occupational group to which the actor belongs.

I.   A.   A merchant [who sells produce in bulk amounts] may buy [grain] from five [different] threshing floors and put [it] into a single storehouse [even though the grain is of different qualities].

     B.   [And he may buy wine] from five [different] wine presses and put [the wine] into a single vat [even though the various types of wine are of different qualities].

     C.   [He may do so] provided that he does not intend (*mtkwwn*) to mix [the produce for fraudulent purposes. That is to say, if he mixes the grain so as to accumulate enough for bulk sale, his action does not constitute a transgression. But if his purpose in combining the produce is to deceive his customers, his act constitutes a violation.]

M. B.M. 4:12

II. A.   [By contrast, householders who sell produce] may not mix produce[27] [from one field] with produce [from another field] even if [both types of produce] are recently [picked, and presumably of the same quality. The sages declare a householder guilty of fraud whenever he mixes produce of two different qualities, regardless of his actual intention.]

M. B.M. 4:11

Combining different types of produce may or may not constitute a violation, depending upon the occupation of the man involved. If the man is a householder, who owns a farming establishment, the Mishnah automatically holds him liable for having transgressed (II A). If, by contrast, a merchant performs the very same act, he has not necessarily violated God's law. In this case, the sages takes account of the merchant's subjective intention. Only if his purpose was to deceive his customers does his action count as a transgression (I C).

The sages treat a merchant's and a householder's action according to different standards because merchants and householders are presumed to abide by different norms. Merchants typically combine produce for one of two reasons. Either they intend to commit fraud or they wish to accumulate enough produce for a bulk sale.[28] As I have previously shown, when two equally plausible interpretations apply to an act, the person's actual intention is decisive. Since a merchant's action is equivocal, his actual intention defines the meaning of his act. Householders, by contrast, normally sell their merchandise in small amounts in the marketplace or to neighbors. Generally, they do not sell produce in bulk. Consequently, when a householder combines produce of differing grades it generally signifies the intention to defraud. The sages routinely ascribe this purpose to any householder who mixes produce, regardless of his subjective intention (II).[29]

The following cases illustrate again how the Mishnah places far greater importance on the norms of a man's occupational group than on the intention he actually formulates. The Mishnah discusses situations in which Israelites are suspected of violating the divine injunction against putting on one's body a garment made from linen and wool (Lev. 19:19, Deut. 22:9-11). Having considered this law in a previous context, we need only briefly review the basic rules concerning garments of mixed weave. In the Mishnah, putting a garment of mixed weave on one's body constitutes a transgression only if one's intention is to use the garment as clothing (i.e., to protect oneself from the elements). But if one dons the garment for some other purpose, for instance to model the fabric for a customer, this does not constitute a transgression.

I. A. Clothes salesmen [may] sell [garments made of linen and wool] in the normal manner [that is, by modeling them on their own person].

    B. [This is the case] provided that the clothes salesmen do not intend (*mtkwwn*) on a hot day [for the garment to serve as protection] against the sun,

    C. and [provided that] on rainy days, [they do not intend to put on the garments to serve as protection] from the rain. [If they don the clothes only for the purposes of their trade, they do not violate the law, for this does not constitute using the fabric as clothing. But if they intend the garment to protect them from the elements, a normal function of clothing, they have transgressed.]

    D. Scrupulous [salesmen, however, do not model the garments on their person under any circumstances] but tie them to a pole [and display them in this fashion. Although by law they are permitted to wear the garments for the purposes of modeling, they will not do so, lest other Israelites misconstrue their action and think they are violating a law.]

                                                                M. Kil. 9:5

II. A. Tailors [may] sew [garments of mixed fabrics] in the normal manner [i.e., by draping them over their knees],

    B. provided that they do not intend on a hot day [for the garments to serve as protection] against the sun,

    C. and [provided that] on a rainy day, [they do not intend that the garments serve as protection] against the rain.

D. Scrupulous [tailors, however,] sew with garments draped on the ground [and not over their knees. They do not drape the garments on their knees lest other Israelites think they are using the garment to protect them from sunburn.]

M. Kil. 9:6

III. A. [By contrast], an [householder] may not wear [garments of mixed weave] even on top of ten [garments of a single fabric. The sages regard this as a violation because householders normally wear garments for protection against the elements.]

B. [And householders may not wear garments of mixed fabrics] even to avoid paying [Roman] customs tax. [One way of avoiding what were considered illegal taxes was by wearing the garments through customs. However, even if this were his intention he transgresses the law.]

M. Kil. 9:2

The Mishnah acribes to householders and merchants the purpose that other people of the same occupation would normally have in mind when donning a garment of mixed weave. Householders almost always employ garments as clothing. They rarely put on clothes for other purposes. Whenever a householder dons a garment of mixed weave, therefore, he has transgressed, even though he may have had no intention of using the garment as clothing.[30] By contrast, a merchant's donning of a garment can bear two equally plausible interpretations. Merchants sometimes put on garments to protect them from the elements. But they also don garments for the purpose of modeling. Since no clearly defined norm exists among merchants, the sages make liability dependent on the purpose the merchant actually has in mind.[31]

Geographic Norms

According to the Mishnah, social norms not only vary by occupation but also with geographic location. Galileans, living in the northern part of the land of Israel, behave differently than Jerusalemites, who live in the southern part of the land. This is because the life experiences of Israelites in one location may differ in important respects from those of people living in other places. The sages believe that one result of such differences appears in the way people use the Hebrew language. A single Hebrew word may have one meaning in the northern regions and an entirely different significance in the south. Consequently, to determine the meaning of a person's vow, the Mishnah considers it important to determine the geographic region in which the votary lives.

In the rule below, a person uses ambiguous language. For example, he vows to treat wine as though it were a Temple donation, without specifying the precise type of donation he has in mind. He may be referring to the donation of the shekel to the Temple chamber, which is a voluntary gift, or to the

agricultural gift (i.e., tithe), which is obligatory. Due to the ambiguity in the
Israelite's language , it is unclear whether a binding vow has been taken, for in
mishnaic law, a vow is only binding if the votary has specified something that
is normally subject to a voluntary donation. However, if the votary specifies an
obligatory offering, the very purpose of a vow is undermined and the vow is
null. In the cases at hand, the sages resolve the ambiguity in the votary's
language by taking account of what people from the same geographic location
normally mean by the language in question:

A. R. Judah says, "[If a person says, 'I vow to treat bread and wine as
   though they were a Temple donation (*terumah*)],' without specifying the
   [particular type of donation (*terumah*) to which he is referring]--

B. "[if he lives] in [the geographic area called] Judah [which encompasses
   the Temple, his vow is understood as denoting the donation to the
   Temple chamber (lit. *terumah* of the Chamber), which is a voluntary gift
   (M. Sheq. 3:1)].

C. "[Since he specifies a substance that Israelites give voluntarily, his vow
   is valid, with the result that the bread and wine] are forbidden.

D. "But [if he lives] in the Galilee [which is a distance from the Temple, his
   vow is understood to refer to the agricultural gift (*terumah*), which
   Israelites are obligated to donate to the Temple priests].

E. "[Accordingly, the vow is considered null with the result the bread and
   wine] are permitted.

F. "[This is] because people of the Galilee [who live a distance from the
   Temple] know nothing of the [voluntary] donation to the Temple
   chamber. [However, as farmers, Galileans are certainly familiar with the
   obligatory agricultural gift].

G. "[If a person says, 'I vow to treat bread and wine like a devoted thing
   (*herem*)],' without specifying [the type of consecrated property to which
   he is referring]--

H. "[If he lives] in [the area called] Judah [which encompasses the Temple,
   his vow is understood as referring to the devoted property for priests,
   which is an obligatory gift (Num. 18:14)].

I. "[Accordingly, the vow is null, with the result that the bread and wine]
   are permitted.

J. "But [if the votary lives] in the Galilee, [his vow is understood as
   referring to property devoted for Temple repairs, which is a voluntary
   gift].

K. "[Accordingly, the vow is considered binding, with the result that the
   bread and wine] are forbidden.

L. "[This is] because people of the Galilee are not familiar with property
   consecrated for priests. [But they are familiar with property devoted to
   Temple repairs]."

M. Ned. 2:4

To decide whether a person's words constitute a binding vow, the sages
ascribe to the votary the meaning those words normally bear in his or her
geographic area. When a Galilean vows to treat wine as though it were a Temple

gift, the sages do not treat this statement as a binding vow. Most Galileans are more familiar with the obligatory agricultural gift than with the voluntary type of Temple donation (F). This rule once more demonstrates how the Mishnah dismisses the idiosyncratic use of language. Even if the Galilean at hand was actually referring to the voluntary kind of Temple gift, his words would not constitute a binding vow. The Mishnah, therefore, implicitly admits that a person may have to abstain from a specified food, even though he or she did not actually intend to take a binding vow. Similarly, there could be cases in which a person's words are considered pure gibberish, even though that person did intend a binding vow. To avoid misinterpreting the divine will, Israelites must choose their words carefully, making sure that their vows bear only the meaning they wish them to convey.

Generational Norms

Thus far we have discovered that within the society imagined by the Mishnah, norms vary according to occupational grouping and geographic location. In discussing these norms, we have focused exclusively on the standard patterns of behavior within a single generation. But the Mishnah also claims that norms of society change over time. Israelites of the present generation abide by a different set of norms than Israelites of previous generations. Here, as elsewhere, the Mishnah idealizes prior generations, claiming that in the "good old days" Israelites performed certain acts out of true religious devotion, while in the current generation, Israelites perform the same act from selfish motives.

The rule to follow illustrates the sages' belief that social norms change over time as well as their conviction that the law must be reformulated in light of such changes. The Mishnah claims, for instance, that the law given by God to Moses was designed with the norms of Moses' generation in mind, but requires reformulation in the present generation. Specifically, the rule at hand involves levirate marriage. According to Scripture, when a man dies without an heir, his brother must marry the widow and produce children who will preserve the dead man's line. Scripture conceives of no circumstance in which the brother may legitimately ignore this obligation. Therefore, if he refuses to marry the widow, he must undergo a humiliating rite of release, in which the widow removes his sandal, spits in his face, and says, "Thus shall be done to the man who will not build up his brother's house (Deut. 25: 5-10)." As we shall now see, the Mishnah claims that this scriptural law requires revision.

A. The obligation to marry the widowed sister-in-law takes precedence over the obligation to undergo the rite of release.
B. [This was the law] in former times,
C. for [when men of that generation married their widowed sister-in-laws], they intended [their action] for the sake of a religious duty.
D. But now, since [men who marry their widowed sister-in-law] do not intend [their action] for the sake of a religious duty --

E.   the obligation to undergo the rite of release takes precedence over the
     obligation to marry the widowed sister-in-law.

M. Bekh. 1:7

The Mishnah could not express more clearly the importance it attaches to
societal norms. This rule implies that God originally formulated the law of
levirate marriage to fit the norms of Moses' generation. Scripture says that a
man should marry his widowed sister-in-law rather than undergo the rite of
release, because in that generation, when men married their late brothers' wives,
they normally did so with the intention of fulfilling God's command (A-C). By
contrast, the sages of the Mishnah believe that in their own generation men
generally marry the widowed sister-in-law for ulterior motives, such as gaining
control over their dead brother's estate (M. Yeb. 4:7) (D-E). Since the norms of
Israelite society have changed, the law itself must also be altered. Otherwise,
God's original intent would be undermined.

This ruling has the same paradoxical implication as the ones previously
examined. Conceivably, a person can act with the intention of fulfilling God's
law, but nonetheless perform a transgression. For example, suppose that in the
generation of the sages a man marries his widowed sister-in-law because he
wants to carry out God's command. However, since the majority of Israelites
perform this act from ulterior motives, the sages routinely ascribe improper
motives to anyone who performs this act. The man in question, therefore, would
be guilty of a transgression even though he acted with the intention of fulfilling
divine law. In this system, therefore, the virtuous individual is one who takes
account of social norms whenever embarking upon a given course of action.

Explaining the Significance of Social Norms

The preceding set of cases amply demonstrates the importance of social
norms in the mishnaic system. On the basis of normal Israelite behavior, the
Mishnah determines the purpose a given action typically serves and imputes that
purpose to anyone who performs the act in question. Intention, therefore, is
routinely subordinated to norms. When the act bears a normal meaning, the
actor's intention has no role in determining liability. The Mishnah falls back on
intention only in cases where the action is ambiguous, namely, if the act in
question serves more than one purpose in Israelite society. Having demonstrated
how these ideas are implicit in the Mishnah's rules, we need now explain their
significance. This question is much broader than it first appears. To a large
extent, the answer will depend upon how we characterize the mishnaic system.
Two obvious alternatives present themselves. First, it is possible to conceive of
the Mishnah as a legal system. The Mishnah not only specifies rules of
behaviors but also courtroom procedure, such as how to interrogate witnesses,
choose judges, and punish the guilty party (Tractates Sanhedrin and Makkot). At
the same time, treating the Mishnah strictly as law ignores the fact that the

Mishnah is a religious system which makes certain theological claims about the nature of the divine-human relationship, as well as specifies rules of behavior for carrying out the divine will. Obviously, these two concerns overlap in the Mishnah and cannot be divorced from one another.

The question, however, is whether we should understand what we have discovered about social norms in terms of the Mishnah's legal character or in terms of its theological concerns. Our interpretation of the facts will be very different depending upon how we deal with this issue. If we emphasize the legal character of the Mishnah, then we will understand the Mishnah's reliance on norms as an expression of the sages' concern with creating a viable legal system. However, if we stress the theological dimensions of the Mishnah, we will want to correlate its ideas about norms with its conception of God and the divine-human relationship. In what follows, I will attempt to treat the facts at hand from each of these perspectives.

Reliance on Norms as an Aspect of the Mishnah's Legal Theory

All legal systems have to deal with the problem of determining an actor's intention. Because people do not have direct access to one another's minds, intentions are unverifiable. An actor's intention, therefore, must be inferred from the facts of the case. The Mishnah's reliance on norms may represent one way in which the sages deal with the problem of determining an actor's purpose. By appealing to Israelite conventions, the sages establish the normal meaning of the act in question. They then ascribe that purpose to the actor at hand. In this way, the sages need not rely on the actor's subjective intention, which is not capable of verification.

The strength of this explanation is that it accords well with what we know about other legal systems. According to Hart, Anglo-American law deals with the problem of intention in a similar fashion.

Another reason limiting the scope of the excusing conditions is difficulty of proof. Some of the mental elements involved are much easier to prove than others. It is relatively simple to show that an agent lacked, either generally or on a particular occasion, volitional muscular control; it is somewhat more difficult to show that he did not know certain facts about either present circumstances (e.g. that the gun was loaded) or the future (that the man would step into the line of fire); it is much more difficult to establish whether or not a person was deprived of 'self-control' by passion provoked by others, or by partial mental disease. As we consider these different cases not only do we reach much vaguer concepts, but we become progressively more dependent on the agent's own statements about himself, buttressed by inferences from 'common-sense' generalizations about human nature, such as that men are capable of self-control when confronted with an open till but not when confronted with a wife in adultery. The law is accordingly much more cautious in admitting 'defects of the will' than 'defect in knowledge' as qualifying or excluding criminal responsibility. Further difficulties of proof may cause a legal system to limit its inquiry into the agent's 'subjective condition' by asking what a 'reasonable man' would in the circumstances have known or foreseen, or by asking whether 'a reasonable man' in the circumstances would have been deprived (say, by provocation) of self-control; and the system may then impute to the agent such knowledge or foresight or control.[32]

It is obvious that what Hart describes here does not precisely match what we have found in the Mishnah. Nonetheless, there are noteworthy similarities. Hart suggests that in order to determine the actor's mental state, Anglo-American law makes "common-sense generalizations" about human nature. In addition, Anglo-American law appeals to the concept of the "reasonable man" and imputes to an actor what the reasonable person would know or foresee in the circumstances in question. The notions of the "reasonable man" or of "common sense generalizations" about human nature are merely another way of referring to what we have called social norms. After all, we generally define as reasonable what most people would do or know in a given situation. This parallel lends validity to the thesis that in mishnaic law social norms provide a method for dealing with the unverifiability of intentions.

The Mishnah also recognizes a second method of determining an actor's intention. In order to convict someone, mishnaic law requires that two people not only witnessed the act in question but also warned the Israelite not to carry out that act (*htr'h*). This admonition serves two important functions in mishnaic law. First, it tells the court that the actor knew the act was a violation. After being warned, an actor obviously cannot claim to have been ignorant of the law. Second, the Israelite can hardly claim to have done the act unintentionally. For example, suppose witnesses said, "Do not kill x" and the actor killed x. Subsequently, however, the actor says he killed x by accident, and that his real intention was to kill y. Here the actor's claim is suspect. The two witnesses had reason to believe his intention was to kill x prior to the action (for example, they saw him aiming in x's direction). Since that result obtained, it is hard to believe that it occurred by accident. Forewarning an actor, therefore, enables the sages to determine whether an Israelite intentionally performed the act in question.

The question naturally arises as to why the sages devised the above two methods for getting at an actor's intention. It seems that each method is designed to determine a distinctive aspect of the actor's mental state. We recall that the Mishnah recognizes two different aspects of intention. The Mishnah takes account of 1) whether the actor performed the act intentionally and 2) the actor's purpose in performing the action. The two methods of determining intention correspond to these two types of intentions. The warning of the actor enables the sages to determine whether he or she acted intentionally. As I explained above, a person who is forewarned can not claim to have performed the act by accident. However, the admonishment fails to indicate another aspect of the actor's mental state, namely, his or her purpose in performing the action. To determine the actor's purpose, therefore, the sages turn to the second method of determining intention. They consider what the act normally means against the backdrop of norms which are presumed to operate in Israelite society. Let me make spell this out through an example.

Consider the following scenario. Two witnesses warn a woman not to put on a garment of mixed weave, but she does so anyway. Here, the admonishment indicates that the woman donned the garment intentionally. She not only knew it was of mixed weave, but she deliberately put it on her body. Nonetheless, it is important to determine her purpose in performing the act. As we recall, donning a garment of mixed weave is only a violation if the garment is worn as clothing. But if the purpose of donning it is to model the garment, this does not constitute a violation (M. Kil. 9:5-6). The fact that the woman was warned not to perform this act indicates nothing about her purpose in acting. This would explain why the sages consider it necessary to take account of Israelite norms. Norms help determine the reason the person performed the act in question. In this case, it is clear that in Israelite society women generally do not serve as merchants. Hence, the above woman's purpose in donning the garment is probably to use it as clothing, not to model it.

Reliance on Norms as an Aspect of the Mishnah's Theological Concerns

Treating the Mishnah's reliance on norms strictly in terms of the Mishnah's legal character leaves a number of questions unanswered. First, and perhaps most importantly, if the sages considered an actor's intention unverifiable, how do we account for the fact that they sometimes rely on the actor's subjective intention? We have seen in case after case that when norms do not provide a definitive interpretation of an action, the sages make liability depend on the actor's subjective intention. What does this mean? Should we assume that in these cases the sages actually rely upon what the individual says he or she intended? I find this interpretation problematic, for there is nothing to prevent the individual from lying in order to avoid culpability. Rather, it seems to me that in these situations, the sages are claiming that God holds people liable for their intentions. The implication, then, is that when a court cannot conclusively determine an actor's intention, God will hold that person liable. In other words, God plays a role complementary to that of the human court.

The Mishnah in fact makes this notion explicit. There are a number of transgressions for which a person is liable to flogging (M. Mak. 3:1-2) or the death penalty (M. San. 7:4, 9:1, 11:1) However, if there is not sufficient evidence to punish the accused, the person incurs the divine penalty of a premature death (M. Ker. 1:1). This means that when the human court cannot convict, the divine court goes into action. If the actor is guilty, God shortens his or her life. Moreover, if there is enough evidence to subject a person to flogging, that person is no longer liable to the divine penalty of premature death (M. Mak. 3:15). Therefore, if the human court has successfully convicted and punished the actor, God has no reason to step in. In the Mishnah's own language, "All those people who are liable to the divine punishment of premature death and who have been flogged --they are no longer liable to a premature death (M. Mak. 3:15)." We see, therefore, that the sages conceive of God as serving as an adjunct to the human system. When the human system fails, God steps in and executes justice.

We must also invoke the Mishnah's theological concerns to explain another significant fact. The Mishnah appeals to Israelite norms even in cases which are not presumed to be adjudicated by a court. Typically, these involve positive duties, such as the obligation to pray to God, the duty of hearing the Scroll of Esther read, the obligation to fulfill one's vow, the duty to keep one's household objects free from contamination, and the like. These duties are strictly between a person and God. To my knowledge, the Mishnah nowhere suggests that a person is brought before a court for not reciting prayers, for not tithing the correct amount of produce, or for selling untithed produce. Similarly, when a person takes a vow, it is up to him or her to fulfill that vow. A person only goes to the sages when seeking dispensation (cf. M. Ned. 2:5). Finally, the rules of purity presuppose that a householder knows how to determine whether something is capable of absorbing impurity. Presumably only doubtful cases are brought to a court (M. San. 4:2).

Significantly, even in these areas of law which are between a person and God, norms play a fundamental role. We saw, for example, that the meaning of a vow depends upon the meaning those words normally bear in Israelite society. In Chapter Three we shall see that norms also play a critical role in determining whether a given object can absorb impurity. Determining whether household objects can absorb impurity apparently is not an issue which is normally adjudicated by a court. A person who wishes to obey the rules of purity must decide for him or herself what can and cannot become contaminated. A person cannot consult the sages to determine the status of every object in the household.

These examples show that norms are important even in cases which are strictly between a person and God. Why then does the Mishnah claim that norms are important in determining liability? Clearly it is not because the court needs to determine the actor's purpose, for the court does not routinely adjudicate such cases. This is why the importance of norms can not be explained as deriving entirely from the sages' concern with developing a reliable method for verifying an actor's intention. Rather, the Mishnah seems to be suggesting that God takes account of social norms in determining liability. In other words, God holds a person responsible for the normal meaning of his or her action or words. This notion, of course, seems counterintuitive. The sages clearly assume that God knows an actor's intention. Why, then, would they claim that God takes account of social norms in determining liability? Let me propose a possible answer.

The notion that God ascribes to an actor the normal meaning of his or her act derives from the conviction that Israelite society itself constitutes an embodiment of the divine will. Israelite society is conceived of as a holy community founded upon divine law. The norms produced by this society assume a sacred status in their own right. By definition, therefore, conformity to norms represents an affirmation of God's will, whereas individualism constitutes a rejection of divine authority. This is why we find that in the Mishnah the norms of society provide the definitive interpretation of human action. In allotting reward and punishment, God always considers the normal meaning of an act to be more important than the actor's subjective purpose.

The rules we previously examined lend support to this interpretation. We saw that the Mishnah implicitly encourages individuals to pay attention to the norm when setting out on a course of action. Indeed, failure to take account of the norms often resulted in an misinterpretation of divine will, if not in an actual transgression. For example, the person who vowed not to derive benefit from "dark haired ones" must realize that the words have an idiomatic meaning. Even if the votary had a literal meaning in mind at the time of the vow, he or she must not derive benefit from all men.

One final piece of evidence suggests that the Mishnah actively discourages individualism: in allotting reward and punishment, the sages totally ignore the individual's prior record of conduct. When a person is suspected of violating a law, the Mishnah never inquires about his or her behavior in similar situations in the past. If the person has previously violated the law, this fact plays no role whatsoever in determining the legal outcome in the case at hand. This is in striking contrast to our own legal system in which the prior behavior of the accused almost always serves as evidence of his or her character. To the best of my knowledge, the Mishnah does not mention a person's prior behavior in any of its discussions of civil or religious law. Rather, the Mishnah treats all Israelites as if they shared the same pattern of prior conduct. The sages do not discriminate between a person who has been negligent in the past and one who has never done anything wrong.

This lack of interest in the prior conduct of Israelites is even more striking given the fact that the framers do take into account the prior conduct of oxen. When an ox causes damage, the framers apply a harsher punishment for an animal that has gored on previous occasions than for one that has never caused damage before (M. B.Q. 1:4). We may infer, since the framers do not indicate otherwise, that a person who has violated God's law on previous occasions does not receive a harsher punishment than a person who has committed a first offense. The total neglect of an Israelite's personal history provides support of the thesis that the Mishnah seeks to downplay and even discourage individualism within Israelite society.

In encouraging conformity to social norms, the mishnaic system, in its own distinctive fashion, takes up a pressing philosophical problem of late antiquity. Like the Cynics, Stoics, and Epicureans, the sages of the Mishnah discuss whether one can achieve a "life of virtue" by conforming to the conventions and norms of society. The Cynics, for example, "developed...an antithesis between the life of virtue and the life according to the laws of the city in which one had been born."[33] In their view, the attainment of virtue involves repudiating the norms of society, which are not founded on reason. The sages of the Mishnah do not work with categories like virtue or reason. Yet they focus on a very similar question. They ask how an individual can live a life in accordance with the divine will. In their judgment, no conflict exists between social conventions and the holy life. On the contrary, in their view, conformity to the norms constitutes a prerequisite for living in accordance with God's law.

In sum, we have interpreted the Mishnah's reliance on norms from two different perspectives. We have related it to the Mishnah's character as a legal system as well as to its theological presuppositions. The two explanations are by no means mutually exclusive. In the context of the Mishnah's legal theory, the appeal to norms solves the problem of determining the actor's purpose. At the same time, the stress on norms seems to have theological significance. The Mishnah claims that God takes account of Israelite norms in determining liability. Since Israelite society lives by divine law, its norms become consecrated, and hence they serve as models for proper behavior.

Conclusion

The laws examined in this chapter amply demonstrate the importance the Mishnah ascribes to an actor's purpose. In mishnaic law, no action is inherently a violation or fulfillment of divine law. It is the purpose of the action, whether objectively or subjectively determined, which ultimately determines its status. For example, Scripture forbids wearing garments woven of linen and wool. But in the Mishnah the violation of this rule depends upon the actor's purpose in donning the garment. By the same token, no action is by definition a fulfillment of divine law. The sages always take account of the actor's purpose in deciding whether to credit the person with having fulfilled a religious duty. Therefore, even if a person recites the words of a given prayer, he or she does not automatically fulfill the duty to pray to God. In addition, his or her purpose in reciting the prayer must have been to fulfill the religious duty. According to the Mishnah, therefore, two different people can perform the very same physical movements, yet one may have transgressed and the other may have performed an act with no legal consequences. By the same token, two different people may perform the same physical movements with the result that one fulfills divine law and the other does not.

In making an actor's purpose an important criterion in evaluating human action, the Mishnah reshapes biblical law in two fundamental respects. First, biblical law, especially the priestly legislation, only takes account of whether an actor has intentionally performed the act in question. But the actor's purpose in performing an act plays little role in determining liability. Second, in biblical law, the actor's intention can only affect the severity of the punishment; it has no role in determining whether the actor has committed a transgression. The Mishnah, by contrast, makes the whole question of culpability dependent on the actor's intention. Precisely the same action may constitute a transgression if done with one purpose in mind, while it may be a permissible act if performed for a different purpose. By stressing a new aspect of intention, therefore, the Mishnah fundamentally reworks biblical law.

The mishnaic emphasis on an actor's purpose stems from the theological assumptions which underlie the system as a whole. As I have argued, the Mishnah conceives of intention as the human counterpart to the divine will. Knowing an actor's purpose, therefore, is critical in determining whether the act in question affirms or repudiates divine authority. When a person performs an act for a purpose which the law forbids, he or she has in effect rejected God's will. However, the performance of the same act for a different purpose does not represent a spurning of God's authority.

Given that the actor's purpose is important, the question naturally arises as to what the Mishnah means by the purpose of an action. The Mishnah makes a categorical distinction between two types of purposes: 1) the purpose the actor has in mind, and 2) the purpose the action normally serves in the context of Israelite society. In some cases, of course, the purpose the actor has in mind coincides with the purpose his or her action normally serves. But in some cases, the actor intends the act to serve an idiosyncratic purpose.

The fact that an actor's subjective intention does not always correspond to the purpose his or her act appears to serve raises a crucial problem for the mishnaic system. What determines the legal outcome in a given case: a person's actual purpose, or the purpose the action normally fulfills? The Mishnah, as we have seen, places most stress on the purpose the act usually serves in Israelite society. If a given act serves a distinctive purpose in Israelite society, the Mishnah ascribes that purpose to the actor at hand, whether or not the actor actually had that purpose in mind. In some cases, however, a given act is simply ambiguous, serving more than one function in Israelite society. Since in this case the sages cannot ascribe a purpose to the actor, they take account of his or her subjective intention.

In making this distinction between the actor's subjective purpose and the normal purpose of the action, the Mishnah confronts a problem which continues to arouse the interest of philosophers today. Central to almost any contemporary discussion of intention is the question of the relationship between the actor's own understanding of his or her action and the interpretation of the action by an observer. Anscombe, for example, discusses the case of a person who is pumping poisoned water into a house. Now, we might say that this person's intention is to poison the inhabitants. However, when asked, the actor says that his intention is only to carry out the job of replenishing the water supply. Anscombe claims that

> there can be a certain amount of control over the truthfulness of the answer. For example, in the case of a man [who said he was merely replenishing the water supply as part of his job and had no intention of murdering the people inside].. part of the account we imagined him as giving was that he just went on doing his usual job. It is therefore necessary that it should be his usual job if his answer is to be acceptable; and he must not do anything, out of the usual course of his job, that assists the poisoning and of which he cannot give an acceptable account...Up to a point, then, there is a check on his truthfulness in the account we are thinking he would perhaps give; but still, there is an area in which there is none.[34]

The similarities between Anscombe's discussion and those of the Mishnah are striking. First, she distinguishes between the actor's subjective account and the intention ascribed to a person on the basis of behavior. Second, she implies that in interpreting another person's action, we always make reference to social norms, that is, normal behavior provides a standard against which the actions of individuals can be compared. Consequently, in the case at hand we assume that the actor intended to poison the inhabitants of the house if in carrying out his job he departed in any significant respect from his normal routine. Searle develops this point even further, claiming that in interpreting an action or statement, we rely upon a "Local Background" or "Network" of assumptions about reality and normal behavior.[35] The local background includes certain cultural assumptions about the normal meaning of an action and what a typical person would mean by this sort of act. Without this background, we could not possibly make sense of another person's action or statements.

The Mishnah's reliance on social norms, of course, stems from its own particular set of problems and assumptions. In part, the stress on norms derives from the Mishnah's concern with verifying an actor's intention. Since people cannot read one another's minds, there is no way to determine whether a person in fact meant to do what he or she claims. Consequently, the sages can only infer an actor's intention from the circumstances. Normal Israelite behavior provides a useful tool for making such determinations. Rather than rely on an actor's subjective intention which is ultimately unverifiable, the sages impute to an act its normal meaning.

This explanation by itself, however, cannot satisfactorily explain the importance of norms in the mishnaic system. First, if the sages were so concerned by the unverifiability of intention, how do we account for the fact that in many cases an actor's subjective intention actually determines whether that person is guilty? Second, the above explanation does not explain why norms play a role in cases which are not typically adjudicated in a human court, for example, in the laws of vows and impurity. If these cases are strictly between a person and God, the sages have no need to determine the actor's actual intention. To resolve these questions, we must appeal to the theological dimensions of the mishnaic system. It appears that the Mishnah takes for granted an active role on the part of God in adjudicating cases. The reason the Mishnah sometimes makes liability depend on an actor's subjective intention, therefore, is because it assumes that God holds actors accountable for the purposes they have in mind. In the Mishnah's conception, therefore, God plays a complementary role to the human court. When humans cannot adequately determine a person's intention from the norm, God holds the person liable for his or her actual intention.

Furthermore, the fact that norms are important in cases which are strictly between an individual and God implies that God takes account of social norms in judging a person. That is, God holds a person accountable for the standard meaning of his or her words or action. On the surface, this idea seems paradoxical. Since God, according to the Mishnah, knows each person's thoughts, why would God sometimes ignore those thoughts and stress instead the normal meaning of the action? As previously suggested, the Mishnah considers Israelite society to be holy. Since this society is founded on divine law, the norms it produces by definition become consecrated. For this reason, social norms provide the definitive interpretation of an Israelite's words or deeds. God ascribes to a person's action the meaning the act normally serves in Israelite society. Only when no clearly defined norm exists does God take account of what the individual actually intended.

The notion that God relies on Israelite norms in evaluating human action has important implications for the Mishnah's conception of the moral life. By insisting that God ascribes to individuals the purpose their action normally serves, the Mishnah expresses its view that living a holy life requires conformity to social conventions. Ignorance of or disregard for social conventions inevitably leads a person to transgression. Moral behavior, then, consists of learning what people of one's occupation and geographic location normally do in given circumstances and learning to act accordingly. By contrast, a person must not rely upon his or her own sense of right and wrong, for one's own judgment as to what is proper or improper in a given circumstance is likely to be idiosyncratic. To be sure, norms alone do not provide the model for virtuous behavior. God's law as recorded in Scripture provides the basic blueprint for moral behavior. In many instances, however, it is unclear whether a given action constitutes a violation of these rules, because each situation is unique. Social conventions, therefore, supplement God's law by clarifying whether the act in question in fact produces legal consequences.

As we now turn to the second part of our study, we shall find that the assumptions which the Mishnah brings to the discussion of human action also underlie the mishnaic rules dealing with the status of objects. Specifically, we shall see that the Mishnah treats objects in precisely the same way that it treats human action. Just as classifying actions as either a transgression or fulfillment of divine law plays an important role in the Mishnah, the classification of objects also arouses the Mishnah's interest. For reasons we shall explore shortly, the Mishnah devotes much space to determining whether a given object falls into the category of a useful or useless thing. It turns out that the Mishnah solves the problem of classification in the same way that it deals with the interpretation of human action. Just as the observable features of an action play only a minimal role, the perceptual characteristics of an object are relatively unimportant in its classification. What defines the classification of an object is how a person intends to use it. Furthermore, the sages believe that determining the object's intended use requires a complex interpretive act which involves reference both to the situation and to the owner of the object. In turning our attention to this problem, we shall see that the Mishnah's method of classifying objects corresponds perfectly to its method of interpreting human actions.

Part Two

THE FUNCTION OF PLANS
IN THE MISHNIAC SYSTEM

Chapter Three

Plans in the System of Purity

A person sometimes intends to perform an action before taking any concrete steps towards its execution. For example, a man may decide to go to the marketplace to sell his produce before he has made any preparations for the trip. When he first forms the intention, he has not yet performed any overt act. He has merely calculated how he will act in a future situation. This type of intention we shall call a person's plan.[1] Two questions form the focus of the present inquiry. First, we wish to know the function that plans serve in the mishnaic system. That is, what type of legal effect do plans produce? Second, our study investigates when and why plans precipitate those consequences. As we shall discover, in some cases the Mishnah stresses the importance of a person's plans, whereas in other contexts, it completely ignores what a person intends to do. By determining how such cases differ from one another, we can adduce the Mishnah's theory as to when and why plans matter.

To answer the above questions, we trace through the mishnaic system the Hebrew word which designates a person's plan, namely, the word *mahshabah*. This word almost always refers to the answer an Israelite would give to the question, "What do you plan to do with the object at hand?"[2] For example, the sages employ a form of the word *mahshabah* when referring to a person's decision to use a piece of leather for sandals. To provide an example in their own language, the sages say the leather is susceptible to impurity "if a man intends it (*hsb ᶜlyw*) for [use] as sandals (M. Kel. 26:9)." By this they mean that the Israelite plans to use the leather in question for shoes.

The 'Magical' Effects of Planning

In the mishnaic system, the plans a person formulates often produce a kind of 'magical' effect. Merely by formulating a plan to use an object in a given way, a person changes the most important property of the object in question, namely, its capacity to absorb or withstand cultic contamination. For example, the intention to eat a given substance makes that item capable of absorbing impurity.[3] Prior to the formulation of the intention, however, the substance could not become contaminated under any conditions.

Let me explain the mechanism by which intention produces such effects. When a person plans to use an object in a given way, his or her plan has the effect of classifying that object. For example, the plan to eat a given substance, automatically places that substance into the category of food. The idea that intention can classify things finds a parallel in our own frame of reference. Suppose you tell your spouse that you plan to drive to Indianapolis to visit a friend. By expressing your intention to use the car, you have effectively classified the car as "yours for the day." If your spouse subsequently wants to take the car, therefore, you would refuse, claiming that the car has already been reserved for your use.

This analogy captures the mishnaic idea that plans have the effect of classifying things. From the Mishnah's standpoint, when an Israelite intends to use an object for a particular purpose, he or she automatically places that object into one of the classifications which are deemed to be important. Objects may fall into opposing categories, such as "sacred" and "profane," or "useful" and "useless." Therefore, an Israelite who plans to put an object to sacred use *ipso facto* classifies it as a sacred thing. For instance, an animal that an Israelite intends to sacrifice becomes a holy thing from the moment he conceives of his plan and puts it into words. Just as a person reserves the car for his or her use by expressing an intention of using it, so an Israelite designates an animal as a holy thing by formulating a plan to sacrifice it. In the mishnaic system, therefore, the mere formulation of a plan effectively determines the classification of the object in question.

In the system of the Mishnah, the classification of an object is extremely important, because it determines whether or not that object can absorb impurity. For example, substances belonging to the category of food can become contaminated by impurity. But objects which fall under the rubric of waste cannot become unclean even if they come in contact with sources of contamination. The same distinction applies to useful and useless objects. When useful objects are brought in contact with sources of impurity, they are rendered unclean. Useless objects, by contrast, cannot become contaminated under any conditions.

Moreover, upon entering a given category an object becomes subject to divinely ordained rules which govern that class of thing. Sacred objects, for example, must be used only in the Temple precincts and only for sacred purposes. Profane things, by contrast, may be used wherever an Israelite wishes and for any purpose. Similarly, the Mishnah expects Israelites to keep useful objects from coming in contact with sources of impurity. This restriction does not apply to useless things. Since God has ordained the rules governing the various classes of objects, an Israelite who wishes to obey the divine will must determine the classification of each object that he or she owns and treat it according to the appropriate rules. If one fails to determine the object's correct classification, one will inevitably violate God's law by obeying the wrong set of restrictions. For this reason, the Mishnah discusses thousands of objects that an Israelite might encounter in one's daily routine, ranging from broken tables to dead cows. In each case, the Mishnah categorizes the object in question and thereby determines the rules governing that object's use.

Let me make the above ideas more concrete by referring to several specific cases. The following rule illustrates both the power of intention to classify objects and the capacity of classification to alter the properties of an object. Here, the Mishnah discusses the power of a person's plan to determine whether a table top belongs to the category of objects that can absorb impurity or to the category of objects that cannot. To understand the role of intention in this case, we first need to familiarize ourselves with the Mishnah's conception of purity, which in many respects derives from Leviticus.

According to Leviticus, God has declared certain objects to be sources of impurity, such as a corpse, a dead reptile, and certain body fluids, such as menstrual blood and semen (Lev. 11 and 15). These sources of impurity, among others, can contaminate various types of objects such as human beings, food, or household vessels. According to the authors of Leviticus, God expects Israelites to maintain the Temple and its cult in a state of cultic purity. Israelites involved in the cult, therefore, must avoid introducing contaminated objects into the Temple precincts, and prevent themselves from becoming comtaminated, so that their entrance into the Temple does not jeopardize the purity of the sacred place.

In appropriating the levitical rules of purity, the Mishnah alters the levitical scheme in two significant respects. To begin with, it extends the rules of cultic purity to the Israelite household. In the Mishnah, God expects each householder to treat his home as he would treat the Temple. Consequently, Israelites must prevent impurity from contaminating household objects and food. Second, the Mishnah grants human beings a central role in determining which objects can and cannot absorb impurity. For reasons we shall explore later, only objects that serve a purpose can become contaminated by impurity. Useless objects, by contrast, cannot absorb impurity under any conditions. A table, therefore, which by definition is useful, absorbs impurity if it comes in contact with a dead reptile. A broken table, however, cannot contract impurity because it is useless.

Turning our attention to the rule at hand, we see that an Israelite's plan serves as a criterion for determining whether a given object falls into the category of useful or useless things. By intending to put an object to use, one *ipso facto* places that object into the category of useful things, with the result that it can subsequently contract impurity. Conversely, if the Israelite intends to discard the object, it falls into the class of useless objects and cannot absorb impurity under any conditions.

A. [Concerning] a table [which normally stands on three legs, and subsequently] one of its legs was removed [with the result that it can no longer function as a table]--

B. it is clean [that is, it is cannot absorb impurity, because it falls into the category of a useless thing].

C.   [If] a second [leg was removed], it is clean [that is, it cannot absorb impurity because it remains useless].

D.   [If] the third [leg] was removed [that is all of its legs]--

E.   it [can contract] impurity only when [an Israelite] intends [to use] it [for some purpose, such as a tray to set upon the knees].[4]

M. Kel. 22:2

In this rule, a person's plan has the power to classify objects around the household. Merely by intending to use a table top, a householder in effect classifies it as "useful." Consequently, the table top can subsequently absorb impurity should it come in contact with one of the sources of contamination (E). A person's mere formulation of a plan, therefore, can produce significant legal consequences, which affect the other members of the household. Since the table top can now contract impurity, all members of the household must prevent it from coming in contact with sources of uncleanness. If they fail to do so, the table top will become contaminated and can no longer remain in the household. We now see why the issue of classification preoccupies the Mishnah's framers. In their system, an Israelite who wishes to live a life in accordance with divine law must know the mishnaic principles of classification. One who does not know these rules cannot determine which possessions are susceptible to contamination.

Just as intention determines whether an object falls into the category of useful or useless objects, it also serves as a criterion for distinguishing "food" from "waste." If a person intends to eat a certain substance or to sell it for human consumption, it falls into the category of food. Conversely, if someone intends to discard it, it is classified as waste. As previously discussed, whatever falls under the rubric of food can absorb cultic impurity, whereas waste products cannot contract impurity. For example, a piece of meat contracts impurity if it comes in contact with a source of impurity, with the result that an Israelite may no longer eat it. By contrast, rotten vegetables cannot become contaminated because they belong to the category of waste. The case at hand involves a pigeon which has died by falling into a wine vat. As we shall now see, the bird's classification depends upon the plan of the person who owns the wine vat.

A.   [As regards] a young pigeon that fell into a wine vat [and died]--

B.   if [the owner] intended to remove it (hsb ᶜlyw) [from the vat] for [sale to] a gentile,

C.   [the pigeon] is impure, [that is, it is subject to the rules governing food impurity.[5] Since the Israelite intends to sell it for consumption, the pigeon falls into the classification of food, and hence, it is subject to the restrictions governing food products].

D.   [If, however, the owner intended to remove the pigeon from the vat] for a dog,

E.   [the pigeon] is clean. [that is, it cannot contract impurity because the Israelite did not intend to use it for human consumption].

M. Toh. 8:6

By deciding what to do with the dead pigeon, the Israelite at hand determines whether it falls into the classification of human food or waste. The intention to sell the pigeon for human consumption makes it fall into the category of food, with the result that it is subject to the laws governing the purity of food (C). [6] If the owner decides to throw it to a dog, it becomes waste, and hence the rules governing the purity of food do not apply (D-E). [7]

Plans play a classificatory role in only one context outside the system of cultic purity, namely, in the laws regulating the sacrificial system. These laws in many respects take up the same sorts of problems examined in the system of cultic purity. In the laws of cultic purity, the Mishnah discusses the procedures for maintaining the home in a state of cultic purity. Similarly, in the laws of sacrifice, the Mishnah takes up the procedures for carrying out the Temple cult in accordance with God's wishes. As we shall now see, plans play a central role in the sacrificial system. Merely by formulating a plan, an Israelite priest determines whether the animal he sacrifices belongs to the category of an holy offering or to the category of a profane slaughter.

A. [Concerning a priest who, while slaughtering an animal, forms the intention] to eat an olive's bulk [of its flesh] outside the place [God has designated for its consumption],

B. and [who while collecting, transferring, and sprinkling the blood forms the intention] to eat an olive's bulk the following day [that is, after the period of time specified for its consumption has elapsed]...

C. [the offering] is invalid.

M. Zeb. 2:5

Here, the priest's plans have the power to desacralize an animal designated for a sacrifice. Since the priest intends to eat the meat at a place of his own choosing, and not in the place specified by God, he has in effect classified the cow as an animal slaughtered for secular purposes. His intention, therefore, effectively removes the animal from its classification as a holy thing, with the result that God repudiates the sacrifice. Once again, merely by forming an intention to put an object to a particular use, an Israelite alters the classification and hence the status of that object.

While intention serves similar functions in the sacrificial system and in the system of purity, there are several important differences. For this reason, we shall discuss the function of plans in the sacrificial system in the subsequent chapter. In the discussion to follow, we focus exclusively on the role of intention in the Mishnah's system of purity. This brings us to the critical question of the present inquiry: how do we make sense of the notion that human intention can determine the status of things?

The Power of Plans to Classify: The Underlying Significance

In the context of the mishnaic system, the capacity of intention to determine whether an object can absorb impurity constitutes an extraordinary power. For the sages, the distinction between pure and impure is constituent of reality. By this I mean that the line dividing clean and unclean things constitutes one of the two fundamental distinctions that give order to the sages' world. According to the Mishnah, the world is neatly divided into two grand dichotomies: 1) clean and unclean 2) sacred and profane. We know these two categories are primary because all other distinctions which the Mishnah makes are related to them. We saw, for example, that the Mishnah distinguishes carefully between useful and useless objects, and between food and waste. But these oppositions are merely a variation on the more basic distinction between pure and impure. Useful things and food can absorb impurity, whereas useless objects and waste are immune.

Perhaps an analogy would be helpful in understanding the significance of these distinctions in the mishnaic system. The dichotomy between pure and impure can be compared to the distinction between hot and cold. Impure objects, like hot things, are dangerous and need to be avoided. Being unable to distinguish between clean and unclean things or between things which absorb and withstand contamination, therefore, would be tantamount to not sensing the difference between hot and cold. One would be able to discriminate between objects on the basis of other criteria such as shape or color. But a crucial feature of the environment would be lacking. Moreover, without a sensitivity to hot and cold, everything would be potentially dangerous, because it would be impossible to know whether one was getting burned. To be sure, the sages of the Mishnah do not consider the risk of contamination to be a health hazard. But it does jeopardize their living a life in accordance with divine law. This analogy, therefore, suggests what the sages' world would be like were they unable to distinguish pure and impure things.

We can now appreciate the importance of intention in the Mishnaic system. In determining whether an object can become contaminated, intention in effect defines an important aspect of the sages' reality; it determines, so to speak, whether objects are hot or cold, and consequently how humans should treat those objects. In this sense, intention plays a critical role in shaping the character of the world. Stated still more abstractly, the Mishnah ascribes to human intention the power to domesticate reality itself. As I will argue in more detail below, the Mishnah thus perceives an analogy between human intention and the divine will. Just as God created the world through an exercise of will, humans impose order on their world by formulating intentions. By so doing, humans carry forward the divine work of creation. Having discussed the importance of planning, we must now consider the extent to which the framers derived their views from Scripture.

The Power of Plans to Classify: Mishnaic Innovation or Scriptural Inheritance?

The idea that a person's plans can determine whether an object absorbs or withstands impurity clearly represents a mishnaic innovation. In biblical law, human intention plays absolutely no role in the system of purity. In fact, in Leviticus, which provides the foundation for the Mishnah's system of purity, the term for human plans (*mahshabah*) does not even make its appearance.[8] This is because according to the priestly writers God alone determines which objects fall into various categories. Whereas in the Mishnah "food" refers to substances which people plan to use for food, in Leviticus, "food" refers to substances which God has designated for Israelite consumption. Thus, when the writers of Leviticus state that "any food that might be eaten" can contract impurity (Lev. 11:34), they mean that any substance which God permits Israelites to eat can become contaminated.[9] By contrast, when the Mishnah says that an object falls into the category of food it is because someone has decided to use it for that purpose. We see, therefore, that the biblical rules of purity do not place any stress at all on human intention.

While the biblical rules of purity place no stress on intention, we need to consider whether other strands of biblical thought shaped mishnaic thinking. In looking for the biblical antecedents of the Mishnah's theory, it seems only natural to examine the term *mahshabah* in its biblical contexts, as this is the term which the Mishnah employs to designate a person's plans. A survey of this term in its biblical setting reveals that aspects of the Mishnah's theory are indeed anticipated in the biblical writings. Specifically, the biblical writers treated the human capacity to plan as an important factor in the divine-human relationship. In the view of the priestly writer, for example, God decided to destroy the world because he "saw how great was man's wickedness on earth, and how every plan (*mahshabah*) devised by his mind was nothing but evil all the time. And the Lord regretted that He made man on earth, and His heart was saddened (Gen. 6:5-6)." Similarly, the writers of Proverbs proclaim, "Evil thoughts (*mhsbt*) are an abomination to the Lord, but pleasant words are pure (Prov. 15:26)." "The purposes (*mhsbt*) of the righteous are just, the schemes of the wicked are deceit (Prov. 12:5)."

These biblical statements anticipate the mishnaic concept of plans in several respects. First, the biblical writers believe that God cares, not only about what humans do but also about what they plan. Furthermore, we note that the biblical writers make an implicit connection between the human capacity to make plans and the divine will, for they use the same word (*mahshabah*) to describe human plans and divine thoughts. People are most like God when they make plans in accordance with divine will. Conversely, when they devise evil plans, they repudiate God, for they have pitted human will against divine will. As we saw previously, the Mishnah expresses similar ideas. In the Mishnah, the human capacity to plan enables humans to carry forward the divine will by categorizing the world into the categories God deems important. Moreover, human intention is like the divine will in that it has the power to shape reality.

While we find some similarities between the biblical and mishnaic conceptions of human plans, we also note an important difference. When the biblical authors invoke the notion of human plans, they frequently refer to situations in which a person repudiates God's will.[10] In addition to the three examples provided above, consider the following. According to Ezekiel, the Lord says, "On that day, a thought will occur to you and you will conceive a wicked design *(hsbt mhsbt r*c*h)*. You will say, 'I will invade a land of open towns (Ezek. 38:10-11).' " Similarly, God says to Jeremiah, "I have heard what the prophets say, who prophesy falsely in My name: 'I had a dream, I had a dream.' How long will there be in the minds of the prophets who prophesy falsehood-the prophets of their own deceitful minds- the plan *(hhsbym)* to make My people forget My name (Jer. 23:25-27)?" The biblical writers, therefore, often equate the human capacity to plan with the inclination to rebel against God. In the biblical literature, when a person forms a plan, it generally signifies the pitting of human will against the divine will. The Mishnah, by contrast, does not employ the term "plan" to designate the human inclination to rebel against God. On the contrary, in the Mishnah it is the capacity to plan which enables people to carry out the divine will by classifying the world into the categories God has defined as important.

Among those biblical passages in which the term *mahshabah* is used, the following reveals the most similarities to the Mishnah's conception of human planning. This passage, written by the priestly authors, describes how God commissioned Bezalel to design the Temple.

> And Moses said to the people of Israel, "See, the Lord has called by name Bezalel the son of Uri, son of Hur, of the tribe of Judah; and He has filled him with the Spirit of God, with ability, with intelligence, with knowledge, and with all craftsmanship, to devise artistic designs *(lhsb mhshbt)*, to work in gold and silver and bronze, in cutting stones for setting, and in carving wood, for work in every skilled craft *(ml'kt mhsbt)*. And He has inspired him to teach, both him and Oholiab the son of Ahisamach of the tribe of Dan. He has filled them with ability to do every sort of work done by a craftsman or by a designer *(hwsb)* or by an embroiderer in blue and purple...by any sort of workman or skilled designer *(hwsb mhsbt)*. Bezalel and Oholiab and every able man in whom the Lord has put ability and intelligence to know how to do any work in the construction of the sanctuary shall work in accordance with all that the Lord has commanded (Ex. 35:30-36:1). [11]

This passage anticipates many of the ideas we have discovered in the Mishnah. First of all, we note that the term *mahshabah* frequently appears in this passage and that it bears a meaning that closely corresponds to its meaning in the mishnaic system. Here, *mahshabah* denotes the human capacity to design an artistic work, which by definition involves formulating plans about how to utilize the various materials at hand. This idea is similar to the mishnaic notion that plans have the power to classify things. More importantly, this story makes explicit the notion that God appoints human beings to carry out divine plans. Here, Bezalel acts as God's partner in a joint venture of creation. God reveals a blueprint of the Temple and asks him to oversee its construction. As I previously suggested, the Mishnah also conceives of humans as acting as God's partner when they categorize the world. According to the Mishnah, God has instructed humanity to implement a divine scheme of classification. Hence, by classifying an object, one carries out the divine will. Of all the passages in Scripture that speak about the human capacity to plan, therefore, this passage bears the most similarities to the Mishnah's conception.

Nonetheless, critical elements of the Mishnah's theory are noticeably absent from this passage as well. We find, for instance, no indication that the classification of an object plays a fundamental role in determining its character. In my judgment, therefore, we need to look elsewhere to find the biblical roots of the Mishnah's theory. In what follows, I will argue that it is the two biblical myths of creation which provide the foundation for the Mishnah's theory of intention.

From Biblical Mythology to Mishnaic Theology: The Creation Stories and the Mishnah's Theory of Classification

The priestly account of creation (Gen. 1-2:4) emphasizes precisely those themes discovered in the Mishnah.[12] The priestly writer, for example, stresses the importance of classification in defining the character of the world.

> When God began to create the heaven and the earth...God said, "Let there be light"; and there was light. God saw that the light was good, and God separated the light from the darkness. God called the light Day, and the darkness He called Night...God made the expanse, and separated the water which was below the expanse from the water which was above the expanse. And it was so. God called the expanse Sky...God said, "Let the water below the sky be gathered into one area, that the dry land may appear." And it was so. God called the dry land Earth, and the gathering of waters He called Seas (Gen. 1:1-9).

According to the priestly writer, one of the central tasks in creation was classifying the world and giving things names. God separated light from darkness, the heavens above from the waters below, and the dry land from the seas. Upon categorizing the world, God named each of the things that was created. This myth anticipates the Mishnah in an important respect. It conceives of classification as instrumental in determining the character of the world. In this account, the divine act of classification is what gives the world its texture.[13] As I argued previously, the Mishnah also conceives of classification as playing a fundamental role in determining the character of reality. When the classification of an object is altered, its basic character changes as well. As we have seen, the Mishnah ascribes these powers to human beings. By implication, therefore, the Mishnah equates the human capacity to classify with the divine work of creation.

This explains why in the Mishnah the act of classifying an object alters that object's basic properties. In the Mishnah, as in Genesis 1, classification is an aspect of creation. Consequently, human acts of categorization, like God's, have the power to change the basic character of reality. When humans classify their world, therefore, they carry forward the divine act of creation.

The idea that human acts of categorization can affect the status of things obviously has no counterpart in the priestly story of creation. This biblical myth nowhere ascribes a role to humanity in classifying the world. For the priests, the basic dichotomies were established by God at creation. This is why in Leviticus, which was also written by the priests, humans have no role at all in classifying the world. In my judgment, the Mishnah based this conception on the other biblical story of creation, which is attributed to the Yahwist (Gen. 2:4-24):

> And the Lord God formed out of the earth all the wild beasts and all the birds of the sky, and brought them to the man to see what he would call them; and whatever the man called each living creature, that would be its name. And the man gave names to all the cattle and to the birds of the sky and to all the wild beasts (Gen. 2:19-20).

The author of this passage conceives of Adam as acting like God when he brings order out of chaos. By giving names to the animals, Adam completes the work of creation by labeling and thereby distinguishing one type of animal from another.[14] As a result, he participates with God in imposing order on the world. Adam, of course, is the prototype for humanity. The Yahwist, therefore, like the writers of the Mishnah, compares the human capacity to classify with God's power to create the world through an exercise of divine will.

This myth anticipates the Mishnah's theory in a second important respect. The biblical idea that Adam names the animals corresponds in fundamental ways to the mishnaic idea that human beings classify objects by planning to use them. To begin with, in planning how to use an object, a person in effect gives that object a name. For example, when a person decides to eat a dead bird, he or she effectively labels the bird "food." In this respect, planning how to use an object and naming an object are two sides of the same coin. More importantly, within the context of their respective systems, naming and planning fulfill identical roles.

The correspondence between naming and planning emerges when we consider the significance of naming in the biblical literature. We noted above that in the biblical myth, God gave names to the various things which were created. In biblical thought, naming is in some sense equivalent to creating. This is why the biblical writers represent a change in a person's character by changing his or her name. The priestly writer claims, for example, that when God formed a covenant with Avram and Sarai , he changed their names to Abraham and Sarah (Gen. 17:15).[15] Furthermore, by giving something a name, one defines its character and thereby gains mastery over it. In several biblical accounts, therefore, an angel refuses to reveal its name to a human being. This prevents the person from gaining control over the angel (see Gen. 32:30, Jud. 13:17-18).

The notion that God permits Adam to name the animals, therefore, implies that God confers on humanity the power to define the character of wildlife and thus master it. This idea thus corresponds to the mishnaic idea that human beings classify the world by planning how to use things. Just as in biblical thought naming an object defines the character of that object, so in the mishnaic system people define the character of objects by planning how to use them. Of all the biblical passages, therefore, the Yahwist story of creation comes closest conceptually to the Mishnah's theory of intention.

Conceptual similarities by themselves are insufficient to demonstrate the Mishnah's dependence on these biblical myths. However, other evidence supports my claim that the biblical stories of creation are at the core of mishnaic theology. The Mishnah cites Genesis 1 a number of times to justify certain rulings and to support certain theological propositions.

First, it appeals to Genesis 1 in clarifying the rule that an animal and its offspring cannot be sacrificed on one day (Lev. 22:28). Specifically, the Mishnah wants to determine what constitutes "one day." Does one reckon a day from sunrise to sunrise or from sunset to sunset? The Mishnah concludes that a day begins and ends at sunset, because Genesis 1 says, "And there was evening and there was morning, one day (Gen. 1:5)." This verse implies that God considered a day as beginning at sunset and continuing until sunset the next day (M. Hul. 5:5).

Second, the Mishnah cites the priestly account of creation in discussing the obligation of Israelites to procreate. According to one sage this obligation applies both to men and women. He bases his view on the fact that Genesis says "God blessed *them* and God said to *them*, 'Be fertile and increase (Gen. 1:28).'" Since the command is addressed to the first man and woman, both men and women fall subject to the obligation. The same Mishnah passage also cites God's activity at creation to support the view that the obligation to procreate is only fulfilled when one has given birth to a son and a daughter. Genesis says that when God created humanity, "male and female He created them (Genesis 5:2, 1:27)." Because God produced a male and female at creation, an Israelite is also expected to have a son and daughter (M. Yeb. 6:6).

Third, the Mishnah specifies blessings which Israelites must say over the food they are about to eat. Significantly, the substance of these blessings refers to God's act of creation. For example, over wine one says, "Blessed art thou...who has created the fruit of the tree," and over vegetables one says, "Blessed art thou...who creates the fruit of the ground (M. Ber. 6:1)." Over items like meat and fish, one says "Blessed art thou...by whose word all things exist (M. Ber. 6:2-3)." We see, therefore, that the Mishnah expects Israelites to reflect routinely upon the divine act of creation. Every meal or snack is an occasion for celebrating God's creation of the world.

Fourth, the Mishnah discusses at some length the significance of the fact that Adam was created alone:

> Only a single person was created to teach that anyone who kills a single soul from Israel, Scripture deems it equivalent to destroying the entire world. Anyone who saves an Israelite life--Scripture deems it equivalent to saving the entire world. [A single person was also created] for the sake of harmony among humankind. This prevents one person from saying to another, "My ancestor was greater than yours [since everyone derives from the same ancestor]." It also prevents sectarians from saying "There are many powers in heaven." [Finally, the creation of a single person] testifies to the greatness of the Holy One, the Blessed, for humans make many coins from a single mold [with the result that] each resembles the other, but the King of Kings, the Holy one the Blessed, made all human beings with one mold and yet no one looks alike (M. San. 4:5).

As the above passages suggest, we have ample evidence that Genesis 1 plays a fundamental role in shaping mishnaic thought.

More significantly, in two instances the Mishnah explicitly links its system of purity to God's activity at creation. First, it claims that materials which are susceptible to impurity were created on alternate days of creation.

A. On the first day [of creation] something was created which is susceptible to impurity [when made into a vessel], but on the second day of creation [nothing was created] which is susceptible to impurity.

B. On the third day [of creation], something was created which is susceptible to impurity, but on the fourth and fifth days, nothing [was created] that is susceptible to impurity...

C. Everything that was created on the sixth day of creation is susceptible to impurity.

M. Kel. 17:14

It is significant that the Mishnah seeks to link the types of materials which are susceptible to impurity to the creation story. In so doing, the Mishnah is claiming that God's act of ordering the world is directly related to the classifications which govern the Mishnah's system of purity. By distinguishing things which can and cannot absorb impurity, therefore, Israelites carry forward a basic distinction that God implanted in the world at creation.

The Mishnah also refers to the priestly version of creation when determining whether seas can serve as as an immersion pool (*mikveh*) for cleansing a person of ritual impurity (M. Par. 8:8, M. Miq. 5:4). One sage cites Genesis 1:10 as evidence that the seas can serve that function. In his judgment, the fact that God called the gathering (*mikveh*) of water "seas" proves that the sea can serve as an immersion pool (*mikveh*) for the purposes of ritual purification. These two sources, therefore, testify that the priestly account of creation functions as a paradigm for the Mishnah's system of purity.

Finally, we find a linguistic connection between the Mishnah's interest in classification and the priestly version of creation. The Mishnah often discusses whether two items belong to the same category of thing. Significantly, one of the expressions the Mishnah uses to express this idea is related to an expression which appears several times in Genesis 1. The Mishnah frequently says that "one type of produce is or is not of the same kind as another (*myn bmynw* or *myn bs'ynw mynw*)." [16] This formula is apparently related to the biblical idiom "according to its own kind (*lmynhw* or *lmynw*). It turns out that it is only in Genesis 1 that Scripture uses this expression in referring to plant life (Gen. 1:21, 24, 25).[17]

It is more difficult to demonstrate the Mishnah's reliance on the Yahwist story of creation (Gen. 2:4-25). In fact, no mishnaic passage explicitly cites this story. Nonetheless, the Mishnah's debt to this biblical myth is suggested by the terminology which the Mishnah employs in articulating its theory of classification. The Mishnah frequently refers to classifying objects as "calling them a name (*lqrw' sm*)" (see, for example, M. Dem. 4:3, 4:4, 7:6, M. Ter. 3:5, 5:1, M. M.S. 4:4, 5:9, M. Pes. 3:3). This is precisely the same expression that appears in the passage regarding Adam's naming of the animals. God brought the animals to Adam "to see what he would call them; and whatever the man called each living creature, that would be its name. And the man gave [lit. called] names (*wyqr' smwt*) to all the cattle and the birds of the sky and to all the wild beasts." In addition, the Mishnah uses the biblical word "name (*sm*)" to mean "category." For example, when two objects do not belong to the same category, the Mishnah says that they do not derive from the [same] name ('*ynw mn hsm*) (M. Ker. 3:4, M. Mak. 3:9).[18] The Mishnah did not have to rely on this biblical expression to express the idea of category. Mishnaic Hebrew provides other words to express the idea of category (i.e., *b' lkll* or *bkll*). The fact that the Mishnah appropriates language from Genesis 2, therefore, strengthens my claim that this biblical myth provides the conceptual foundations of the Mishnah's theory of classification.

In this connection, it is interesting to note that the Mishnah frequently refers to God as "The Name (*hsm*)." [19] At the simplest level, this expression is a circumlocution for the tetragrammaton. But given the importance of the word "name" in the Mishnah's theory of classification, one wonders whether this expression resonates on another level for the Mishnah's sages. As we have seen, the Mishnah uses precisely the same expression when referring to an object's category. For example, when the Mishnah says that two objects do not belong to the same category, it says they "are not [from] the name" (*hsm*) (M. Ker. 3:4, M. Mak. 3:9). It is as if the sages give linguistic expression to an idea which we have shown is at the heart of the mishnaic system, namely, the idea that God is the ultimate classifier or the ultimate source of classification. This point, however, is impossible to prove and must remain a matter of speculation.

To return to the main point of our inquiry, one final piece of evidence substantiates a connection between the story of Adam naming the animals and the Mishnah's theory of intention. The Mishnah, as we shall now see, conceives of human beings as serving as God's agent when they categorize things. Indeed, the Mishnah implies that God actually commissioned humanity to complete creation by sorting various things into their respective categories.

Humanity as an Agent of God

In the biblical myth, God asked Adam to give the animals names. In appropriating this conception into their own system, however, the framers of the Mishnah develop an idea which is only implicit in the biblical narrative, namely, the idea that God appointed human beings as agents to carry out the work of classification. To be sure, the biblical account conceives of Adam as being a partner of God in completing the work of creation. The sages of the Mishnah, however, give this idea a distinctive twist. In the Mishnah, appointing someone as an agent has a technical sense.[20] It means that both the principal (i.e., the person who appoints the agent) and the agent resemble one another in certain fundamental respects and are legally bound by certain reciprocal rights and duties, which I shall spell out below. In what follows, I will argue that the mishnaic conception of agency provides the conceptual framework for all that the Mishnah says about the role of humans in the system of purity. In making this claim, I am ascribing to the Mishnah a view which is never explicitly stated. However, an inductive study of the Mishnah's rules shows that the mishnaic conception of agency informs the sages' discussion. In other words, we find that the mishnaic laws which govern the relationship between a principal and agent in other parts of the mishnaic system correspond to the rules governing the divine-human relationship in the Mishnah's system of purity.

In the mishnaic system, the problem of agency forms an important topic of discussion in its own right. The Mishnah discusses numerous situations in which one Israelite appoints another to act on his or her behalf. For example, the sages consider cases of an Israelite man who asks someone to carry out his obligation of setting aside produce for the temple (M. Ter. 4:4), or to deliver a writ of divorce to his wife (M. Git. 1:4, 4:1), or to espouse a woman on his behalf (M. Qid. 9:4). In contemplating these situations, the sages discuss the reciprocal rights and duties that an agent and the principal have to one another. Specifically, three rules govern the relationship between principal and agent.

First, the Mishnah states unequivocally that by appointing someone as an agent, an Israelite transfers his or her own legal powers to that person. For example, a child has neither the duty nor the right to dedicate heave-offering to the Temple. But if a householder, who by definition has such a right, appoints his son as an agent, the son may carry out this task (M. Ter. 3:4). By assigning this task to his son, the householder in effect confers on the child the legal power to sanctify produce. An agent, therefore, can create the same legal consequences as the principal.

A similar idea appears to underlie the sages' conception of the human role in classification. Because the Mishnah conceives of humans as acting as divine agents, it ascribes to human beings powers which are analogous to God's. In the mythic story of creation, it was the divine acts of classification which gave shape to reality. The sages treat human acts of categorization as tantamount to creation. This is evident in the fact that the Mishnah attributes profound consequences to human acts of classification. When a person puts an object into a given category, he or she determines its most fundamental characteristic, namely, whether it can absorb or withstand impurity. In appointing humanity to classify the world, therefore, God in effect transferred divine powers to human beings.

This brings us to the second way in which the Mishnah's conception of agency is implicit in its system of impurity. In mishnaic law, an agent must resemble the principal in certain fundamental respects. In particular, the agent must be permitted to perform for his or her own benefit what the principal has requested. If the law does not permit a person to perform a given act, then such a person cannot perform that act for someone else. The Mishnah says, for example, that by hearing a minor, a deaf-mute, or retarded person blow a ram's horn, an adult Israelite male does not fulfill his religious obligation to hear the ram's horn on the New Year's day. Since these Israelites do not have the religious obligation to hear the horn blown, they cannot perform that act on behalf of someone who has this obligation, namely, an adult male (M. R.H. 3:8, M. Meg. 2:4). For similar reasons, a minor, deaf-mute, and retarded person cannot serve a writ of divorce. Since these people lack the legal capacity to enter into a marital relationship, they cannot act on behalf of someone who has that power. The Mishnah treats these Israelites differently from others because it conceives of them as lacking certain rational faculties.[21] Because they do not have the capacity to understand the full implications of the task involved, they cannot act as agents for Israelites who have such capabilities. From the Mishnah's standpoint, therefore, a person can transfer legal powers only to someone who has the capacity to understand the full implications of the assigned task.

In the Mishnah, humans can act on God's behalf because they are fundamentally like God in that they have the capacity to think, or more specifically, the capability of analysing the world around them. It is this rational capacity which enables human beings to understand the order of creation and to imitate God's act of classifying the world. We have seen, for example, that in the mishnaic system an Israelite who wishes to fulfill divine law must learn the rules governing the classification system. Failure to understand the divine theory of classification will result in an infraction of divine law. The laws of blessings also illustrate the importance of the rational faculty in carrying out God's will.

We recall that the Mishnah requires Israelites to recite certain blessings over the foods which they eat. In order to choose the correct blessing, an Israelite must identify the item's proper category. For example, one must learn to distinguish "fruit of the ground" from "fruit of the tree." In addition, an Israelite must understand the relationships among the various categories. One must know that fruit of the trees is a subcategory of fruit of the earth. Therefore, one satisfies one's religious obligation by saying "Blessed are You...who creates the fruit of the ground" over an apple, because an apple is included in the category "fruit of the ground." But one does not satisfy one's religious duty by saying "who creates the fruit of the tree" over a potato, because a potato is not included in the category "fruit of the tree." The Mishnah, therefore, expects one to have mastered the various classifications which God established in nature. Failure to understand the divine order makes one incapable of praising God. Insofar as humans have the mental capacity to understand and therefore imitate the divine ordering of the world, they have powers like God's.

It follows that Israelites who lack rational faculties will not have the power to classify the world. This explains why in the mishnaic system the plans of children, deaf-mutes, and retarded persons have no power to classify objects. From the Mishnah's standpoint, these persons do not resemble God in the same way as a mentally fit adult, for they lack full mental capacities. Since they do not resemble God in this critical respect, they cannot serve as God's agent for classifying the world. Accordingly, the plan formulated by any of these persons has no power whatsoever to determine the classification of an object (M. Kel. 17:15, M. Toh. 8:6, M. Makh. 3:8).

A third mishnaic principle governing agency also finds a parallel in the Mishnah's theory of classification, namely, the principle of vicarious liability. Vicarious liability means that the principal assumes responsibility for his or her agent's action, as long as the agent follows the principal's instructions. Suppose, for example, that a man appoints an agent to espouse a woman on his behalf. If the agent carries out that task as he was directed, the principal is betrothed to the woman in question (M. Qid. 4:9). We see, therefore, that as long as an agent executes his task as instructed, he produces legal effects binding upon the principal. In this respect, the agent exercises power over the principal. Consider, for example, the case of a man who appoints an agent to divorce a woman, but while the agent is en route, the man changes his mind and decides he does not want the divorce. Unless he reaches the agent before the writ of divorce has been delivered, the divorce is valid. As long as an agent acts in good faith, the principal must accept the legal consequences of the agent's action.

If, however, an agent disobeys instructions, no legal effects are produced. Thus if a man asks an agent to espouse a particular woman in Jerusalem, but the agent espouses her in Tiberias, the betrothal is invalid (M. Qid. 2:4). Since the agent violated the terms of his agency, his action produces no binding legal consequences.

A parallel conception underlies the mishnaic theory of classification. In the sages' view, human acts of categorization alter an object's status only when divine instructions have been obeyed. But if people ignore the terms of their agency, their intentions lack the power to affect the status of objects. To fully understand this idea, we must first consider what, from the Mishnah's standpoint, constitute the terms governing human agency.

The framers believe that God's instructions to humanity are recorded in Scripture, especially in the book of Leviticus. In that book, God specified a scheme of classification and assigned humans a role in implementing that scheme. In the Mishnah's understanding of Leviticus, God assigned people the task of determining which objects would be capable of absorbing impurity. This is why in the Mishnah, humans determine whether objects fall into the following two pairs of categories: food and waste, and useful and useless things. As we have already seen, the objects that fall into the first category of each pair (i.e. food and useful things) can contract impurity, whereas objects that fall into the second category in each pair (i.e., waste and useless things) cannot absorb impurity. By giving humanity this particular assignment, the Mishnah asserts that God empowered people to decide what objects would contract impurity and which objects would be immune.

We find, however, no mishnaic cases in which humans determine whether something is a source of impurity. Certain substances, such as flesh from a corpse, semen, and certain types of dead animals are by definition sources of impurity. Humans cannot affect the status of these things. The implication of this fact is self-evident. According to the sages, God did not commission humankind to determine what objects are sources of impurity. That task was reserved for God alone.[22] God has said that these things impart impurity and humanity has no input into the matter (Lev. 11:29-32). Whereas God determines which objects are sources of impurity, humans determine which objects can contract impurity from them. This, then, constitutes the terms of human agency.

On what do the sages base this understanding of Leviticus? Apparently, they pick up on an ambiguity in the levitical law. The writers of Leviticus did not bother to enumerate the types of substances that can absorb impurity. Leviticus says that "as to any food that might be eaten, it shall become unclean if it came in contact with water; as to any liquid that might be drunk, it shall become unclean if it was inside any vessel (Lev. 11:34)." Similarly, Leviticus says that "anything on which [a swarming thing] falls when dead shall be unclean: be it any article of wood, or a cloth, or a skin, or a sack-any such article that can be put to use ...(Lev. 11: 32). "Leviticus does not provide an extensive list of what constitutes food and useful things. This is in striking contrast to the way in which Leviticus enumerates *ad nauseam* the types of things which are sources of impurity (Lev. 11:2-32; 13;15). The sages of the Mishnah apparently understood this to be a mandate for humanity to determine what constitutes food and useful objects. In their view, since Leviticus did not spell out in detail the kinds of items that constitute food or useful things, God must have meant for human beings to define these categories.

Having now spelled out the terms of human agency as the Mishnah understands it, we shall see that this plays a fundamental role in determining whether a person's intention can produce legal consequences. The Mishnah ascribes powers to human intention only when people carry out the task that God assigned them. But when they ignore divine instructions, their intentions produce no consequences at all.

The following mishnaic passage illustrates this point. The Mishnah contrasts two cases: one in which human intention has the power to determine the status of an object, and a parallel case in which intention is ineffective. Specifically, the first case involves an Israelite who slaughters a pregnant cow according to the correct ritual procedure. Upon cutting open the carcass, he discovers the fetus of a baby cow. The contrasting case also involves an Israelite who finds a fetus inside a slaughtered cow. Here, however, the Israelite has slaughtered the mother cow improperly.

Separate questions of classification occupy the sages in the two cases. In the first case, they wish to know whether the fetus of the cow belongs to the category of food or waste. The answer to this question, as we now expect, determines whether the fetus can become contaminated by impurity. In the second case, the sages want to know whether the fetus belongs to the category of the animal's meat, or to the category of its entrails. This distinction is important because in mishnaic law the meat and entrails of an improperly slaughtered animal have a different status. The meat of the animal is a source of uncleanness and makes anything it touches impure. The entrails, however, do not impart impurity (Lev. 7:24, M. Hul. 9:1). By asking whether the fetus belongs to the category of meat or entrails, therefore, the sages wish to know whether it is a source of impurity.

A. [As regards an Israelite] who slaughters an animal [according to the correct procedure] and finds a fetus within it--

B. a person with a strong stomach (*nps hyph*) may eat it. [Since the animal was properly slaughtered, Israelites are permitted to eat the fetus just as they are permitted to eat the meat of the animal. Therefore a person who can tolerate such food is permitted by law to eat it if he or she so desires].

C. [Although Israelites are permitted to eat a fetus, it falls into the category of waste, with the result that it] cannot contract food impurity. [This is because most Israelites consider the fetus repulsive and do not eat such things. Since Israelites do not regard a fetus as food, it does not contract the impurity of food].

D. And [in the case of a fetus that was discovered in a cow that had been slaughtered improperly, the fetus does not transmit] the impurity of carrion, [because only the meat of carrion transmits uncleanness. The fetus, like the bones, sinews and fat does not (see Lev. 7:24, and M. Hul. 9:1)].

E. [If, however, in the case of the properly slaughtered cow, the slaughterer] planned [to eat] the fetus (*hsb* ^C*lyb*) [before carrying out the slaughter] --

F. [the fetus falls into the category of food with the result that it] can contract food impurity. [In this case, the intention of the slaughterer determines the status of the fetus].

G. But [in the case of the improperly slaughtered cow, if the slaughterer plans to eat the fetus and thus clearly regards it as part of the beast's meat, it nonetheless does not fall into the category of meat, and hence] does not [transmit] the impurity of carrion. [In this case, the intention of the slaughterer is irrelevant. The fetus is treated as part of the cow's entrails even if the slaughterer considers it to be meat].

M. Hul. 4:7

The important point emerges from the contrast between the two cases at hand. In the first case, the Israelite's intention has the power to classify the fetus. By formulating a plan to eat it, he effectively classifies it as food, and hence must treat it according to the rules of cultic purity (E-F). In the contrasting case, however, the Israelite's intention is powerless to affect the classification of the fetus. Although he clearly regards it as meat, it does not fall into that category. It retains its status as entrails and hence does not transmit the impurity of carrion (G).

We can make sense of this rule by appealing to the Mishnah's conception of agency. In the Mishnah, human beings have the power to classify things only when they carry out the task that God initially assigned them. As I argued previously, in the Mishnah's understanding humans are only commissioned to determine what things can absorb impurity. But it is God alone who determines what is a source of impurity. It is for this reason that the Israelite's intention has no power to determine whether the fetus at hand is meat or entrails. Otherwise, the Israelite would be overstepping the bounds of his authority by determining whether the fetus is a source of impurity. The Israelite's intention, however, does have the power to determine whether it is food or waste. In this instance, the Israelite is carrying out God's mandate to determine whether something is capable of absorbing impurity.

This passage is important in another respect as well. It indicates that as long as human beings obey the terms of their agency, they have absolute power to determine the classification of the object in question. For having assigned to humankind the specific task of determining what things can absorb impurity, God totally relinquished control over how humans carry out that function. The Mishnah makes this point by noting that an Israelite may classify an object in a different way than God! In the case at hand, the sages obviously believe that God considers a fetus to be legitimate food for Israelites. Otherwise, they would forbid Israelites to eat it (B). Nonetheless, the fetus is not necessarily susceptible to impurity. This is because humans alone determine what constitutes food and waste. The Mishnah, therefore, recognizes the paradoxical conclusion that God and humans have different conceptions of food. God specified a range of substances that Israelites may and may not eat. Yet these substances do not automatically constitute food. Ultimately, their status depends on whether the Israelite community treats them as food.

The Mishnah makes the same striking point in a case which we have considered elsewhere. Here, the sages discuss whether a pigeon which has died by falling into a wine vat belongs to the category of food. According to Scripture, God does not permit Israelites to eat any animal which has died of natural causes (Lev. 7:24, 17:15, 22:8, Deut. 14:21).[23] But consider what happens once an Israelite plans to sell the dead pigeon as food:

A. [As regards] a young pigeon that fell into a wine vat [and died]--
B. if [the owner] planned to remove it (*hsb* *^{c}lyw*) [from the vat] for [sale to] a gentile, [the pigeon] is impure. [Since the Israelite intends to sell it for consumption, the pigeon falls into the classification of food, and hence, it becomes subject to the rules governing the purity of food].[24]
C. [If, by contrast, he intended to remove it from the vat] for a dog, [the pigeon] is insusceptible to impurity [because the Israelite did not intend to use it for human consumption].

M. Toh. 8:6

According to Scripture, God has forbidden Israelites to eat any animal that has not been ritually slaughtered. Hence, the pigeon that died by falling into a wine vat cannot be consumed by an Israelite. However, according to the Mishnah, an Israelite who plans to sell the dead bird in the market place effectively puts it into the category of food, with the result that it is now subject to the restrictions governing the purity of food (A-B).

This rule, therefore, is the mirror image of the previous example. In that case, an Israelite classified as waste something that in the sages' judgment God conceives of as food. Here, an Israelite classifies as food something which the framers believe God forbade Israelites to eat. Both rules, therefore, illustrate the respective roles of God and humans in the process of classifying the world. The Mishnah claims that God specified the general categories into which the world would be divided (in this case the categories of "food" and "waste") and ordained the rules that would govern those categories. But the Mishnah also maintains that God authorized humanity to determine what items actually would fall into the designated categories. As long as people obey the divine terms of agency, therefore, they have absolute control over the classification of objects. Translated into theological language, the sages believe that when human beings properly execute their agency, they fulfill the divine will. In these circumstances, therefore, their intentions have powers which are analogous to God's. However, a person who violates the divine terms of agency, in effect repudiates the divine will. Consequently, this person cannot exercise the powers which were conferred by God.

Having explained why human plans have such dramatic effects in the mishnaic system, we now take up the second important question of the present study: in what specific contexts does intention serve as a criterion for classification?

When and Why Plans Have the Power to Classify

In classifying an object, the Mishnah sometimes takes account of how a person plans to use it, while in other contexts, it completely ignores what the person plans. What induces the Mishnah to appeal to plans in some cases but not others? Examination of the Mishnah's rules shows that the sages appeal to a person's plans only when an object's status is equivocal. But if the status of the object is self-evident, they completely ignore how the owner plans to use it.

Let me provide an example illustrating each aspect of this theory. Suppose that an Israelite householder finds a dead cow lying in his field. Since the farmer has so far done nothing with the carcass, it is unclear whether it falls under the rubric of food or waste. On the one hand, he may sell it as food. On the other hand, he may let it rot in his field. To resolve the ambiguity, the Mishnah will appeal to the householder's plan. If the householder intends to sell the cow, the sages treat it as food, whereas if he plans to discard it, the cow falls into the category of waste. An Israelite's plan, therefore, enables the sages to predict an object's use before the Israelite has actually done anything with it. Consequently, by knowing the Israelite's plans, the sages can settle the ambiguity in the object's status.

In some cases, however, the sages consider the status of an object to be self-evident and therefore deem irrelevant what the owner plans to do with it. For example, if the cow mentioned above had died in the marketplace rather than in the field, the sages would automatically classify it as food. They would do so on the assumption that the householder would sell the cow since it was already in the marketplace. In this case, since the status of the cow is unequivocal, the sages would ignore the owner's intention. Even if he decided to let it rot, the cow would remain in the category of food and hence be susceptible to contamination.

In sum, therefore, intention only classifies an object if its status is equivocal. But if it clearly belongs to a particular category, the owner's intention is powerless to affect that item's status. Let me now demonstrate how these points actually emerge from the Mishnah's rules.

The Power of Plans To Resolve Ambiguity: The Case of Household Objects

We turn first to the familiar case of the broken table. Here, the sages consider whether a table, as it gradually loses each of its legs, can absorb cultic impurity. The answer depends upon whether the broken table has fallen under the rubric of a useless thing. If so, then the table can no longer contract impurity. In examining this rule, we wish to know why the Mishnah invokes the householder's plan only at the point at which the table loses all of its legs:

> A. [Concerning] a table [which stands on three legs, and subsequently] one of its legs was removed [with the result that it can no longer function as a table],
> B. it is clean [that is, it cannot contract impurity, because it clearly falls into the category of useless objects].
> C. [If] a second [leg] was removed,
> D. it [remains] clean [that is, it still cannot contract impurity, because it remains useless].
> E. [If] the third [leg was removed, that is, it is now missing all of its legs],
> F. it [becomes susceptible] to impurity [only] when [the householder] plans [to put] it (*yhsb* ^{c}*lyw*) [to use].
> G. Rabbi Yose says, "[In order to absorb impurity] it is not necessary [that the householder formulates] a plan [to use the table top. Whether or not the householder actually plans to use it, the table can absorb impurity.]"
>
> M. Kel. 22:2

This rule illustrates both aspects of the Mishnah's theory. When a table loses some of its legs, it obviously becomes useless. For this reason, the Mishnah automatically declares it insusceptible to impurity. The owner's intention plays no role whatsoever in defining its status (A-D).

A dispute arises, however, over the status of a table which has lost all of its legs. The unnamed sages think its classification is equivocal. On the one hand, the householder may eventually use it as a tray. On the other hand, he may also discard it as trash. To clear up the ambiguity, therefore, the sages turn to the householder's plan (E-F). Yose, by contrast, claims that once a table loses all its legs it automatically re-enters the class of useful things. Since a table top can effectively function as a tray, Yose assumes that the householder will use it for that purpose. He takes for granted that Israelites normally do not throw away things which can serve a household function. For this reason, Yose considers the householder's intention to be irrelevant. We see, therefore, that although Yose and the sages disagree about the status of the table top, they subscribe to the same underlying theory. Intention is only of consequence when an object's status is ambiguous.

The following rule makes essentially the same point. Here, however, ambiguity arises not because the item in question has fallen apart, as in the case of the table, but because the householder has so far done nothing with the object that might indicate its status. Specifically, the Mishnah discusses whether various leather goods can absorb impurity. In order to understand this rule, we first need to familiarize ourselves with the complex laws governing the cultic purity of leather.

The sages divide leather goods into three distinct categories. First, they make the familiar distinction between useful and useless objects. Useful leather goods can absorb cultic impurity, whereas useless leather goods cannot. Second, the sages further subdivide useful leather goods into two classes: 1) those which are large enough to sit on and 2) those which are not. Different rules apply to small and large leather goods. Small leather goods, like other household objects, can absorb impurity only if they come in direct contact with a source of impurity. The larger goods also absorb impurity through contact. But in addition, they become contaminated even if they should bear indirect pressure from a source of impurity. For example, if a corpse falls on a rock that touches a leather rug, the leather becomes contaminated, even though the intervening rock is immune from impurity. Since the corpse has indirectly exerted pressure on the leather, the leather is rendered impure. In the rule at hand, the sages discuss the status of various leather objects. For our purposes, one critical question arises. Why does the Mishnah invoke the owner's intention in classifying only one of the leather goods in the list below?

A. These are the [types of] leather goods which contract impurity through the exertion of pressure:
B. a hide which [a householder] planned [to use] for a rug,
C. a tablecloth [with straps by which it attaches to the table, (see M. Kel. 16:4)],
D. a [leather] bedspread [which ties to the bedframe (see M. Kel. 16:4)],
E. a hide [used by] ass-drivers [for a saddle],[25]
F. a hide [used by] flax-workers [to protect their hands (M. Kel. 16:6)],
G. a hide [use by] a porter [to protect his shoulders from the object he carries (M. Kel. 28:9)],
H. a hide [used by] a physician [as an apron during blood letting],
I. a hide [used for a baby's] crib (M. Par. 12:8),
J. a hide [which protects] a child's heart [a euphemism for a child's diaper],[26]
K. a hide [which can be stuffed to serve as] a mattress (see M. Kel. 15:4, M. Miq. 7:6),
L. a hide [which can be stuffed to serve as] a cushion (see M. Kel. 16:4, M. Miq. 7:6).
M. [All of these leather goods absorb impurity] through [the exertion of] pressure.

M. Kel. 26:5

The Mishnah takes account of a householder's intention to determine the status of a leather hide (A) but not the status of the other leather goods (B-L). This is because the classification of a leather hide is equivocal, for the householder has so far done nothing with it. He may eventually use it as a rug, as a cover for a vessel, or simply cut it into sandal straps. Unless the sages appeal to the householder's plan, they have no way of predicting whether the hide will fall under the rubric of large or small leather goods. The householder's plan to use the hide as a rug, therefore, has the effect of placing it into the category of a large useful hide. Hence, it subsequently absorbs impurity if it bears the slightest pressure from a source of impurity. Presumably, although sages do not say this explicitly, if the householder intends to use the hide as a cover for a vessel, it would fall under the rubric of a small, useful leather object. Like other small leather goods, it would contract impurity only by coming in direct contact with sources of impurity.

Intention plays no role in deciding the status of the other leather goods listed here, because their function is self-evident. Some of the objects, such as the tablecloth (C), bedspread (D), mattress (K), cushion (L), the hide for the crib (I), and the leather diaper (J) have distinguishing physical characteristics such as straps or cavities for stuffing, which indicate their purpose (see M. Kel. 16:4). Similarly, the function of the other hides (E-H), can be deduced merely by determining the profession of the person who owns them. A hide owned by a porter, for example, obviously serves to protect his shoulders (G). In each case, it is obvious that the hide in question falls into the category of a large, useful leather product.[27] Accordingly, these hides can absorb cultic impurity through the mere exertion of pressure.

This case, therefore, like the one before it, implies that the Mishnah ignores a householder's intention when the function of the object is obvious. In the following passage, the Mishnah spells out this point explicitly. Here, the sages discuss a case of a householder who plans to cut a useful leather hide into straps or soles for sandals. In mishnaic law, straps and soles of sandals by definition fall under the rubric of useless things. This is because Israelites normally make straps and soles from leftover scraps of leather. Since these leather goods generally derive from waste, the sages always regard them as useless (M. Kel. 24:12). When a householder intends to cut a leather hide into straps, as in the case at hand, he in effect plans to convert a useful object into a useless one. As we shall now see, in this situation his intention is powerless to alter the status of the object.

A. [Concerning] a [large useful] leather hide [such as an apron or bedspread] which may contract impurity through pressure--

B. [even if the owner] planned [to cut] it (hsb ᶜlyw) into straps or [into soles for] sandals, [the leather remains in the category of a useful object and hence may still contract impurity through the exertion of pressure].

C. "[But] once he touches the knife to the hide [as he begins to cut it], the hide [immediately falls into the category of useless objects, and hence] it becomes clean [that is, it can no longer contract impurity at all]," [these are] the words of Rabbi Judah.

D. Sages say, "[It falls into the category of useless objects only when the rug has been cut into pieces] smaller than five handbreadths. [When it is this size, it can no longer serve most household functions and hence it falls into the category of useless things with the result that it can longer absorb impurity (see M. Kel. 27:2).]"

M. Kel. 26:9

If an object clearly serves a designated function, the householder's intention is powerless to change the status of that object. Even if the householder plans to break or cut the object into pieces, the sages continue to treat it as a useless thing. This is why in the case at hand the householder's plan to cut a rug into useless scraps has no effect on its status. The Mishnah continues to treat the rug as useful, as is evident by the fact that it can absorb impurity. As in previous laws, the Mishnah apparently takes for granted that Israelites do not destroy valuable things. The sages, therefore, doubt whether the householder at hand will in fact carry out his plan to destroy the hide. For this reason, they simply discount the intention he has formulated.

But what happens if the Israelite actually implements his intention? Judah maintains that once the householder applies the knife to the hide, one can safely assume the householder will carry out the intended act. At the moment the knife touches the leather, therefore, the hide enters the category of useless things. The sages, by contrast, regard the hide as useless only if the householder actually cuts it into pieces. In their view, only at this point can one know for certain that the householder will no longer change his mind. This law thus draws our attention to the respective roles of plans and actions in the Mishnah's system of classification. We see that actions possess a far greater power than plans. By cutting an object into pieces, an Israelite can convert a useful thing into a useless one. The mere plan to carry out this act does not affect the status of the object at all.

We now turn to the sages' own abstract, albeit rather cryptic, formulation of their theory. In most respects, this law will tell us nothing we have not already discovered inductively. However, it is interesting to see how the Mishnah itself attempts to rise above the details of the cases to formulate its theory in abstract form. The sages begin by explaining when and why plans have the power to classify, and then proceed to contrast the respective powers of plans and actions:

A. All objects can contract impurity [once an Israelite formulates] a plan (*mahshabah*) [to put them to use].
B. But [objects] lose their susceptibility to impurity [only] through an act that modifies [their appearance.[28] That is, a useful object only becomes useless once an Israelite destroys it].
C. [The underlying assumption of A-B is that] an action may annul [the effects of a prior] act or [the effects of a prior] plan (*mahshabah*).
D. But a plan (*mahshabah*) cannot annul [the effects of a prior] action or [even the effects of a prior] plan (*mahshabah*).

M. Kel. 25:9

The Mishnah expounds in its own idiom the principles we have already teased out of its rules. Let us work our way through the sages' formulation of their theory. The important point emerges from the contrasting statements at A-B. In the sages' words, plans have the power to "make objects susceptible to impurity," but have no power to make objects "lose their susceptibility to impurity." As previously discussed, only useful objects are susceptible to impurity. Translating the Mishnah's words into more abstract language, therefore, the sages are saying the following: when a person plans to use an object, he or she assigns it to the class of useful things (i.e. makes it susceptible to impurity). But once an object falls under the rubric of useful things, plans no longer can alter its status (i.e., plans cannot make the object lose its susceptibility).

The framers also contrast the respective roles of action and intention. In their own language, "an action can annul the effects of a prior act or plan (C). " But "a plan cannot annul the effects of either prior actions or plans (D)." To understand what the sages mean by this statement, we must imagine the following scenario. Suppose a person places an object into the category of useful things either by actually using it or by intending to use it. The question the sages address is this: can the Israelite subsequently alter the status of the object? In their view, he can do so only by destroying it. To return to their words, "an act [of destroying an object] can annul the effects of a previous action or intention." By contrast, a plan to destroy the object does not have the power to render the object useless, or in the Mishnah's own words, "an intention [to destroy an object] cannot annul the effects of a prior action or intention."[29]

In formulating their theory, the framers have articulated one point that we have not yet encountered, namely the idea that a person's plan cannot annul the effects of a prior plan. That is to say, if one intends to use an object and thereby defines it as a useful thing, one cannot alter its status by subsequently deciding to discard it. This notion, however, is merely a variation on a principle we have already discovered. Intention only matters when the classification of an object is equivocal. Since the Israelite's first intention resolves the ambiguity in the object's status, any subsequent intention is irrelevant.

We have focused thus far upon the role of intention in sorting household objects into their respective classes. Turning now to rules involving the classification of food substances, we find that intention serves precisely the same function in this context. The Mishnah appeals to a householder's plan only when an ambiguity is detected in the status of a substance.

The Power of Plans to Resolve Ambiguity: The Case of Food Substances

When a substance does not fall clearly under the rubric of food or waste, the sages take account of how the owner plans to dispose of it.[30] The intention of eating or selling it places that substance into the category of food. Consequently, from the moment the Israelite formulates an intention, the substance can absorb impurity. On the other hand, if he or she plans to discard the item, it falls into the category of waste and can not contract impurity. To illustrate the role of plans in resolving ambiguity of this sort, we turn once again to the case of a person who discovers a fetus inside a properly slaughtered cow:

A. [As regards an Israelite] who slaughters an animal [according to the correct procedure] and finds a fetus within it--

B. a person with a strong stomach may eat it.

C. [Although Israelites may eat it, the fetus falls into the category of waste, with the result that it] cannot contract food impurity. [This is because most Israelites consider the fetus repulsive and do not eat such things.]...

D. [If, however, the slaughterer] planned [to eat] the fetus [before slaughtering the cow],

E. [the fetus falls into the category of food with the result that it] can contract impurity.

M. Hul. 4:7

The Mishnah determines the status of the fetus by making reference to the slaughterer's plan. If while sacrificing the animal, he or she intends to eat the fetus, the sages assign it to the category of food substances (D-E). The sages take account of the Israelite's intention in this case because the status of the fetus is ambiguous. It is uncertain whether the fetus falls under the rubric of food or waste. On the one hand, Israelites are permitted to eat the fetus from a properly slaughtered cow, just as they are permitted to eat other parts of a cow's body (B). On the other hand, most Israelites regard a fetus as a repulsive thing. Intention, therefore, decides into which of these two categories the fetus belongs.

The Mishnah articulates the same principle in the following rules which involve the classification of substances which Israelites are forbidden to eat. In the first case, an Israelite improperly slaughters a permitted species of bird. Since he or she carried out the rite incorrectly, the bird may not be eaten. In the second case, the sages discuss an Israelite who kills a forbidden species of bird (see Lev. 11:13-19). For our purposes, one fact stands out. In either case, if the Israelite decides to sell the fowl in the marketplace, the Mishnah treats these substances as food.

I. A. [In order for] the carrion of a permitted species of bird [to enter the category of food and thus to become subject to the restrictions governing food substances],

B. it is necessary [that an Israelite form] a plan [to sell it to a gentile as food.[31] That is, the Mishnah refers to a case of an Israelite who captures a species of bird which Scripture permits Israelites to eat. However, the Israelite slaughters the bird improperly. Since it falls into the category of fowl-carrion, he cannot eat the bird, because by doing so, he would become impure. If, however, the Israelite formulates the intention of selling the fowl to a gentile, it enters the category of food with the result that it can now contaminate other food products].[32]

M. Toh. 1:1 (M. Oh. 13:5)

II. A. [In order for] the carcass[33] of a bird of a forbidden species [to enter the
         category of food and thus to becomes susceptible to the impurity]
     B. it is necessary [that an Israelite formulate] a plan (*mahshabah*) [to sell it
         as food to a gentile].

                                                        M. Toh. 1:3 (M. Oh. 13:6)

Israelites typically dispose of a forbidden substance in one of two ways.
Either they treat it as waste by throwing it to their dogs, or they sell it to
gentiles for food (see M. Toh. 8:6). Since the Israelite may choose either of
these alternatives, there is no way of knowing whether the fowl at hand falls
under rubric of food or waste. The Mishnah solves the ambiguity in its
predictable fashion, namely, by appealing to intention. If the owner decides to
sell it, the bird enters the category of food. By the same token, if one decides to
toss the bird to a dog, it is regarded as waste.

The Role of Social Norms in Classifying Objects

Thus far, we have found that intention is only invoked when the sages need
to clarify an ambiguity. It turns out, however, that the Mishnah recognizes a
second means of resolving ambiguity. Sometimes, rather than relying upon the
Israelite's intention, the Mishnah bases its classification of an object on the
behavioral norms which are presumed to exist in Israelite society. For example,
the Mishnah claims that most Israelites will use a dead cow as food, because it is
too expensive to waste. If most Israelites are presumed to put a particular object
to use, the Mishnah automatically treats all objects of the same kind as useful.
The sages make reference to normal Israelite behavior for the same reason they
sometimes appeal to a person's plan. By knowing how other people typically
use an object, the sages can anticipate how the individual at hand will use it and
thereby resolve any ambiguity in the object's status.

The Mishnah, therefore, employs two strategies for clarifying the
ambiguities in an object's classification. Either it appeals to what the owner
actually plans to do, or it takes account of what Israelites typically do with
objects like the one in question. These two strategies, however, may potentially
produce contrary results. Sometimes, a householder intends to toss out
something which most Israelites put to use. Alternatively, a person may plan to
use an object which most Israelites treat as useless. In either case, if the
Mishnah turned to the householder's plan, it would assign the object to one
category, but if the Mishnah stressed what Israelites normally do, the item would
fall into the opposite category.

The fact that these two strategies of classification sometimes produce
contrary results generates the fundamental issue that the sages examine in the
following rules. In turning to these rules, we wish to know when the Mishnah
appeals to a person's plans, and when it relies strictly on normal Israelite
behavior.

The Relative Importance of Plans and Social Norms: The Case of Household Objects

It turns out that the Mishnah always subordinates intention to norms in its system of classification. By this I mean that when the sages can solve an ambiguity by appealing to normal Israelite behavior, they completely ignore what the individual in question actually intends to do. If most people are presumed to use a particular kind of object, all objects of that type are by definition considered useful, regardless of the owner's actual intention. Consequently, even if the owner plans to destroy or dispose of the item in question, it retains its status as a useful thing. In some instances, however, the sages cannot determine the object's status by appealing to the norm, because in their judgment no clearly defined norm exists. In such a case, the sages cannot resolve the object's status by appealing to typical Israelite behavior, and thus intention becomes decisive. Intention, therefore, constitutes a last resort in the sages' classification scheme. Let us now see how the Mishnah actually articulates these points.

In the rule to follow, for example, the Mishnah appeals to normal Israelite behavior to decide whether an untanned hide falls into the category of useful or useless things. As we shall now see, the sages appeal to the owner's plan only when the other strategies of classification prove inadequate.

A. [Concerning untanned] hides belonging to a householder--
B. [the householder's] plan (*mahshabah*) [to use them classifies them as useful things and hence] makes them susceptible to impurity.
C. But [the untanned hides] belonging to a tanner--
D. [the tanner's] plan (*mahshabah*) [to use them does not have the power to classify them as useful. Despite his intention, they remain in the category of useless things and hence cannot absorb impurity.]

M. Kel. 26:8

The Mishnah takes account of the owner's occupation in classifying an untanned hide. Since tanners almost never use untanned hides for any purpose, the sages automatically treat such hides as useless when they are owned by a tanner. Consequently, a tanner's intention to use an untanned hide has no power to place it into the category of useful things (C-D).[34] The sages, however, do take account of a householder's intention (A-B). This is because some householders use untanned leather, whereas others do not. Consequently, the sages cannot determine the status of an untanned hide merely by appealing to the norm among householders, and so they rely on intention.

Although the sages cannot infer from the norm precisely what a householder will do with a leather hide, they sometimes can narrow the range of possibilities. By appealing to the normal behavior of householders, one may learn that householders usually put hides to certain kinds of uses and not others. The Mishnah considers such information important, because it provides a test for

determining whether the householder is likely to act on his intention. If a
householder intends to use a hide for a purpose that it normally does not serve,
the framers believe it unlikely that he will act as he planned. However, if he
plans to use a hide the way other householders use them, the sages assume he in
fact will put his plan into effect.

This point emerges from the following case which involves a hide which
requires cleaning, stretching, and tanning. According to the Mishnah, the status
of such hides is ambiguous because some householders put unprocessed hides to
use, whereas others consider them useless. Nonetheless, by appealing to the
norm, the sages do derive a useful piece of information: when householders put
an unprocessed hide to use, they almost always employ it as a saddle cover, a
function for which the quality of the leather is unimportant. Unprocessed hides
rarely serve any other purpose. Accordingly, the Mishnah reaches the conclusion
that an unprocessed hide must be one of two things: a useless object which
requires further processing or a saddle cover. Note how this assumption
influences the Mishnah's classification of the hide:

A. In any case [involving leather hides] which require no further
workmanship [such as cleaning and stretching and hence are suitable for
a variety of household uses]--[35]

B. [if the householder formulates] a plan [to use them, he effectively
classifies them as useful things, with the result that] they become
susceptible to impurity.

C. [By contrast] in any case [involving leather hides which] require further
workmanship [such as cleaning or stretching, in order to prepare them
for household use]--

D. [if the householder formulates] a plan [to use the hides, they do not fall
under the rubric of useful things and hence] do not become susceptible to
impurity,

E. unless [he plans to use them as] a saddle cover. [If, he plans to use an
unprocessed hide as a saddle cover, it does fall into the classification of
useful things, and hence can absorb impurity.]

M. Kel. 26:7

When a householder plans to act in an idiosyncratic manner, his intention
has no power to classify the object. This explains why an unprocessed hide
remains in the status of a useless thing, despite the householder's intention to
use it as a rug, apron, or bedspread (C-D). The sages believe that householders
almost never use an unfinished hide for a purpose other than a saddle cover.
Consequently, when the individual at hand plans to use it as a rug, the sages do
not believe that he will actually carry out his plan. But if he intends the hide to
serve as a saddle cover, there is good reason to assume that he will put his plan
into effect. After all, other householders use unprocessed hides for that purpose.
In this case, therefore, his intention places the hide into the category of useful
things (E).

For obvious reasons, the Mishnah cannot invoke the same line of reasoning in the case of a fully processed hide (A-B). Householders employ fully manufactured hides for a variety of purposes. Therefore, no matter what a householder intends to do, whether to use the hide as a rug, an apron, or bedspread, the Mishnah takes for granted that he will carry out his plan. Consequently, the intention to use a fully processed hide always has the effect of making it a useful object. In summary, then, social norms provide a standard against which the Mishnah compares an individual's intention. The sages ignore the intention of one who plans to act idiosyncratically, because they assume that that individual will ultimately act like other people.

To infer from societal norms how a householder or tanner will use a leather hide in his possession may seem relatively simple. But in the rule to follow, the sages claim they can even predict through which door a person will remove a corpse from his house. That is to say, if a person dies in a house, the Mishnah insists it knows ahead of time which exit the householder will use to remove the corpse. In order to follow the sages' line of reasoning, we must briefly consider the Mishnah's somewhat unusual notions of corpse uncleanness. Based on Numbers 19:14-16, the Mishnah claims that when a person dies in a house, the corpse exudes impurity into the air and thus contaminates other household things. Any permanent division in the house, such as a wall, can prevent corpse impurity from passing from one room to another, or from inside the house to the outside. A temporary division, such as a partition which can be easily removed, does not stop impurity from flowing to the other side.

Closed doors and windows, however, present a special problem. Do they fall into the category of permanent or temporary divisions? The answer depends upon whether someone will remove the corpse through the door or window in question. If that door or window will be opened, it is treated as a temporary division. Hence, from the moment of the person's death, that door or window allows impurity to pass outside the house.[36] If it will remain shut, the door or window falls under the rubric of a permanent division, and so contains the spread of impurity. The distinction just described is but another variation on the familiar dichotomy between useful and useless objects. Here, a door or window that will serve as an exit allows impurity to pass beyond the walls of the house. Conversely, a door or window which will not function as the exit for the corpse does not permit the passage of impurity. For the present inquiry, one fact draws our attention: by appealing to normal Israelite behavior, the sages sometimes claim they know which exit a householder will use. In such circumstances, as we have learned to expect, the Mishnah completely ignores the plan that the householder actually formulates:

I.   A.   [Concerning] a person who dies in a house with many doors [all of which are closed]--
     B.   all [of the doors immediately] become impure [and allow the passage of impurity to the outside. This is because the door through which the

corpse will be removed from the house transmits impurity from the moment that the person has died. Since all the doors potentially may serve as the exit for the corpse, all convey impurity outside the house].

II. A. [But if] one [of the doors] was opened,

    B. it becomes impure, and the other [doors revert to a] clean [state. A door that is opened automatically absorbs impurity from the corpse. Hence, the sages assume that the householder will remove the corpse through this exit so as not to contaminate one of the other doors.]

III. A. [If in a case where all the doors are closed as at A] he plans *(hsb)* to remove [the corpse] through one of them [in particular],

    B. or [in the case where all the windows are closed and he plans to remove the corpse] through [one particular] window that is [at least] four handbreadths wide--

    C. he [effectively classifies that door or window as a temporary division, with the result that] he rescues the other doors [from contamination. That is, by deciding which door or window he will use, he indicates that the other exits will not be opened. Hence, they do not contract impurity].

    D. The school of Shammai say, "[In order to save the doors from becoming contaminated as at G] the householder must [formulate his] plan [to open a particular door] before the person has died." [If, however, he formulated his plan after the person died, then he cannot save the other doors from becoming unclean. This is because plans do not have the power to restore something which is impure to a pure state, (see M. Kel. 25:9).]

    E. The school of Hillel say, "Even [if he formulates his plan to open a door] after the person has died, [his plan restores the other exits to a pure state." The Hillelites agree with the Shammaites that plans cannot restore to a clean state something which has already become contaminated. But in this case, the doors were deemed unclean only because it was unclear which exit would be used. Once the householder resolves the ambiguity by intending to open a specific exit, we know that the other exits were never unclean to begin with.]

IV. A. [In the case of a house with several doors], one [of which] is sealed [with stones]--

    B. [even if the householder] changes his mind [and decides] to open [the sealed door, that door remains pure. Despite the householder's intention to open the sealed door, the sages assume that he will not do so because that would require a great deal of effort.]

    C. The school of Shammai say, "[The sealed door allows the passage of impurity] only if he [actually] opens it four handbreadths. [At this point, the opening is wide enough to permit the passage of corpse uncleanness.]"

    D. The school of Hillel say, "[The sealed door allows the passage of impurity as soon as] the householder begins [to remove the stones. At this point, it becomes obvious that, despite the effort required, the householder will in fact open this door.]"

M. Oh. 7:3

One single point emerges from the four cases at hand. The householder's intention matters only when the sages cannot predict from normal Israelite behavior which door he will open. If, however, they can make such a determination, they ignore any plan that he may actually formulate. Let us see how this theory works itself out in the cases under discussion. In the first and third cases, the sages discuss a house in which all the doors are shut. Here, one cannot predict which door the householder will open, because in this situation different people would choose to open different doors (I A). By appealing to normal behavior, therefore, the Mishnah cannot resolve the ambiguity inherent in the situation. For this reason, knowing the householder's plan becomes critical. If he plans to use a specific door then only that door allows impurity to pass outside the house (III A-C).

The second and fourth cases, by contrast, illustrate instances when the sages need not take account of the householder's intention. In these situations, by appealing to normal Israelite behavior, one can anticipate which door will serve as the exit. The second case, for example, involves a situation in which one of the doors has already been opened (II A). An open door automatically falls under the rubric of a temporary division, and therefore it permits impurity to pass outside the house. In this situation, the sages assume the householder will remove the body through the open door. They base this assumption on the belief that the householder, like other Israelites, wishes to obey God's law. Accordingly, they take for granted that he will do everything in his power to keep the other doors free from contamination. Since one door is already impure anyway, he invariably will remove the corpse through that door rather than open and thereby contaminate a second door.

A similar line of reasoning is invoked in the fourth case. Here an Israelite intends to remove the corpse through a door which is sealed by stones (IV). By intending to open the sealed door, the householder has formulated an intention to act in an atypical manner, for most householders would not take the trouble to open a sealed door. Since he intends to deviate from the norm, the Mishnah simply discounts his intention. Unless he actually puts his plan into action, the sages assume he will act like other people normally do (IV C-D).

In the rules thus far examined, the sages claim they can predict how an individual will respond to the particular situation he or she faces by appealing to the norms which are presumed to operate in Israelite society. But how exactly do the sages make such a determination? The rule to follow permits us to see the sages' method at work. To begin with, the Mishnah realizes that no two situations are exactly alike. Consequently, to determine how the typical person would respond under the conditions in question, the sages take account of all the various factors which normally influence an Israelite's behavior. Only after weighing the relevant evidence can the sages infer how the typical person would act in the situation under discussion.

To understand this rule, we again must rehearse certain facts which the Mishnah takes for granted. Here, the Mishnah discusses whether various cracks or fissures in the wall of a house allow corpse uncleanness to pass through the walls to the outside. To answer this question, the Mishnah appeals to the familiar criterion of usefulness. Any hole that serves a household purpose is also large enough to permit uncleanness to pass out of the house. A light-hole (i.e., a hole that admits light to the house) or a niche for storing household goods, therefore, falls under the rubric of useful holes and hence permits impurity to pass through the walls of the house. On the other hand, useless openings prevent impurity from flowing outside.

Turning to the rule at hand, we find that the Mishnah classifies a hole in the wall in the same way that it categorizes other household things, namely, by determining whether the typical householder would employ the hole in question for some purpose. In answering this question, however, the sages first need to know two important facts: 1) the size of the hole, and 2) its origin. Only when the sages have this information in hand can they determine whether the crack under discussion would normally serve a useful purpose.

A. [If a] householder makes a light-hole [in the wall of his house, and a person subsequently dies in his house],

B. [the hole permits the passage of corpse impurity if it has attained the size of] a hole made by the large drill of the [Temple] chamber [i.e., a very small hole about the size of a coin (see M. Kel. 17:12)].

C. [By contrast], a partially sealed light-hole [permits the passage of corpse uncleanness if it is at least] two finger-breaths high by a thumb-breath wide.

D. What constitutes "partially sealed light-holes?"

E. [An example is] a window [which an Israelite] partially sealed [with dirt and stones].

F. [Concerning holes created by natural causes, for example,] when water or small animals eat through the walls,

G. or [when] salt [in the soil] corrodes [a hole through the wall]--

H. [such holes automatically permit the passage of corpse uncleanness if they attain] the size of a fist.

I. [However, if] the householder planned [to put] it to use [by employing it as a niche in which to store household goods, it allows the passage of corpse uncleanness even if it is only] a hand-breath wide. [Since he planned to use it, it enters the category of useful things even before it reaches the size of a fist as at H].

J. [If he] planned [to use] it as a light-hole, [it conveys uncleanness even if it only reaches the negligible] size of a hole [produced by] the [Temple] drill [as at A].

M. Oh. 13:1

Below, I have provided a diagram of this rule to aid us in following the Mishnah's reasoning.[37] As we examine this chart, we shall discover that at several points, the Mishnah takes for granted that it knows whether the typical

householder would put the hole in question to use. To make such a determination, the Mishnah appeals to two criteria. To begin with, it distinguishes
cracks produced by human activity from those produced by natural causes. The
sages almost always treat a man-made hole as useful, because most householders
make a hole in their wall only when they need it for some purpose (I A). By the
same token, when householders fill in a window they normally seal up the entire
opening. If they leave a crack bigger than a finger-breadth, it is generally because
they intend to use it for some purpose (I B).

Types of Holes	Size at which hole falls into the category of useful things and allows corpse uncleanness to pass through the wall	Reference to Mishnah passage
I. Holes produced by human activity		
a. made from scratch	drill hole [smallest]	A
b. partially sealed light hole	finger-breadth wide [largest]	C-E
II. Holes produced by natural causes		
a. cases in which householder did not intend to use hole	fist [largest]	H
b. cases in which householder formed intention to use hole		
1. intended to use it for a light hole	drill hole [smallest]	J
2. intended to use it for a niche	hand-breadth	I

Cracks produced by natural causes, however, pose an ambiguity. Since a
person did not make this hole, one cannot automatically assume that the hole is
functional. Some householders use such holes for bringing light into the house
or as a niche for storing household goods. Other householders simply regard the
hole as a nuisance. To help resolve this ambiguity, the Mishnah turns to the
second criterion: the size of the hole. If it is smaller than a drill hole, the sages
treat it as useless, because most householders do not use cracks of this size for
any purpose, not even for light-holes. Consequently, even if the householder at
hand plans to use it as a light-hole, it remains in the category of a useless hole
(II B 1). If, however, the hole widens to the size of a fist, the framers
automatically classify it as useful (II A). The assumption is that the typical
householder never permits a hole to reach this size unless he considers it useful.

Accordingly, even if the Israelite at hand does not specifically form the intention of using it, it nonetheless falls under the rubric of useful things (II A).

When a crack produced by natural causes falls between the size of a drill hole and the size of a fist, the Mishnah cannot resolve the ambiguity by appealing to the norm (II b 1-2). On the one hand, it is now large enough to serve a useful purpose. Yet on the other hand, householders sometimes regard such holes as useless. To settle the ambiguity, the sages have no choice but to appeal to the householder's intention. If he plans to use the hole, it falls into the category of a useful thing as soon as it is large enough to serve the designated purpose (II b 1-2).

The Relative Importance of Plans and Social Norms: The Case of Food Substances

The Mishnah appeals to behavioral norms not only to decide the status of household objects but also when sorting substances into the categories of food and waste. If most people typically discard a given substance, the Mishnah automatically assigns any substance of that type to the category of waste. If a particular individual plans to eat such a substance, therefore, the sages discount his or her intention. They assume, until proven otherwise, that the Israelite ultimately will conform to normal Israelite behavior. The Mishnah adopts the same line of reasoning in classifying substances which people normally eat. Such substances automatically fall under the rubric of food, no matter what the owner intends to do. We turn first to the sages' own explanation of how they go about assigning substances to categories. As we shall now see, they explicitly draw attention to the fundamental role of social norms in their system of classification.

A. [The sages] stated the [following] general principle concerning food purity:

B. Anything that is [normally] designated for human consumption [falls into the category of food, and hence] can absorb impurity, unless it becomes so putrid [that it is not even] fit for dog food.

C. But anything that is not [normally] designated for human consumption is insusceptible to impurity, unless [an Israelite] designates it [by thought or action] for human consumption. [If he or she indicates that it will be used for food, it is classified as food and hence it can absorb impurity.]

D. What is an example [of a case in which an Israelite classifies something as food by intending to use it for that purpose]?

E. [An example is the case of] a young pigeon that fell into a wine vat and died].

F. If [the owner] planned to remove it (*hsb* ^{c}*lyw*) [from the vat] for [sale to] a gentile, [the pigeon] is impure. [That is, since the Israelite intends to sell it for consumption, the pigeon falls into the classification of food, and hence is subject to the rules governing food purity.]

G. [If, by contrast, he or she intended to remove it from the vat] for a dog, [the pigeon] is insusceptible to food impurity [because the Israelite did not intend to use it for human consumption].

H. Rabbi Yohanan son of Nuri [classifies the pigeon as food and hence declares it] susceptible to food impurity [whether or not the householder actually formed the intention of selling it to a gentile. Yohanan assumes that the householder will sell the pigeon to a gentile because most Israelites would attempt to make a profit from the dead bird.]

I. If a deaf-mute, retarded person, or minor planned [to remove the pigeon from the vat to sell as food to a gentile, but has not yet given it to him, the pigeon falls into the category of waste, and hence] cannot absorb impurity.

J. But if [a deaf-mute, retarded person, or minor actually] removed the pigeon from the vat [and sold it to a gentile][38] the pigeon is [classified as food and hence] can contract impurity.

K. This is because the actions [of deaf-mutes, retarded persons and minors] produce legal consequences, but their plans do not.

M. Toh. 8:6

To place substances into the categories of food and waste, the sages appeal to the normal behavior of Israelites. Substances that most people eat or sell in the marketplace are automatically treated as food. An individual's intention to toss out such a substance, therefore, has no effect on its status. In fact, the only way food can actually enter the category of waste is by becoming so putrid that even a dog would not eat it (A).

Following the same logic, the Mishnah treats as waste any substance which Israelites normally do not eat (C). Here, however, we note one important difference. By intending to use a substance as food, an Israelite has the power to remove that substance from the category of waste and place it in the category of food. This would seem to contradict our prior findings. Previously, we said that when the status of a substance is self-evident, the Mishnah ignores a person's intention. Why then can an Israelite classify as food something which most Israelites do not or cannot eat? The sages realize that gentiles often buy the very foods which Israelites do not eat. This is why the unnamed sages consider the status of a dead pigeon to be ambiguous (D-G). On the one hand, the Israelite might decide to throw it to a dog. Yet, on the other hand, he or she might sell it to a gentile. To determine, therefore, whether the bird falls under the rubric of food or waste, the sages appeal to the Israelite's plan.

Yohanan, however, registers a dissenting opinion (H). He treats the pigeon as food even if the Israelite does not specifically form an intention of selling it. Yohanan takes for granted that Israelites who live near a marketplace almost always sell the substances which they cannot eat. He therefore assumes that no matter what the householder intends he ultimately will sell the pigeon in the marketplace.

The Mishnah brings this rule to a conclusion by making a point we have also discussed in a previous context. Minors, deaf-mutes, and retarded persons under no circumstances can place a substance into the category of food by intending to sell it. In the sages' view, only people who resemble God can classify things. Since a minor, deaf-mute, and retarded person lack certain mental capacities, God does not confer on them the power to classify the world. However, while their intentions do not produce legal consequences, their actions do, as actions by definition are observable. Hence, when they actually hand the pigeon to a gentile, it becomes obvious to all that the bird belongs to the category of food.

We turn now to a long series of cases which provide a fitting climax to the Mishnah's entire discussion of classification. Here, the sages illustrate how they infer from a given situation whether a typical Israelite would choose to sell a substance as food or simply dispose of it as waste. As in the case of household objects, they weigh all the relevant factors which might influence the behavior of a typical person. In this context, the Mishnah considers crucial the following three factors: 1) the location of the food stuff (whether in a marketplace or in a village), 2) its value (can the Israelite afford to discard it?) and 3) its marketability (will gentiles buy it?). The sages claim that by analysing a situation in terms of these three criteria, they can often deduce how the typical person would act. Sometimes, however, even after taking account of these three criteria, the substance's status nonetheless remains ambiguous. In such instances, the Mishnah predictably solves the ambiguity by turning to the owner's intention.

In turning to the rules themselves, we shall find that the Mishnah also addresses a problem which lies outside the immediate focus of our inquiry, namely, the way in which food substances can absorb impurity. Some edible substances can absorb impurity simply by falling under the rubric of food. [39] Other edible substances, however, can absorb impurity if, in addition to entering the category of food, they are also moistened by water. [40] Since this distinction does not bear on the question of intention, we simply ignore this issue as we consider the cases at hand. Our task, as I spelled out above, is to examine the way the framers decide whether a person will use a given substance as food.

I.   A.   [The Mishnah specifies four classes into which food substances may fall based on the answer to the following two questions, 1) Do they automatically fall into the classification of food or do they enter the classification of food only when a person has first intended to use them for that purpose? 2) Do they require moistening in order to absorb impurity?]

     B.   (1) Some [substances] require moistening but not intention.

     C.   (2) [A second group of substances requires] intention and moistening.

     D.   (3) [A third group of substances requires] intention but not moistening.

     E.   (4) [A fourth group of substances requires] neither moistening nor intention.

     F.   [The sages now provide examples of substances that fall into each of the categories mentioned above. The following fall into the first category at

1]: All edible [things generally] designated for human [consumption] require moistening but not intention. [Since most Israelites eat these items, they are classified as food whether or not the owner intends them for that purpose].

M. Uqs. 3:1

II. A. [The following are examples of substances that fall into the second category described at I C: A sliver of flesh that] one cuts from

      1) a [living] person, or

      2) from a [live] domesticated animal or

      3) from a [live] wild animal

      4) from [live] fowl or

      5) from the carcass of a forbidden[41] species of fowl [such as a vulture], and [likewise],

      6) the fat [Israelites cut from properly slaughtered animals while] in villages--

B. and [as regards] 7) all wild vegetables except the truffle and mushroom--

C. Rabbi Judah says, "Except for wild spices [i.e. allium ampleoprasum] and pursulane and ornithogalum."[42]

D. Rabbi Simeon says, "Except for gundelia."

E. Rabbi Yose says, "Except for wild figs."

F. the [items listed at A-B are classified as food only if] there is an intention [on the owner's part to use them for human consumption], but they do not require moistening [in order to absorb impurity. These substances only fall into the category of food if someone intends to use them for food because their classification is ambiguous. The substances listed at II A, Israelites are forbidden to eat. Accordingly, the sages are uncertain as to whether the Israelite will discard them or sell them to a gentile for food. Likewise, the classification of wild vegetables is equivocal. Israelites may utilize them as spices, as fodder for their animals, or as kindling wood (see M. Sheb. 8:1). Consequently, the Israelite's plan serves as the criterion for classification].[43]

M. Uqs. 3:2

III. A. [The following items fall into the third category of substances: As regards]

      1) the carcass of a forbidden species of animal [such as a camel] regardless of its location [whether in a village or marketplace], and

      2) an improperly slaughtered bird of a permitted species [such as a pigeon that an Israelite has] in a village --

B. [These items are classified as food[44] only] if there is an intention [on the owner's part to use them for human consumption], but they require no moistening [in order to absorb impurity. The Israelite is forbidden to eat the substances at hand either because they are a forbidden species of animal or because he slaughtered them improperly. Accordingly, the status of these objects is uncertain. Will the Israelite throw them away or sell them to a gentile? To resolve the ambiguity, the sages therefore take account of his intention].

C. [The following items fall into the fourth category of substances: As regards]

1) an improperly slaughtered animal of a permitted species [such as a cow] regardless of its location [i.e., whether in a village or market place], and

2) an improperly slaughtered bird of a permitted species [such as a pigeon that an Israelite has] in the marketplace, and

3) the fat [Israelites cut from a properly slaughtered animal] in the marketplace.

D. These [items at III C may absorb impurity even] if there is no moistening, and [they are classified as food even] if there is no intention [on the owner's part to use them for human consumption. The Israelite is forbidden to eat the animals at hand. The sages, however, automatically classify the substances at hand as food because they assume the Israelite will sell them. Why so? In the one case he is in the marketplace and in the other case the animal is too valuable to toss out.]

E. R. Simeon says [in disagreement with the sages at A-B] "Also [forbidden species of animals, such as] the camel, rabbit, fox, and pig [that an Israelite has] in the marketplace [are classified as food whether or not the owner forms an intention to use them for human consumption. Simeon claims that the Israelite will not throw such animals away because gentiles routinely buy them in the marketplace. Hence, if the Israelite has them in the marketplace, the presumption is that he will sell them.]"

M. Uqs. 3:3

IV. A. Fish and grasshoppers of a forbidden species (see Lev. 11: 9-12, 22-23) [that are found] in a village [are classified as food only if] there is an intention [on the owner's part to use them for human consumption. Since he cannot eat these, the sages are uncertain whether he will throw them away or look for a buyer. Therefore, the sages take into account his intention. If, by contrast, he has these substances in a marketplace, there is no ambiguity. The sages assume that he will sell them to a gentile. Hence, even if he does not actually form this intention, they fall into the category of food.]

M. Uqs. 3:9

What draws our attention is the strategy the Mishnah adopts to determine how a typical Israelite would respond to the situation under discussion. As I said above, the sages consider three criteria important: 1) the location of the foodstuff, 2) its value, and 3) whether gentiles will buy it for food. If on the basis of these three criteria the sages can deduce what an Israelite will do with a given item, they simply ignore his or her actual plans. To understand how these points actually emerge from the data at hand, we turn to the chart provided below. Here I have catalogued all the substances mentioned by the sages. For our purposes, I place them into three groups illustrating when intention is crucial and when it is not.

In the first category, the Mishnah takes account of an object's location. If an Israelite is carrying any of these substances in a marketplace, it is automatically classified as food. Since the Israelite stands not in a village but in the marketplace, the sages assume the substance will be sold rather than thrown away. When, by contrast, the Israelite carries the same item in the village, the framers can no longer be certain what will be done. On the one hand, the owner may decide to look for a gentile buyer. On the other hand, since the marketplace is not immediately accessible, the owner may simply decide to toss it out. Since the sages cannot predict what the Israelite will do, they rely upon intention (I A, B, C).

Location: Type of item	In a marketplace	In a village
I. Category One		
A. improperly slaughtered bird of a clean species	classified as food regardless of owner's intention (III C, 2)	classified as food only if owner intends to sell it for food (III A, 2)
B. fat of an animal	classified as food regardless of owner's intention (III C, 3)	classified as food only if owner intends to sell it for food (II A, 6)
C. fish and grasshoppers of an unclean species	classified as food regardless of owner's intention (IV A)	classified as food only if owner intends to sell it for food (IV A)
II. Category Two		
A. improperly slaughtered animal of clean species (such as a cow)	classified as food regardless of owner's intention (III C, 1)	classified as food regardless of owner's intention (III C, 1)
III. Category Three		
A. dead fowl of unclean species (such as a vulture)	classified as food only if owner intends to sell it for food (II A, 5)	classified as food only if owner intends to sell it for food (II A, 5)
B. flesh from living animals	classified as food only if owner intends to sell it for food (II A, 1-4)	classified as food only if owner intends to sell it for food (II A, 1-4)

| C. dead animals of unclean species (such as camel, rabbit, fox, pig) | classified as food only if owner intends to sell it for food (III A) | classified as food only if owner intends to sell it for food (III A) |
| D. dissenting opinion of Simeon: (camel rabbit, fox, pig) | classified as food regardless of owner's intention (III E) | classified as food only if owner intends to sell it for food (III E) |

The Mishnah also stresses the pecuniary value of the substance in question. This is why it automatically classifies an improperly slaughtered cow as food, regardless of where the Israelite has killed it (II A). The sages assume that an Israelite cannot afford to throw the cow away as with animals of lesser value like grasshoppers and fish (I C). Therefore, even if one killed the cow in a village rather than in the marketplace, the sages assume that every effort will be made to take the meat to market in order to sell it to a gentile. Even if the Israelite does not specifically form this intention, therefore, the meat of the animal falls under the rubric of food.

The sages also take account of each item's marketability. They believe that even gentiles normally do not eat certain substances, such as flesh cut from a living animal. Accordingly, even if an Israelite brings such things to the marketplace, doubt remains as to whether it falls into the category of food or waste (III A-C). The sages, therefore, must take account of the owner's plans if they wish to classify the items in question.

In conclusion, we see that the Mishnah's method for classifying food substances corresponds in most respects to its strategy for categorizing household objects. Whenever possible, the sages determine the status of either a household object or edible substance by appealing to the behavioral norms which are presumed to exist in Israelite society. Only when this method fails do the sages actually take account of an individual's plan. However, we do discover one important difference in the way that the Mishnah classifies household objects and food substances. When assigning an object to a category, the sages often make reference to the occupation of the owner. We recall, for example, that an untanned hide belonging to a tanner by definition falls under the rubric of useful things, whereas an untanned hide belonging to a householder can fall either into the category of useful or useless things. The Mishnah never invokes a person's occupation to determine whether he will use a substance for human consumption. The reason for this is not far to seek. In the society imagined by the framers, a person's occupation (whether tanner, merchant, or householder) does not influence the way he disposes of edible substances. Other factors, such as an object's value, location, and marketability, play a more decisive role.

The Image of the Typical Israelite

Because the Mishnah places so much stress on Israelite norms, we may extrapolate from the various rules we have examined the image of the typical person that lies behind the Mishnah's discussion. The Mishnah takes for granted that the typical Israelite always wishes to act in accordance with God's law. If a person is faced with a choice between two different courses of action, the sages always assume he or she will chose to act in the way that meets with God's approval. For example, if a householder has to remove a corpse from a house, the Mishnah claims that he will invariably use the door that is already contaminated, the assumption being that the householder will do everything in his power to contain the spread of impurity. Since removing the corpse through a second door would create further contamination, the sages conclude that he will not adopt this course of action.

In many situations, however, a person must choose between two courses of action, neither of which involve violating God's law in any way. For example, suppose a man finds a dead animal in his field. In the mishnaic system, God does not care whether he decides to sell it or give it to his dog. Yet, even in cases such as these, the sages sometimes claim to know how the normal Israelite will act. This is because the sages picture the typical Israelite as a rational person, primarily concerned with his economic well-being. In case after case, the framers assume that a householder will not waste something that he could readily sell for a profit (M. Toh. 8:6, M. Uqs. 3:1-3, 9).[45]

In addition, the Mishnah regards the typical Israelite as a practical person who always chooses the most sensible or easiest course of action. He or she will consider, for example, the amount of energy that must be expended to pursue a given action and will choose the path of least resistance. For this reason, they assume that a householder generally will not take the trouble to unseal a door closed with stones (M. Oh. 7:3). In the conception of the Mishnah, Israelites do not act without analysing all the relevant facts. They take account of all aspects of a situation, weighing the benefits and losses of each possible course of action. In the Mishnah, therefore, the ideal Israelite is a rational, practical person whose behavior is always predictable. In stressing this point, the sages return to the one point which consistently draws their attention: it is the exercise of one's mental capacities, whether to formulate a plan or to analyse a situation, which enables human beings to fulfill the divine will.

The Subordination of Intention to Actions and Norms in the Mishnah's Classification Scheme

The rules previously considered provide a fully worked out theory of classification. In the Mishnah's system, actions provide the most important criterion for determining an object's status. Actions override all other criteria. Therefore, once an Israelite puts an object to use, it automatically falls under the rubric of a useful thing. It remains in that category until the Israelite performs another action which makes it useless, for example, by cutting it into pieces. However, for one reason or another an Israelite might not yet have done anything with the item in question. In this case, an ambiguity arises in determining whether the object belongs to the category of useful or useless things. To resolve ambiguities of this sort, the sages first appeal to normal Israelite behavior. If most Israelites use such objects, the sages automatically classify the object at hand as useful. Conversely, if it turns out that most people treat objects like this one as waste, it enters that category.

In some instances, the Mishnah cannot determine an object's status even by appealing to Israelite norms, because Israelites treat such objects in a variety of ways. It is only in circumstances such as these that the sages actually turn to the owner's intention. We have now discovered a paradoxical fact about the role of intention in the mishnaic system. Intention is the least important of the criteria the sages use in classifying things. However, this does not mean intention is unimportant in the mishnaic system as a whole. On the contrary, as the cases above have demonstrated, the sages frequently cannot decide an object's status on the basis of other criteria, and consequently, often have no choice but to rely on intention.

In the Mishnah's classification scheme, therefore, plans play a less important role than either a person's action (i.e., what he or she does with an object) or normal Israelite behavior (i.e., what most people do with such an object). It is obvious why the sages consider actions more important than plans. Once a person has either put an object to use or thrown it away, the sages know its status. For this reason, the person's plan is of no consequence.

But why do social norms play a more prominent role in the Mishnah than an individual's plans? We have already examined this problem in the previous chapter. The cases examined here support the theological interpretation I proposed in that context. Specifically, I argued that the emphasis on norms derives, at least in part, from the sages' conception of Israelite society as a holy community founded on divine law. Consequently, the norms produced by this community by definition embody God's will. The model "citizen" is the person who adheres to the conventions of God's holy society. By the same token, a person who deviates from the norm in effect repudiates God. This proposition is evident in the fact that these laws implicitly encourage Israelites to take account of social norms at various points in their daily routine. In fact, the Mishnah implies that the failure to do so will result in an infraction of divine law. We saw, for example, that if most Israelites treat a substance as food, that substance is automatically defined as food, even if the owner of the substance decides to let it rot. Consequently, an Israelite must never base his classification of an object on his own idiosyncratic plans. Although he intends to discard it as waste, it may in fact belong to the category of food and hence be susceptible to impurity. The failure to pay attention to the norm, therefore, may lead a person to treat something as insusceptible to impurity when it in fact can become contaminated. These rules, therefore, suggest that the norms of society are prescriptive for Israelite behavior in general.

Classifying Actions and Classifying Objects: A Comparison

Having analysed the Mishnah's scheme for classifying objects, we see that the Mishnah treats objects in precisely the same fashion that it treats actions. The theory of classification exposed in this chapter corresponds to the theory we discovered in Chapter Two. The following diagram illustrates the similarities between the two schemes of classification. Column A represents the method which the Mishnah uses to determine whether an action constitutes a transgression of divine law. Column B represents the sages' strategy for classifying objects.

	A. Scheme for classifying actions	B. Scheme for classifying objects
I. Most important criterion:	purpose	function
II. Secondary:	social norms (purpose an action normally serves)	social norms (function an object normally serves)
III. Least important:	actor's subjective purpose	person's plan

We begin our comparison by noting that intention occupies the least important role in both schemes (III A, B). In deciding whether to treat an action as a transgression or fulfillment of divine law, the sages take account of an Israelite's subjective purpose only as a last resort. Similarly, in placing objects into categories, the Mishnah appeals to an Israelite's plan only when all else fails. In both cases, therefore, the intention an Israelite actually formulates plays the least important role in the overall strategy of classification.

Second, in both schemes societal norms play a more important role than an individual's intention. If an action normally serves a distinctive purpose in Israelite society, the Mishnah automatically ascribes that purpose to the actor at hand, and simply ignores the purpose the person actually had in mind (II A). The sages carry out a similar operation when assigning objects to their respective categories. If people typically put an object to a specific use, the framers assume that the Israelite at hand will utilize that kind of object in precisely the same way. They therefore automatically place the object into the category of useful things, regardless of the plan the owner actually formulates.

Finally, both schemes of classification ultimately rest on the same standard. The sages evaluate an action by appealing to its purpose (I A). Similarly, they determine an object's status by appealing to its function (I B). The criteria of function and purpose are essentially identical. To begin with, in our everyday speech, the terms purpose and function are sometimes interchangeable. For example, we can speak about either the function or purpose of an object. Moreover, both terms are teleological. By this I mean that when we refer to the function of an object or the purpose of an action, we are describing both the object and the action in terms of its end or *telos*. When we say that the function of an object is "x", we mean that the object can or will bring about x. Take, for example, the statement that "the function of the heart is to convey oxygen to extremities of the body." By the heart's function, we refer to the end which is being realized, namely, the transfer of oxygen. Similarly, when we describe an action in terms of its purpose, we refer to the end towards which the action is directed. For example, if we say that the purpose of an action is to commit murder, we mean that that action is meant to bring about someone's death.

There is, to be sure, one important difference between the two schemes of classification. Whereas one may determine the function of an object by knowing what a person does with it, one cannot determine the purpose of an action without appealing to either social norms (what people normally mean by that kind of act) or the purpose the actor has in mind. So while we can point to mishnaic cases in which the sages deduce the function of an object from how a person uses it, we find no corresponding cases which speak about an actor's purpose. Whenever the Mishnah refers to an actor's purpose, it is speaking either about the purpose as deduced from normal Israelite behavior or the purpose the person actually has in mind.

Nonetheless, we find a near perfect correspondence between the method the sages use to evaluate human action and their strategy for assigning objects to categories. This is significant, because it demonstrates a link between the Mishnah's theory of actions and its more general theory of taxonomy. Moreover, in both instances, we have detected the same tendency to relativize the priestly view of the world as recorded in Scripture. To repeat what I said in Chapter Two, the Mishnah departs dramatically from the biblical theory of liability by making the actor's purpose the decisive criterion for determining whether a transgression has occurred. In the biblical laws, especially the priestly legislation, the actor's purpose plays no role at all. Consequently, in Scripture the same action performed on two different occasions is always treated in the same way. For example, donning a garment of mixed weave will be a transgression regardless of the actor's purpose. In the Mishnah, however, an action has no fixed status. It may or may not be a transgression, depending upon the purpose with which it was done.

We see the same effort to relativize Scripture in the Mishnah's theory of taxonomy. According to the priests, the classification of objects is established by God at creation. Consequently, the classification scheme is rigid and fixed; humans play no role at all in deciding an object's status. But in the Mishnah, humans are given the definitive role over at least one part of the system. What they do and think determines what kinds of things can absorb impurity and what kinds of things remain immune. Consequently, the same kind of object may or may not absorb impurity depending upon the intention of the owner. In sum, the mishnaic emphasis on the *telos* of objects and actions serves to undermine the conception of reality articulated in the priestly writings of Scripture.

Conclusion

The capacity to formulate plans is one expression of human beings' rational faculties. In formulating a plan, one weighs various aspects of the situation and forms a judgment about what would constitute an appropriate course of action under those conditions. The Mishnah treats the capacity to formulate rational plans as analogous to the exercise of divine will in the mythic story of creation. Just as in the mythic story of creation God willed the world into existence, so by planning an action a person has the power to turn substances into food, or objects into useful things. The Mishnah claims, therefore, that like God, humans have the power to change the character of the world merely by exercising their intellectual capacities. At the core of the Mishnah's system of classification, therefore, we find the priestly story of creation. The very texture of reality stems from divine acts of classification. Because humans share the capacity of classifying things they too can determine critical aspects of their reality. Human acts of categorization can transform the world because classification is tantamount to creation itself.

Despite the remarkable similarities between the Mishnah's theory of classification and the priestly version of creation, one fundamental difference emerges. The priestly writer nowhere assigns humans a role in classifying the world. As I argued, the Mishnah derived this notion from the other biblical account of creation in which Adam is given the task of naming the animals. In the Mishnah humanity continues to carry out the task that God had originally assigned to Adam in that mythic story of creation. In that story God asked Adam to name the animals. In the Mishnah, Israelites carry forward that mandate by naming the objects and substances around their homes. They decide whether to call them food or waste, useful or useless. Paraphrasing the words of Scripture (Gen. 2: 19), "Whatever a person calls an object that will be its name."

In absorbing this biblical myth into their own system, however, the sages interpreted it in light of their own understanding of agency. They thus speak about the human role in classifying the world in precisely the same terms they use to discuss agency in general. Let us briefly review what this means. To begin with, in the mishnaic system an agent must resemble the principal in certain fundamental respects. For this reason, a man cannot appoint a minor, deaf-mute, or retarded person as his agent, because they lack the mental capacity, and hence, the legal power to act on his behalf. In the mishnaic system, God appoints human beings as divine agents because the human capacity to think and plan makes humans able to understand and imitate the divine work of creation.

In the Mishnah, furthermore, God and humanity are both bound by the same reciprocal rights and duties which bind a human principal and agent. First, by appointing another person to be an agent, one confers on that person one's own legal powers. In commissioning humanity to classify the world, God confers on human beings the power to affect the basic properties of reality. Second, an agent has complete autonomy of the principal as long as the terms of the agency have not been violated. The same principle underlies the sages' discussion of classification. If people obey the divine instructions, they have complete control over the classification of an object. Although the sages' assert that God deems a substance to be food, its ultimate classification for the purposes of defining its status in the system of purity depends upon what people think and do.

Finally, in mishnaic law, an agent's actions or words do not produce legal effects if the agent has violated the terms of appointment. The sages also invoke this principal in their discussions of classification. In their view, God assigned people the task of determining which objects can absorb cultic impurity. Consequently, a person's intention can change the property of a substance only if that intention relates to the object's status as either food or waste, or as a useful or useless thing. But if a person repudiates the divine instructions by trying to determine which objects constitute sources of impurity, that person's intention has no power whatsoever. Since the terms of agency have been broken, the person ceases to exercise the powers which were conferred by God.

The Mishnah also recognizes other limitations on the power of human intention. It turns out that the sages appeal to a person's plans only if they have first exhausted two alternative methods of classifying an object. First, they take account of what a person has actually done with the object in question. If he or she has previously put the object to use or thrown the object into the trash, they need not appeal to plans because the object's status is self-evident. If the Israelite has so far done nothing with the item in question, the sages turn to a second criterion, namely, behavioral norms of Israelite society. If the object normally serves a function, the sages automatically assign it to the class of useful things. By the same token, if people typically toss out objects of this type, the Mishnah treats it as useless. When the sages are unable to determine an object's status by either of the two methods just mentioned, they resort to human plans. At this point, what the owner of the object intends to do is decisive in defining the object's status. Among the criteria the Mishnah uses in classifying things, therefore, intention is the least important. This does not mean, however, that intention is unimportant in the mishnaic system. On the contrary, the sages often find that their other strategies of classification are inadequate. Consequently, we find numerous cases in which plans are the decisive criterion in deciding an object's status. In sum, the Mishnah asserts that human intention plays a critical role in maintaining the order which God established once upon a time.

Chapter Four

Plans in the Sacrificial System

Intention plays equivalent roles in the sacrificial system and in the system of purity. In both systems, a person's intention determines the classification into which a given object falls. To be sure, the contexts in which classification matters and the types of objects requiring categorization differ in the two systems. In the rules of purity, as we have seen, the Mishnah speaks about the power of Israelite householders to define the status of objects around their homes and on their farms. Merely by formulating a plan, a householder assigns an object to a given category. In the sacrificial system, by contrast, the Mishnah discusses the role of Temple priests in determining the status of animals which they sacrifice to God. Furthermore, the Mishnah invokes different, although related, categories in the two sets of laws. In the system of purity, the sages consider whether a given object falls under the rubric of useful or useless objects, and whether an edible substance belongs to the category of food or waste. In the laws of the sacrificial system, on the other hand, the sages take an interest in whether an animal slaughtered in the Temple falls under the rubric of a sacred or profane thing.

On the surface, the sacrificial system and system of cultic purity would appear quite different. But at a deeper level, we find that one is the mirror image of the other. To begin with, the dichotomy between useful and useless things parallels the distinction between sacred and profane things. By dividing objects into the categories of useful and useless items, the Mishnah in effect distinguishes objects which belong to the domain of human beings (useful) from objects which belong to nature (useless). Similarly, by assigning things to the categories of sacred and profane, the sages separate objects which belong to God (sacred) from those which belong to human beings (profane). It turns out, moreover, that the priest and householder perform similar roles in their respective domains. Just as a householder presides over the home and ensures that household things are maintained in a state of cultic purity, the priest oversees the Temple cult and safeguards the sanctity of that place.

To return to the main point of the present inquiry, we also discover that intention serves the same function in the two systems. A householder, we recall, places an object into a given category simply by formulating an intention to use it in a particular way. Analogously, the plan a priest formulates determines the status of an animal he is sacrificing. For example, the priest's intention to use an animal for secular purposes has the effect of classifying the animal as a profane thing.

Before proceeding to spell out the role of a priest's intention, we first need to familiarize ourselves with some basic facts about the Temple cult and the function of the priest within the cult. In the Mishnah, as in Scripture, the Temple serves as the axis around which Israelite religious life revolves. When Israelites wish to offer an animal to God, they must bring it to Jerusalem and sacrifice it in the Temple. Israelites offer animals to God for a variety of purposes. Sometimes they dedicate an animal as expiation for a sin they have inadvertently committed (Lev. 4:27). At other times they bring sacrifices in honor of certain festivals (Lev. chap. 23). Offerings, therefore, may fall into various categories. Some offerings are obligatory. For example, when an Israelite unintentionally violates the law, he or she must bring a offering to expiate the sin. Obligatory offerings also include the sacrifices God commanded the people to offer on special festival days, such as the festival of Passover. In addition to the obligatory offerings, an Israelite may of his or her own volition consecrate an animal for an offering. For example, a person may designate an animal for a burnt-offering (Lev. 1:3-14) or for an offering of well-being (Lev. 3:1-17).

Upon bringing any of these offerings to the Temple, an Israelite householder must turn them over to a priest, a temple functionary descended from the line of Aaron. The priest, as the following passage from Leviticus indicates, plays the central role in carrying out the actual sacrifice:

> The Lord spoke to Moses, saying: Speak to Aaron and his sons and to all the Israelite people and say to them: This is what the Lord has commanded: If any man of the house of Israel slaughters an ox or sheep or goat in the camp, or does so outside the camp, and does not bring it to the entrance of the Tent of Meeting to present it as an offering to the Lord, before the Lord's Tabernacle, bloodguilt shall be imputed to that man: he has shed blood; that man shall be cut off from among his people. This is in order that the Israelites may bring the sacrifices which they have been making in the open - that they may bring them before the Lord, to the priest, at the entrance of the Tent of Meeting, and offer them as sacrifices of well-being to the Lord; that the priest may dash the blood against the altar of the Lord at the entrance of the Tent of Meeting, and turn the fat into smoke as a pleasing odor to the Lord (Lev. 17:1-6).

The Mishnah interprets this passage to mean that only a priest, and not a mere Israelite, can perform the rite of tossing the blood on the altar (M. Zeb. 2:1). In order to sacrifice an offering to God, therefore, an Israelite householder has no choice but to ask a priest to perform the offering on his behalf. As I will argue below, the Mishnah thus conceives of the priest as the agent of the Israelite householder. In turning over an animal consecrated for sacrifice to a priest, the Israelite householder effectively appoints the priest to act on his behalf. Consequently, all the rules that normally govern a principal and an agent also govern the relationship between priest and householder. As an agent, a priest has the power to execute a valid sacrifice only if he carries out the instructions of the householder who appointed him. Conversely, if a priest ignores the terms of the agency, his act of slaughter is invalid. I shall return to these points at a later stage in my argument. At present, we must establish how animals become consecrated for sacrifice in the first place.

The Householder's Power to Consecrate an Animal

In the mishnaic system, each Israelite householder possesses the power to consecrate his livestock. Merely by intending to offer an animal to God, an Israelite confers on it the status of a sacred thing. If an Israelite takes an unconsecrated cow and says, "This will be an offering of well-being," the cow immediately becomes holy. The following passages presuppose the householder's capacity to turn an unconsecrated animal into a holy thing:

I.   A.   "[If] a man said, 'The offspring of this animal will be a burnt-offering and the animal itself will be an offering of well-being,' his words are valid [i.e., the pregnant animal falls into the category of an offering of well-being and the offspring falls into the category of a burnt-offering].
     B.   "[If he said], 'This [animal] will be an offering of well-being and her offspring a burnt-offering,'
     C.   "[the animal falls into the category of an offering of well-being and the offspring also falls into the category of an offering of well-being, " the words of Rabbi Meir.

                                                        M. Tem. 5:3

II. A.   [Concerning a householder who intends to say, "This animal] will be a burnt-offering,"
     B.   but who [accidentally said], "an offering of well-being"--
     C.   and [concerning an householder who intends to say, "This cow will be an offering of] well-being"--
     D.   but [who accidentally] said, "a burnt-offering"--
     E.   he has said nothing unless his words and heart correspond. [That is, his words have no legal effects unless he says what he intended. Hence, the animal enters neither the category of an offering of well-being nor the category of a burnt-offering].

                                                        M. Ter. 3:8

These cases take for granted the householder's power to consecrate one of his livestock. The first case (I A-D) involves a householder who dedicates a pregnant cow and her unborn calf for two different types of offerings. Once he expresses his intention to consecrate the pregnant cow as an offering of well-being, it automatically falls into that category. He subsequently is obligated to take that animal to the Temple and have a priest sacrifice it as an offering of well-being. The householder also has the power to consecrate an unborn animal. Here, however, the situation is more complicated, because the unborn calf is still part of its mother's body. Therefore, if the householder consecrates the mother animal first, the unborn animal automatically falls into the same category as its mother (I B-C).[1] The second case, like the first, presupposes the householder's power to sanctify his livestock. The reason that the householder is unable to consecrate the animal in this context is because he fails to express the intention he originally formulated. By implication, however, if his words and intention correspond, the animal becomes consecrated (II A-E).

For our purposes, the cases just considered contribute one important point. Merely by formulating an intention an Israelite householder has the power to sanctify an unconsecrated animal. So here, as in the previous chapter, we discover that the thoughts and intentions of an Israelite householder define the character of objects around him. Holiness is not inherent in any of his livestock. Any animal can potentially serve as either food for his family (profane) or as a holy offering to God (sacred). It is the householder who determines into which of these categories a given animal will fall. If he plans to dedicate it to God, it automatically enters the category of sacred things, whereas if he intends to use it for food, it remains in an unconsecrated state. Sanctity, therefore, is a status which an Israelite confers on an object by intending to use it for holy purposes.

This capacity is part of the householder's overall power to define the character of objects around his home. We have already seen how a householder can determine whether a given object absorbs impurity. The ability to consecrate an animal is equally impressive. By sanctifying an animal, a householder changes its very character. Once it assumes the properties of a holy thing, it must be used only for sacred purposes. If the householder subsequently puts it to profane use, he incurs divine wrath.

The idea that an Israelite can consecrate an animal is scriptural in origin. According to Leviticus, if an Israelite takes a vow to dedicate an animal to the Temple, that animal is consecrated and hence cannot be put to profane use (Lev. 27:9). This biblical rule anticipates the major elements of the Mishnah's theory. Vowing to donate an animal to the Temple is similar to formulating an intention of sacrificing an animal. There is, however, one significant difference between the biblical and mishnaic conceptions. In Scripture, an Israelite's vow merely determines that the animal in question is holy. But in the Mishnah, an Israelite not only sanctifies an animal but defines the precise category of offering for which that animal will be used. Moreover, if that animal is sacrificed for any other type of offering, the sacrificial rite is invalidated. For instance, if an Israelite formulates an intention to offer the animal as a burnt-offering, the animal falls into the category of a burnt-offering and cannot be used for another type of offering. The Mishnah, therefore, goes beyond Scripture by claiming that an Israelite's intention not only consecrates an animal but classifies it as a particular type of sacred offering.

I would suggest once again that this mishnaic innovation is shaped by the Yahwist story of creation. Conceptually, there is a remarkable similarity between the mishnaic notion that an Israelite places an animal into a specific category and the biblical account which says that Adam gave the animals names. Moreover, the biblical story states explicitly that God pays attention to the names which Adam gave to the creatures. God brought the animals "to the man to see what he would call them; and whatever the man called each living creature that would be its name (Gen. 2: 19)." As we shall see, the sages of the Mishnah advance a similar claim. In their view, God takes account of how a householder labels a given animal. Once a householder designates an animal as an offering of well-being, God expects that animal to be sacrificed as an offering of well-being. If it is sacrificed as a different category of offering, God repudiates the sacrifice.

Finally, we again find a linguistic connection between the Mishnah's sacrificial system and the biblical myth. When a householder classifies an animal, the Mishnah says he "calls it a name (*lqrwt sm*)." [2] This is precisely the same expression used in the biblical story of Adam's naming the animals: "And the man gave names (*wyqr' smwt*) to all the cattle and to the birds of the sky... (Gen. 2:20)." Moreover, when a priest has in mind the correct category of offering, the Mishnah says he sacrifices it "in its own name." The Mishnah's sacrificial system, therefore, supports the thesis that Genesis 2: 19-20 played a role in shaping mishnaic theology and law. Having explained how an animal becomes consecrated in the first place, we can return to the main focus of the present discussion, namely, the role of a priest's intentions in the sacrificial system.

The Role of a Priest's Plans in the Sacrificial System: Desacralizing a Consecrated Animal

When a priest performs a sacrifice, his plans have the power either to reaffirm the classification given to the animal by the householder or to alter the animal's status. Depending upon the particular plan he formulates, the animal either retains its sacred status or reverts to its original classification as a profane thing. For example, the animal retains its sacred status if the priest plans to perform the rite within the span of time and location specified in Leviticus for that type of sacrifice. [3] By planning to perform the rite in the correct place and within the designated period of time, the priest indicates that he conceives of the animal's slaughter as a sacred act. On the other hand, if the priest plans to carry out the rite in another location or after the designated period of time has elapsed, he desacralizes the animal. Because he intends to perform the rite at the place and time of his own choosing, he clearly regards the rite as a secular act of slaughter, which Scripture says may take place where and when a person pleases (Deut. 12:20-24).

Four acts comprise the sacrificial rite: slaughtering the beast according to a prescribed procedure, collecting the animal's blood, transferring the blood to the altar, sprinkling the blood on the altar, and in some cases, eating the meat of the animal. As we shall now see, if the priest plans to perform any part of the rite at the wrong place or after the designated time, he spoils the rite.

> A. [As regards a priest who, while slaughtering an animal, plans] to eat an olive's bulk [or more of its flesh] outside [the place designated for eating the offering] and [who also plans, while collecting, transferring and sprinkling the blood, to eat] an olive's bulk [of its flesh] during the following day [that is, after the designated time for eating the sacrifice has elapsed]--
>
> B. [or as regards a priest who, while slaughtering an animal, plans to eat] an olive's bulk [of its flesh] during the following day and [who also plans, while handling the animal's blood, to eat] an olive's bulk [of its flesh] outside [the designated place]--
>
> C. [or as regards a priest who, while slaughtering an animal, plans to eat] half an olive's bulk [of its flesh] outside [the designated place] and [who also plans, while handling its blood to eat] half an olive's bulk on the following day--
>
> D. [or as regards a priest who, while slaughtering an animal, plans to eat] half an olive's bulk the following day and [who, while handling the blood, plans to eat] half an olive's bulk outside the designated place--
>
> E. [in all of these cases, the offering] is invalid.
>
> M. Zeb. 2:5

This rule involves a priest who intends to eat the animal outside the designated place or after the specified period of time has elapsed. Because the priest formulates this plan, he obviously does not regard the animal as a sacred thing, which must be eaten at a specific time and place. On the contrary, he apparently conceives of it as profane food, which he may consume at a time and place of his choice. As a result, his intention desacralizes the animal. By turning a sacred animal into a profane one, the priest has in effect brought an unconsecrated object into the Temple precincts, an act which is forbidden. For this reason, the Mishnah claims that God repudiates the offering.

For precisely the same reasons, a priest invalidates an offering when he intends to perform other parts of the sacrificial rite, for example tossing the blood or burning the entrails outside the Temple precincts or after the proper time has already elapsed:

> A. [Concerning a priest] who slaughters [an animal consecrated for] an offering [with the intention of] sprinkling its blood outside [the designated place] or [with the intention of sprinkling] part of its blood outside [the designated place] --

B. [and as regards a priest who slaughters an animal consecrated for an offering with the intention of] burning its entrails outside [the place designated for this rite] or [with the intention of burning] part of its entrails outside [the designated place]--

C. [and as regards a priest who intends] to eat its meat outside [the designated place], or an olive's bulk of its flesh outside [the designated place], or an olive's bulk from the skin of the fat-tail outside [the designated place]--

D. [in each of these cases the act of slaughter] is invalid, but one does not incur the divine punishment of premature death [if one eats it].

E. [By contrast, if a priest plans] to toss its blood during the following day [that is, after the time designated for consuming the animal has elapsed], or [intends] to toss part of its blood on the following day,

F. [and if a priest intends] to burn its entrails during the following day, or [intends] to burn part of its entrails during the following day--

G. [and if a priest intends] to eat its flesh during the following day, or [intends to eat] an olive's bulk of its flesh during the following day, or [intends to eat] an olive's bulk from the skin of the fat-tail during the following day--

H. [in all of these cases the slaughtered animal falls into the category of] refuse and [anyone who eats] it incurs the divine punishment of a premature death.

M. Zeb. 2:2

In this rule, a priest intends to sprinkle the animal's blood or burn its entrails outside the Temple or after the designated period of time. The fact that the priest formulates this plan indicates that he does not conceive of the animal as a sacred thing. If he did, he would plan to carry out the rite in the proper place and at the proper time. Instead, the priest obviously thinks of it as a profane act, which he may perform where and when he chooses. Consequently, the animal reverts to the status of a profane thing, and hence, God rejects the offering.

It is important to note that different legal consequences occur depending upon the particular intention which the priest formulates. The intention to perform part of the rite at the wrong time not only spoils the rite but also places the animal into the category called "refuse" (E-H). Refuse is the name given to any offering which is not completed by the specified period of time. If a person eats anything which falls into this category he or she incurs the divine penalty of premature death (Lev. 7:18). The intention to violate the rules governing where the sacrifice should take place produces less severe consequences. In this case, the rite is spoiled but the animal is not deemed to be refuse (A-D). Consequently, a person who eats this offering does not incur a premature death.

The reason one plan has more severe legal effects than the other is simple. The Mishnah equates the intention to perform an act with the actual performance of that act. When a priest intends to perform part of the rite after the specified time, the sages treat the animal as if the priest had actually put his plan into effect. Leviticus specifies that any offering which is not completed by the specified time falls under the rubric of refuse (Lev. 7:18). Consequently, the plan to perform that act also places the animal into the category of refuse. But when a priest sacrifices an animal outside the designated place, Leviticus says only that the rite is invalidated. It does not claim that the animal falls under the rubric of refuse (Lev. 17:1-12). Therefore, the plan to perform the rite at the wrong place has precisely the same legal effects as the act itself: the rite is invalidated but the animal does not enter the classification of refuse. We see, therefore, that in determining the status of an animal, the Mishnah equates the priest's intention to perform an act with the very performance of that act.

In one respect, however, the priest's intention is not treated as equivalent to the performance of an act. According to Leviticus, a priest incurs divine punishment either for taking an offering outside the Temple, or for not completing the rite within the specified period of time (Lev. 17:3, M. Zeb. 13:1). But as we see from the rules just cited, the priest incurs no liability at all for merely planning to perform these acts. We here expose a fundamental principle underlying the Mishnah's theory of intention. In the mishnaic system, plans have the power to classify objects. But a person never incurs liability merely for formulating an intention to violate God's law. Whether an Israelite intends to violate a sacrificial procedure or to kill a fellow human being, he or she incurs no punishment as long as no steps are taken toward that goal.[4] The Mishnah thus differs from a system such as the Gospel of Matthew in which the mere intention to violate God's law precipitates divine punishment (Matthew 5:21-30).

Ruling Out Alternative Explanations

I have claimed thus far that a priest's intention spoils the sacrificial rite because he puts the animal into the category of a profane thing. I must now defend this position. At first reading, a far simpler explanation also accounts for the data so far discussed. From the cases already examined, one might argue that a priest invalidates the rite because he plans to violate a rule governing the sacrificial procedure. Since he performs the rite with the intention of violating God's law, God rejects the offering. The following rule shows this interpretation to be incorrect. This rule states unequivocally that an intention to violate a sacrificial law does not necessarily invalidate the offering.

I.   A.   [If a priest] slaughtered an animal with the intention of sprinkling [the blood] on the ramp [of the altar] but not on the base of the altar itself [where by law the blood must be sprinkled (M. Zeb. 2:1)],

     B.   [or if he intended] to sprinkle above [the red line which divides the top of the altar from the base] the blood that [by law] must be sprinkled below [the red line, (M. Zeb. 2:1)],

     C.   [or if he intended] to sprinkle below [the red line] the blood that [by law] must be sprinkled above [the red line (M. Zeb. 2:1)],

D. [or if he intended] to sprinkle on the outer [altar, i.e., the altar in the Temple court], the blood which [by law] must be sprinkled on the inner [altar, that is, the altar within the Temple itself],

E. [or if he intended to sprinkle] on the inner [altar], the blood which [by law] must be sprinkled on the outer [altar, (M. Zeb. 2:1)],

F. [or if the priest intended to let an] unclean person eat [from the offering of well-being which he is offering, an act which is forbidden (Lev. 7:20)],

G. [or if the priest intended to let] unclean persons sacrifice it [and thus handle its blood, an act which is forbidden (M. Zeb. 2:1)],

H. [or if the priest intended to let] uncircumcised persons eat [the Passover offering he is sacrificing, an act which is forbidden (Ex. 12:48)],

I. [or if the priest intended to let] an uncircumcised person offer up a sacrifice [and thus handle its blood, which is forbidden (M. Zeb. 2:1)],

J. [or if the priest intended] to break the bones of a Passover offering [an act forbidden by Ex. 12:46],

K. [or if the priest intended] to eat from [a Passover offering which is raw or boiled in water, an act forbidden by Ex. 12:9],

L. [or if the priest intended] to mix its blood with blood unfit [for sprinkling on the altar, an act forbidden by M. Zeb. 8:7],

M. [the offering is] valid, [despite the fact that the priest planned to perform an act that is forbidden by law].

N. This is because [a priest's] intention (*mahshabah*) invalidates [an offering] only [if he intends to eat the flesh of the sacrifice] after the time [designated for eating it], or outside the place [designated for its consumption, but not if he intends to violate one of the other rules governing the sacrificial procedure].

M. Zeb. 3:6

II. A. [As regards a priest who] slaughtered [an animal] with the intention of leaving either its blood [unsprinkled] or its entrails [unburned] until the following day --

B. or [as regards a priest who slaughtered an animal with the intention] of taking [the blood or the entrails] outside [the proper place, but does not actually plan to sprinkle the blood or burn the entrails there]--

C. Rabbi Judah declares the offering invalid.

D. But the sages declare the offering valid.

M. Zeb. 3:6

A priest's intention to perform part of the sacrificial rite at the wrong time or place spoils the rite (I N). But the intention of violating one of the other laws governing the sacrificial procedure, such as the rules governing where the blood should be sprinkled, or who should eat the offering, does not invalidate the ritual (I A-M). As previously suggested, a simple explanation accounts for why one type of plan spoils the rite but another does not. The rite is disqualified only when it is obvious that the priest conceives of the animal as a profane thing. Specifically, it is the intention to perform part of the rite at the wrong time or place which indicates that the priest regards the rite as a secular act of slaughter, which by definition may take place where and when a person pleases.

By contrast, none of the other plans listed here prove unequivocally that the priest conceives of the offering as a profane thing. For example, one cannot conclude that a priest has in mind a secular act when he intends to sprinkle the blood in the wrong place *within* the Temple precincts. On the contrary, the fact that he plans to sprinkle the blood within the sacred precincts at all indicates that he regards the animal as a consecrated thing. He has merely confused one type of sacred offering with another type of sacred offering, the blood of which is sprinkled in a different place. Since he conceives of the cow as a sacred thing, his intention does spoil the rite.

The same principle is operative in the case of a priest who intends to let an unclean or uncircumcised person perform part of the rite, or eat some of the flesh. By law, such persons are forbidden to eat most types of offerings and to handle the blood of the sacrifice. They are, however, permitted to perform the ritual act of slaughter (M. Zeb. 3:1)[5] and to eat the flesh from an offering of well-being (M. Zeb. 5:7).[6] Consequently, an ambiguity arises when the priest forms the intention of letting such a person participate in the rite or eat part of the animal. It may be that the priest thinks of it as a profane thing, which even unclean and uncircumcised people can eat. On the other hand, it may simply be that he has in mind the type of holy offering which such persons can consume, or the part of the holy rite which these people are permitted to perform. Since his intention is susceptible to alternative interpretations, it does not desacralize the animal.

The same ambiguity emerges in the case of a priest who intends to boil a Passover offering or break its bones. His intention may indicate that he has confused the Passover sacrifice with a secular act of slaughter. However, it is also possible that he only confused the Passover offering with another type of holy offering, the bones of which he may break and flesh of which he may boil. Again, due to the ambiguity involved, his intention has no legal consequences.

We may now understand the rather interesting dispute between Judah and the sages (II A-D). Judah and the sages discuss two cases. The first involves a priest who does not intend to sprinkle the blood or burn the entrails during the specified period of time. The second discusses a priest who intends to take the blood outside the specified place. In both of these cases an ambiguity arises. On the one hand, the priest does not intend to complete the offering within the proper span of time or within the designated area. For this reason, Judah argues that he conceives of the animal as if it were a profane thing. Yet, on the other hand, the priest has not actually formed an intention of performing part of the rite (slaughtering the animal, sprinkling its blood, burning its entrails or eating it) after the specified period of time or outside the designated place.[7] The sages, therefore, conclude that he has not confused the offering with a profane act of slaughter. In their judgment, only if he imagines performing one of the sacrificial acts at the wrong time or place does one know for certain that he confused the holy rite with its secular counterpart.

The Plan to Offer the Wrong Type of Holy Offering

We have seen thus far that a priest spoils a sacrificial rite by planning to put a consecrated animal to secular use. But what happens if, while sacrificing an animal consecrated for one type of holy offering, a priest thinks about a different type of holy offering? In the rules to follow, the sages explicitly address this question. In these cases, a householder initially consecrates an animal for one type of offering. But while sacrificing the animal the priest intends to offer up a different type. As we shall see, sometimes the priest's intention invalidates the rite but in other cases it does not.

I. A. [As regards] all animals [which were originally consecrated as one type of offering and] which were sacrificed under different names [that is, the priest who killed the animal had in mind a different type of offering, for example, he had in mind a burnt-offering while sacrificing an animal the householder has consecrated as an offering of well-being]--

B. [the offerings] are valid, but they do not satisfy the householder's obligation. [That is, the priest can complete the rite by sprinkling the blood on God's altar. However, since the priest had in mind the wrong type of offering, God does not credit the householder who brought the offering with having fulfilled a religious duty].

C. [The above rule applies to all offerings] with the exception of the Passover offering and the sin-offering. [If an animal designated as a Passover or sin-offering is sacrificed under a different name, God totally repudiates the offering. It does not fulfill the obligation of the householder and the priest may not complete the rite by sprinkling the blood on God's altar. The sages now spell this out:]

M. Zeb. 1:1

II. A. [As regards animals consecrated as a] Passover or sin-offering which [a priest] sacrificed under other names [that is, during the sacrificial procedure, he had in mind the wrong type of offering],

B. [and if the same priest] collected [the blood of the offering], or transferred [the blood of the animal to the altar] or sprinkled [the blood on the altar] under some other name--

C. or [if the priest slaughtered these animals] under their own name, but [collected, or transferred, or sprinkled their blood] under some other name--

D. or [if the priest slaughtered these offerings] under some other name but [collected, or transferred, or sprinkled the blood] under their own name--

E. [in each case the offerings] are invalid. [Since during at least one of the sacrificial acts, the priest intended to offer the animal for the wrong type of sacrifice, the offering is declared invalid, as specified at I C.]

M. Zeb. 1:4

III. A. Yose son of Honi says, "[Animals designated as either peace or burnt-offerings which were] slaughtered under the name of a Passover or sin-offering,

B. "are invalid, [that is, God totally repudiates the sacrifice. Hence the priest cannot sprinkle its blood on the altar]."

C. Rabbi Simeon brother of Azariah says, "[If a priest] slaughtered [animals] under the name of [an offering which has a] higher [degree of sanctity],

D. "the [offerings] are valid, [that is, God accepts the offering and hence the priest is permitted to complete the rite.]

E. "[But if a priest slaughtered animals designated for one type of offering] under the name of [an offering which has a] lesser [degree of sanctity],

F. "the offerings are invalid. [In this case, God totally repudiates the offering, which means that the priest cannot complete the rite by sprinkling the blood on the altar].

G. "What [are examples of C-F]?

H. "[In the case of] most holy offerings which were slaughtered under the name of lesser holy things--

I. "[the offerings] are invalid.

J. "[By contrast, in the case of] lesser holy offerings which were slaughtered under the name of most holy offerings--

K. "[the offerings] are valid.

L. "[By the same token in the case of an animal consecrated as] a firstling, or as tithe [offerings] which were slaughtered under the name of offerings of well-being--

M. "the offerings are valid, [because these are of higher degree of sanctity].

N. "[And, in the case of] offerings of well-being which were slaughtered either under the name of a firstling, or under the name of a tithe [offering]--

O. "the offerings are invalid, [because these are of lower degree of sanctity]."

M. Zeb. 1:2

All of the cases at hand take up a single question: if a householder designates an animal for one type of offering and a priest sacrifices it with the intention of offering up a different type of offering, is the offering valid? The answer depends upon two factors: 1) the type of offering for which the householder originally consecrated the animal, and 2) the type of offering the priest has in mind when slaughtering the animal. To understand these rules, therefore, we first need to discuss how the Mishnah subdivides the category of holy sacrifices into classes.

The sages break down holy offerings in two different ways. First they distinguish voluntary offerings (e.g., burnt-offerings and offerings of well-being) from obligatory ones (e.g., sin-offerings and Passover offerings). Second, the sages also distinguish offerings according to their grade of sanctity. Some offerings fall into the category of most holy offerings (e.g., burnt-offerings, sin-offerings, and guilt-offerings). Others fall into the category of lesser holy offerings (e.g., offerings of well-being, the sacrifice of the firstling and tithe of cattle).[8] Below, I have schematized the relationships between the various categories of holy offerings. In the the vertical columns (A, B), I list the types of offerings according to their degree of sanctity. The horizontal columns (1,2), by contrast, divide the offerings between the categories of voluntary and obligatory.[9]

Offerings:	A. Offerings of Higher Grade of Sanctity	B. Offerings of Lower Grade of Sanctity
1. Voluntary:	burnt	well-being
2. Obligatory:	sin	Passover, first born, tithe of cattle

With this diagram in hand, let us now work our way through the sages' discussion. We begin with the statement of Simeon (III C-O). Simeon considers most important the distinction between offerings of higher and lower grades of sanctity. In his view, a priest is expected to have in mind an offering of at least the same grade of sanctity as the householder originally conferred on it. If the priest intends to sacrifice an offering of lesser sanctity, he invalidates the rite. Simeon, therefore, espouses a theory similar to the one we have already discovered in previous rules. Just as a priest spoils an offering by planning to use a consecrated animal for secular purposes, he also invalidates the rite if he has in mind an offering of a lower grade of sanctity.

The anonymous sages (I A-C, II A-E) and Yose (III A-B) consider the distinction between voluntary and obligatory offerings to be most important.[10] If while sacrificing an animal originally designated as an obligatory offering (i.e., a sin or Passover offering), a priest intends to offer a voluntary offering (such as an offering of well-being), he totally invalidates the rite (I C, II A-E). By the same token, a priest spoils the rite by intending to sacrifice as a voluntary offering an animal originally designated as an obligatory offering (III A-B). In either case, by having in mind the wrong category of offering the priest invalidates the sacrifice.

The anonymous sages also raise a further complication. What happens if a priest has in mind the correct general category of offering, but the wrong sub-class of that category? For example, suppose a householder has designated an animal for one type of voluntary offering, for example as an offering of well-being. But when the priest sacrifices it, he intends to offer up a different type of voluntary offering, for example, a burnt-offering (I A-B).[11] Here, the priest has in mind the correct category of offering (i.e., voluntary offerings), but the incorrect class of voluntary offering (a burnt-offering instead of an offering of well-being, both of which are voluntary offerings).

The sages claim that in this situation the priest only partially invalidates it. Since the priest has in mind the wrong class of voluntary offering, the householder who brought it to the Temple receives no credit for having dedicated an offering to God. According to the Mishnah, however, since the priest had in mind the correct general category of offering, God does not repudiate the sacrifice. This is evident in the fact that the Mishnah permits the priest to sprinkle its blood on the Temple altar, an act which symbolizes the acceptability of the offering to God.

Having teased out the principles underlying these rules, we see the same basic theory we found previously. Whenever a priest has in mind the wrong category of offering, whether he confuses a sacrifice with a profane act of slaughter, or one type of sacrifice with another, he invalidates the rite. The mere thought of the wrong type of offering, therefore, alters the animal's status and thus ruins the sacrifice.

This basic theory generates an interesting secondary question. If a priest spoils the sacrifice when he has in mind the wrong category of offering, is it also true that he ruins the sacrifice if he fails to have in mind the correct category of offering? Suppose, for example, that while slaughtering an animal, a priest lets his mind wander and does not concentrate at all on what he is doing. In this situation, the priest has not formed an intention to sacrifice the wrong category of offering. Yet, at the same time, he also does not have in mind the correct category of offering. As we shall now see, the sages dispute whether in this situation a priest spoils the rite:

A. [In order to constitute a valid sacrifice] an offering must be sacrificed [by a priest][12] with the following six things in mind:

B. 1) with the intention of (lit. for the sake of) [offering the particular category of holy] offering [for which the householder designated it],
2) with the intention of [offering the animal on behalf of] the person who supplied the animal for the offering,
3) with the intention of [offering the animal] to God,
4) with the intention of [burning the animal in] the fires [of the altar but not with the intention of burning them at some other place],
5) with the intention of [sending up] an odor [to God, as specified by Lev. 1:9)],
6) with the intention of [producing] a pleasing [smell for God, again as specified by Lev. 1:9],

C. [Moreover, in the case of] a sin-offering or guilt offering [i.e., sacrifices offered after a person has committed a sin, the priest must offer them] with the intention of [expiating] the particular sin [that the householder who brought the animal had committed].

D. Said R. Yose, "Even [if a priest] did not have in mind [even a single] one of the [intentions listed at B 1-6]--

E. "[the offering nonetheless] is valid.

F. "[This leniency] is a stipulation of the court."

G. [The rationale for the rule at hand is supplied by the following]: [The laws regarding] proper intention [listed at A-E] apply only to the officiant [i.e., the priest. During the sacrificial rite, the intention of the householder who supplied the animal for slaughter cannot invalidate the offering.] [13]

M. Zeb. 4:6

The critical issue in this law is whether a priest invalidates an offering if he does not have in mind the category of offering for which the householder originally designated it. In Yose's view, as long as the priest does not have the wrong category of offering in mind, it is irrelevant what he thinks about. Even if he lets his mind wander to other matters, the rite is valid (D-E). The sages disagree. They consider the rite to be valid only if it is self-evident that the priest intends to offer the correct type of holy offering. This is why the sages require the priest to have in mind six specific intentions. Only when a priest has these intentions in mind is it obvious that he offers up the correct type of offering.

Four of these intentions show that the priest conceives of the sacrifice as a holy offering to God. When he intends to send up a pleasing odor to God (3, 5-6) he obviously regards the offering not as a secular thing to be used for human purposes but as a sacred offering. By the same token, the intention to burn the animal in the fires of God's altar demonstrates that he considers the animal to be sacred, and not a substance which he can cook at home (4). In line with the law previously examined, the sages also require the priest to offer the particular type of holy offering that the householder originally designated.

Of the six intentions listed here, only one does not involve the classification of the animal, namely, the intention to offer it on behalf of the householder who brought the cow to the Temple. As I will argue below, the priest must keep the householder in mind because he acts as the agent of the householder. If the priest fails to do so, he in effect repudiates the terms of his agency, and therefore loses the right to perform the sacrifice. The idea that the priest serves as the householder's agent also explains why the intentions of the householder who initially brought the cow to the Temple have no effect upon the validity of the offering (G). When a householder appoints a priest to sacrifice an animal, he turns his own power to determine the status of that animal over to the priest. Having conferred this legal capacity on the priest, the householder relinquishes any further control over the animal's status, and hence, his intention cannot spoil the rite.

We have thus far isolated one factor that determines whether a priest's intention invalidates a sacrificial rite, namely, whether the priest has in mind the wrong category of offering. As we shall now see, a second factor also plays a role in determining whether the priest's intention affects the validity of the rite. The Mishnah also takes account of whether the priest has formulated a plan which he is likely to carry out.

The Appeal to Social Norms in Evaluating a Priest's Plans

A priest's plan spoils a sacrifice only if there is a reasonable possibility that he will put that plan into action. The question naturally arises as to how the Mishnah distinguishes between reasonable and unreasonable plans. A simple test serves this purpose. If the priest intends to act in a manner consistent with the behavioral norms assumed to exist in Israelite society, the sages conclude that he will act as he intended. Such plans, therefore, have the power to invalidate an offering. However, the sages consider it unlikely that a priest will deviate from the norm. Consequently, if a priest intends to act in an atypical manner, they simply ignore his intention. These points emerge from the following rules in which a priest intends to eat parts of an animal which people do not normally treat as food.

I. A. [In the case of a priest] who sacrifices an [animal consecrated as an] offering [with the intention of] eating [outside the designated place or after the specified time] part [of the animal] which typically is not eaten—

    B. and [in the case of a priest who sacrifices an offering with the intention] of burning [outside the designated place or after the specified time] something which one normally does not burn [on the altar]--

    C. [the offering is] valid.

    D. Rabbi Eliezer declares it invalid.

                                                    M. Zeb. 3:3

II. A. [In the case of a priest] who sacrifices an [animal consecrated as an] offering [with the intention of eating]

    B. an olive's bulk from its hide, [or] from the grease [of the meat], [or] from the coagulation [of the meat], [or] from the fatty substance, [or] from the bones, [or] from the sinews, [or] from the hooves, [or] from the horns

    C. after its [designated] time or outside its [designated] place--

    D. [the offering] is valid.

                                                    M. Zeb. 3:4

III. A. [In the case of a priest] who sacrifices a [mother cow consecrated as] an offering [with the intention of eating the] fetus or the placenta, outside [the designated place],

    B. he does not place the animal into the category of refuse, [because most people do not eat the fetus or placenta of an animal, (see M. Hul. 4:7)].

    C. [In the case of a priest] who wrings [the neck of] turtle-doves inside the Temple,

    D. with the intention of eating their eggs outside [the designated place in the Temple]--

    E. he does not place the animal into the category of refuse, [because he has formulated an unreasonable intention].

                                                    M. Zeb. 3:5

The intention to eat part of the sacrifice at the wrong time and place usually invalidates an offering. In these cases, however, it does not. This is because the priest intends to act in a manner which is inconsistent with normal Israelite behavior, for example, by intending to eat the hooves, horns, or fetus of an animal. The Mishnah, therefore, regards these intentions as unreasonable, or perhaps even absurd, and therefore deprives them of their power to determine the status of the offering (I, II, III).[14]

The Mishnah also appeals to Israelite conventions to predict the order in which a priest is likely to carry out his plans. For example, the cases to follow involve a priest who formulates two intentions. He both intends to eat part of an offering outside the designated place and to eat part of the offering after the specified time. The fact that the priest has formulated two intentions creates an ambiguity, for as we recall, each of these intentions has different effects on the status of the offering (see my discussion of M. Zeb. 2:2). The plan to eat the offering after the specified time gives the animal the status of refuse. Eating refuse is a transgression of divine law and incurs a penalty. By contrast, if the priest plans to eat the animal at the wrong place, the sacrifice is invalidated, but the animal does not fall under the rubric of refuse.

In this rule, the sages discuss which of the priest's two intentions determines the animal's status. The answer depends upon the order in which a priest will implement those plans. The plan he is most likely to carry out first determines the classification of the animal. As we shall see, the framers appeal to normal Israelite behavior to predict the order in which a priest will implement his plans.

A. Said Rabbi Judah, "This is the general principle: If the intention (*mhsbt*) [to eat the animal after the proper] time precedes the intention (*mhsbt*) [to eat it outside the designated] place, [the offering falls into the category of] refuse, and [eating] it invokes the divine penalty of a premature death."

B. "But if the intention (*mhsbt*) [to eat it outside the designated] place precedes the intention (*mhsbt*) to eat it after the specified time, it is invalid [but eating it] does not incur the divine punishment of premature death."

C. The sages say, "In both cases it is invalid, and [eating it] does not incur the divine punishment of premature death. [That is, in the sages' view the order in which the priest formulates his intentions is unimportant. No matter which plan he formulates first, the animal is treated as if the priest took the animal outside the designated place before the specified time has elapsed].

M. Zeb. 2:5 (M. Zeb. 6:7, M. Men. 1:4)

The Mishnah does not explain the issue under debate between the sages and Judah. However, based on what we have found elsewhere in this study, we may speculate as to the nature of the dispute in question. It seems that both the sages (C) and Judah (A-B) appeal to normal Israelite behavior to determine which plan the priest will carry out first. The dispute arises because they disagree about how people normally behave.

Judah believes that people tend to execute their intentions in the order in which they formulate them.[15] The sages, by contrast, claim that this is not necessarily so. They argue that, regardless of the order in which the priest conceives of his plans, he probably will transgress the rules governing place before he violates the laws governing time. The sages base this conclusion on their image of the typical Israelite. In their view, if a person intends to perform two actions, he will perform them in the most convenient order. Now a priest can take an animal outside the proper place as soon as he formulates that intention. But in order to eat the offering after the specified time, the priest by definition has to wait until a given period of time has elapsed (one to three days depending on the type of offering in question). The sages, therefore, assume that the priest will violate the rules governing place before those governing time. For this reason, they do not regard the animal as refuse (C).

It turns out, therefore, that norms fulfill the same function in the sacrificial system as in the system of purity. In both cases, normal Israelite behavior serves as a criterion for predicting what an individual will do. When it is possible to predict a person's action in this manner, the Mishnah simply discounts the actual intention the person has in mind.

While norms serve the same function in the two sets of laws, one significant difference emerges. The Mishnah appeals to normal Israelite behavior far more often in the system of purity than in the laws of sacrifice. We cited a half dozen pericopae from the laws of purity in which normal behavior was an important consideration. In the sacrificial system, by contrast, there are only two examples.

Let me propose an explanation of this difference which fits what we have found elsewhere in this study. In the laws of purity, the sages need to predict whether a householder will use or dispose of certain objects or substances. This is precisely the type of question one can answer by appealing to the norm. There tends to be a consensus in society about what things are "food" or "waste," "useful" or "useless." This is why social norms play such a decisive role in the system of purity laws.

But from the Mishnah's standpoint, there exists an intrinsic ambiguity in the sacrificing of an animal. In the society presented by the Mishnah, the killing of an animal can serve one of two purposes. It can either be a sacred act, the purpose of which is to worship God, or a profane act designed to prepare the animal for consumption. Moreover, sacred and profane slaughters are performed according to similar procedures. From the act of slaughter alone, therefore, it is impossible to determine whether the slaughterer conceives of the killing as a sacred or profane act. Since the act of sacrificing an animal is by definition ambiguous, the sages must resolve the doubt by appealing to the subjective intention of the slaughterer. Social norms generally cannot help to determine the meaning of the slaughterer's action. For this reason, Israelite norms play a relatively minor role in the laws of sacrifice.

In summary, we have now determined the circumstances in which a priest's intentions will invalidate the sacrificial rite. First, and most importantly, he spoils the rite if he has the wrong category of offering in mind. Second, an intention ruins the ritual only if it is one which the Israelite is likely to carry out. This now brings us to the next important question for the present study. Why does a priest's intention have the power to define the status of the animal in the first place? I suggested earlier that the Mishnah conceives of the priest as an agent of an Israelite householder. In assigning a priest the task of sacrificing an animal, a householder transfers to the priest the power to define the status of the offering. Let me now substantiate this claim by showing that the Mishnah's conception of agency accounts for the relationship between householder and priest.

Priests as Agents of Householders

The idea that priests serve as agents for other Israelites is implicit in Scripture. God tells the people to bring their sacrifices "to the Lord, to the priest at the door of the tent of meeting, and slay them as sacrifices of peace offering to the Lord; and the priest shall sprinkle the blood on the altar of the Lord at the door of the tent of meeting, and burn the fat for a pleasing odor to the Lord (Lev. 17:1-6)." The biblical writer clearly conceives of the priest as the functionary who performs sacrifices on behalf of other Israelites.

In appropriating this biblical idea, however, the Mishnah interprets it in light of its overall conceptions of agency.[16] Specifically, I will show that the three principles governing agency in general also apply to the relationship between householders and priests. These three principles were discussed in some detail in Chapter Three. Consequently, we need only briefly review them in this context. First, an agent must resemble the principal in certain fundamental respects. Adult male Israelites, for example, generally cannot appoint a child, deaf-mute or retarded person to act as an agent, because these Israelites lack the mature mental capacities of an adult. Second, an agent has the power to produce legal consequences only because the principal has transferred those legal capacities to the agent in the first place. For example, a person can consecrate produce for another person only if instructed to do so (M. Ter. 3:8). Third, an agent can produce legal consequences only by following the instructions of the principal. However, by repudiating the terms of the appointment, the agent loses the powers which the principal originally conferred on him. In what follows, I will show how these ideas govern the relationship between householder and priest.

Householders and Priests: A Fundamental Correspondence

In the Mishnah, a householder can appoint a priest to act on his behalf because a priest resembles a householder in all important respects. To begin with, householders and priests are both adult, male, mentally mature Israelites. The correspondence between priest and householder, however, runs deeper than this, for both serve a similar function in society as a whole. The householder, by definition, is the master of an Israelite household. As master, he has responsibility for overseeing the proper functioning of the household. One of his most important tasks involves making sure that members of his household obey the rules of purity. A priest plays an analogous role in the Temple. He presides over the Temple cult and ensures that the rules of cultic purity and laws of sacrifice are obeyed. The priest, in a sense, is the householder of God's Temple.

By the same token, the householder serves as a kind of priest who presides over the household.

The fact that priests and householders fulfill similar roles does not in and of itself prove that the priest acts as the householder's agent. It remains to be shown that by turning one of his animals over to a priest, the householder confers on the priest the power to determine the status of that animal. What would constitute evidence that priests derive the capacity to define the status of an animal from householders? First of all, we would expect the legal powers of priests to correspond point for point with those of householders. If it turns out that their respective powers do not correspond, it is then obvious that householders are not the source of the priestly powers. Second, if priests derive their powers from Israelite householders, we would expect to find that they lack these powers when acting on behalf of someone other than an Israelite householder.

The Power of Householders to Classify Animals

In the mishnaic system, we find a perfect correspondence between the powers of Israelite householders and priests. To begin with, both householders and priests slaughter animals. Priests, as we have seen, sacrifice consecrated animals in the Temple. Householders, for their part, slaughter unconsecrated animals for food. Furthermore, as the rule below indicates, a householder's intention can spoil a secular act of slaughter in precisely the same way that a priest's intention invalidates a holy offering.

I. A. [Concerning an householder] who slaughters [an unconsecrated animal as a voluntary offering, as for example when he slaughters it] as a burnt-offering, [or] as a [peace-] offering, [or] as a doubtful-guilt offering [i.e., an offering sacrificed when a person suspects but is not certain that he has committed a sin], [or] as a Passover-offering, [or] as a thank-offering,--

   B. his act of slaughter is invalid.

   C. Rabbi Simeon declares [the act of slaughter] valid, [and hence, the householder may eat the meat from the animal]...

   D. [Concerning a householder] who slaughters [an unconsecrated animal as any type of obligatory offering, for example] as a sin-offering, [or] as an offering for certain guilt [i.e., those offerings listed at M. Zeb. 5:5], [or] as a firstling, [or] as a tithe-offering, [or] as a substitute [offering]--

   E. his act of slaughter is valid [and hence he may eat the animal].

   F. This is the general rule:

   G. An offering which is offered in fulfillment of a vow, or voluntarily [i.e., those listed at A]--

   H. [if a householder offered his cow] under its [name, that is under the name of any offering voluntarily given to the Temple],

   I. the animal is forbidden. [The offering has been invalidated and hence he cannot eat the meat of the animal.]

J.   But an offering which is not offered in fulfillment of a vow or voluntarily [i.e., obligatory offerings, such as those listed at C]--

K.   [if the householder offers his cow] under its name,

L.   the act of slaughter is valid [and therefore the animal may be consumed].

M. Hul. 2:10

II. A.   [Concerning a householder] who slaughters [an animal] in honor of mountains, [or] in honor of hills, [or] in honor of the seas, [or] in honor of rivers, or in honor of the deserts--

B.   his act of slaughter is invalid.

M. Hul. 2:8

We see from this rule that the intentions of householders and priests fulfill equivalent functions in their respective domains. A priest spoils a sacrificial rite when he intends to use a consecrated animal for secular purposes. Analogously, a householder spoils a secular act of slaughter if he either intends to offer it to God as a voluntary offering (I A-B, G-I) or intends to honor the mountains or other natural phenomena (II A-B). In either case, he has in mind the wrong category of offering. By intending it for a voluntary offering, he classifies it as a sacred object. Since he slaughters it outside the Temple, he has in effect killed a consecrated thing in a profane place, and for this reason he invalidates the slaughter. Similarly, when he intends to honor the natural phenomena, he places the object into the category of things used for idolatrous purposes. This too spoils the rite.

Only in one case does a householder's intention fail to invalidate the act, namely, when he intends the animal to serve as an obligatory offering (I D-E). Here his thoughts have no legal consequences because householders are permitted to consecrate animals for obligatory offerings only if they previously incurred an obligation to make that sort of sacrifice. A householder can set aside an animal for a sin-offering, for example, only if he has first committed an inadvertent transgression. Since the householder at hand has incurred no obligation, he does not have the right to consecrate the animal for an obligatory offering. Consequently, his intention to use the animal for that purpose is nullified. Since it has no effect on the animal's status, the act of slaughter is considered valid.

For our purposes, the cases just examined illustrate one point: the intentions of householders and priests have similar effects on the animals they slaughter. A priest desacralizes a consecrated animal by forming an intention to use it for secular purposes. A householder, by intending to sacrifice an animal to God, puts an unconsecrated animal into the category of a sacred thing. The fact that householders and priests possess precisely the same legal capacities supports my claim that priests derive their legal powers from Israelite householders. But additional evidence must also be mustered. If, in fact, priests acquire their legal powers from householders, the converse should also be true. We should find that a priest cannot exercise such powers when acting as the agent of someone other than an Israelite householder. This is in fact what we discover.

When slaughtering an animal for a gentile, a priest's intention cannot invalidate the offering. This is because gentiles themselves cannot classify things by forming intentions. Since a gentile lacks this power to begin with, he obviously cannot transfer it to a priest. This proves that the power to classify an animal is not intrinsic to the priestly office. The legal powers which he has are conferred on him by another person. If a priest acts on behalf of someone who has those powers (an Israelite householder), he acquires them. But if he sacrifices an animal for someone who lacks those legal rights (such as a gentile), the priest also lacks those powers.

In order to substantiate this interpretation, let me begin by showing that the intentions a gentile actually formulates produce no legal effects. This point emerges from a case involving a gentile who slaughters an animal according to the prescribed ritual of Israelite law.

A. An act of [profane] slaughter performed by a gentile [automatically places the animal into the category of] carrion and hence it contaminates any person who lifts it. [Even if the gentile followed the correct procedure, the act of slaughter is invalid. This is because when a gentile slaughters an offering, the sages always assume that he intended it for idolatrous purposes, as stated in M. Hul. 2:7].

M. Hul. 1:1

The sages automatically impute to all gentiles the intention of sacrificing the animal to their gods. Therefore, any animal which a gentile slaughters by definition falls under the rubric of an improperly slaughtered animal (carrion). The actual intentions of a gentile, therefore, do not affect the status of the animal. Indeed, even if he had no religious motives in mind, the rite would still be invalid.

Because a gentile's subjective intentions can produce no legal effects, he cannot confer such powers on another person. This point emerges from a rule which discusses a priest who sacrifices an animal which a gentile has brought to the Temple. While sacrificing the animal, the priest formulates an intention to eat it after the time specified for its consumption. We recall that if a priest formulates such an intention while sacrificing an Israelite's animal, the animal would become refuse. But in this case, precisely the same intention has no effect on the animal's status.

A. The holy offerings of gentiles --
B. are not subject to [the rules governing] refuse. [That is, if a priest intends to eat a holy offering brought by a gentile after the specified period of time has elapsed, the offering does not fall into the category of refuse. By extension, the intention to eat the animal at the wrong place also does not invalidate the offering.]...

C.   [If a priest] slaughters [the offerings brought by gentiles] outside [the place designated for the sacrifice of holy things]--

D.   "he is not liable [for having violated the law]," the words of Rabbi Meir. [In Meir's view, gentiles do not have the power to consecrate animals. Hence, if a priest slaughters the animals of gentiles outside the designated area, he does not incur liability for having taken a consecrated thing from the Temple, because the animal was never a holy thing.]

E.   Rabbi Yose declares [the priest] liable. [Yose believes gentiles have the power of consecrating animals by bringing them to the Temple. Therefore Yose considers a priest liable for sacrificing the animal in the secular domain.] [17]

M. Zeb. 4:5

Both Meir and Yose agree that when sacrificing a gentile's cow, a priest's intention has no power to change the status of the offering (A-B). For example, the intention to eat part of the offering after the specified span of time does not place the animal under the rubric of refuse. Meir's logic is self-evident. He believes that gentiles have no power to consecrate an animal even if they bring it to the Temple. Since the animal is not a sacred thing, it does not matter what the priest intends or even does with it (D).

Yose's position is more difficult to understand. On the one hand, Yose clearly believes that gentiles can consecrate offerings by bringing them to the Temple. This is evident from his statement that a priest incurs liability for slaughtering such an animal outside the designated area (E). Although Yose thinks the animal is consecrated, he nonetheless claims that the priest's intention of slaughtering it at the wrong time or place does not invalidate the offering. [18] Apparently Yose believes that the priest's intentions are of no import, because he acts on behalf of a gentile. Since a gentile's intentions lack the power to determine the status of an animal, he cannot confer that power on the priest. In conclusion, therefore, it appears that a priest's intentions can invalidate an offering only when he acts on behalf of a person who has those powers at the outset.

A similar point emerges from the following case, which involves a gentile who asks an Israelite householder to slaughter one of his animals. In mishnaic law, as we saw previously, there is a presumption that gentiles sacrifice their animals to their gods. A problem thus arises when a gentile asks an Israelite to slaughter the animal. On the one hand, the gentile presumably intends to honor his gods by having the beast slaughtered. On the other hand, the Israelite conceives of the killing as strictly a secular act of slaughter. This gives rise to a dispute over the status of the slaughtered animal. One sage argues that the gentile's presumed intent to worship his gods is decisive. From the outset, the animal falls into the category of something used for idolatrous worship. [19] Other sages disagree. In their view, the animal's status depends exclusively upon the person who slaughters the animal. Since an Israelite, and not a gentile, performs the rite, the act of slaughter is valid.

A. [An Israelite] who slaughters [an animal] on behalf of a gentile--
B. his act of slaughter is valid.
C. But Rabbi Eliezer declares the act of slaughter invalid.
D. Said Rabbi Eliezer [explaining his view at C], "Even if an Israelite slaughtered the animal in order that the gentile eat only from the lobe of the animal's liver [i.e., a negligible amount], the rite would be invalid,
E. "for there is a presumption that the thoughts of a gentile are directed to idolatry."
F. Said Rabbi Yose [in disagreement with Eliezer], "[The proper ruling may be derived from an argument] a fortiori.
G. "Now, if in a case where intention has the power to invalidate the rite, [namely] in [cases involving the sacrifice of] holy things, the legal outcome depends exclusively upon the person who sacrifices the animal [i.e., the priest and not the owner of the animal, see M. Zeb. 4:6],
H. "then in a case where intention does not have the power to invalidate the rite, [namely], in [the cases involving the killing of an] animal for profane purposes, it stands to reason that the legal outcome depends exclusively upon the slaughterer."

M. Hul. 2:7

What requires explanation is Yose's claim that the intentions of Israelites do not have the power to invalidate a secular slaughter (E-H). Yose's position here is unclear. In the rules which immediately follow this one in the Mishnah, we learn that the intentions of Israelites can invalidate a profane act of slaughter (see the above discussion of M. Hul. 2:8, 10). What, then, does Yose mean when he states that intentions do not invalidate a secular act of slaughter? It would seem that Yose subscribes to the view that Israelites' intentions are inert when they act on behalf of gentiles.[20] Since the intentions of gentiles do not produce legal effects, they cannot transfer such powers to Israelites who act as their agents.

By way of summary, let me review the strategy of argument until this point. I claimed at the outset of this discussion that a priest's intention can invalidate an offering because he acts on behalf of an Israelite householder who conferred those powers on the priest. Two sets of facts were adduced to support this thesis. First, the householder and priest have precisely the same powers. Second, when the priest sacrifices an animal for a gentile, his intentions become powerless. Turning now to the third piece of evidence, we shall find that a householder's intentions produce legal effects only when he abides by the terms of his appointment.

The Terms of Agency

As I said at the beginning of this discussion, an agent's actions produce legal consequences as long as the agent obeys the principal's instructions. For example, if a woman said to an agent, "Accept a writ of divorce for me in Jerusalem," and the agent accepted it in Tiberias, the divorce would not be valid (M. Git. 6:3). The sages invoke the same line of reasoning in the following case which involves a priest and a householder. A priest can exercise the powers conferred on him by a householder only when he is actually performing his assigned task. When the priest is not involved in carrying out his instructions, however, he lacks the power to define the status of the offering:

I. A. This is the general principle: anyone who slaughters [an animal] or collects [its blood] or transports [its blood to the altar] or tosses [its blood on the altar],

   B. [with the intention of] eating a substance which [people] normally eat,

   C. or [with the intention] of burning a substance which is normally burned [i.e., the entrails],

   D. outside of its [designated] place--

   E. the offering is invalid but [for eating] it [a person does not] incur the divine punishment of premature death.

   F. [If he performed any of the above acts with the intention of eating or burning the offering] after the [specified period] time [has elapsed]--

   G. it falls into the category of refuse and [for eating] it [people] incur the divine penalty of premature death.

                                        M. Zeb. 2: 3

II. A. An [animal designated as a] Passover offering or [an animal designated as] a sin-offering

   B. which [a priest] slaughtered with the wrong category of offering in mind,

   C. [and he] collected, transported, and tossed [the blood of the offering] with the wrong category of offering in mind,

   D. and [concerning a priest who slaughtered the animal] with the correct category of offering in mind, but [collected, transported and tossed the blood] with the wrong category of offering in mind,

   E. and [concerning a priest who slaughtered the animal] with the wrong category of offering in mind, but [collected, transported and tossed the blood] with the correct category of offering in mind--

   F. [in all of these cases, the offerings] are invalid...

   G. For an offering may become invalid [as the result of a priest's intention] during [the] four [essential] acts: during the slaughtering [of the animal], the collection [of blood], the transporting [of the blood to the altar] or [during the] tossing [of the blood on the altar].

   H. Rabbi Simeon declares [an offering] valid [even if during] the transporting [of the blood, the priest had in mind the wrong category of offering].

   I. For Rabbi Simeon did say, "It is impossible [to perform a valid offering] without [the ritual] slaughter, and without the collection [of the blood] and without the tossing [of the blood on the altar].

   J. "But it is possible [to perform a valid offering] without the transporting [of the blood. How so?]

   K. "One may slaughter [the animal] next to the altar and sprinkle [the blood on the altar without needing to transfer it at all. Since one can perform a valid sacrifice without transferring blood, this does not constitute an essential act]."

   L. Rabbi Eleazar says, "One who transports [blood] in circumstances in which he must transport [the blood in order to get it from the animal to the altar, his improper] intention invalidates [the offering].

M. "But in circumstances in which he need not transport [the blood in order to get it to the altar, his improper] intention does not invalidate [the offering]."

M. Zeb. 1:4

When a householder delivers one of his livestock to the priest, he does so with the expectation that the priest will sacrifice it. Consequently, it is precisely during the essential acts of the sacrifice that the priest acts on behalf of the householder, namely, when slaughtering the animal, collecting and tossing its blood. During the performance of those acts, therefore, the priest's intentions have the power to define the status of the animal (I A-G, II A-G). But when the priest performs an unnecessary act, for example, by not carrying the blood directly to the altar, he does not act as the householder instructed. On the contrary, at that moment he is no better than a thief who has stolen an object from a householder. Since he has violated the terms of his agency, he temporarily loses the powers the householder has conferred on him. In this case, therefore, his intention cannot spoil the rite (H-M).

To support my claim that the Mishnah equates a priest who performs an unnecessary sacrificial act with a person who has stolen property,[21] we turn to a rule which discusses the intentions of thieves and robbers. This pericope, drawn from the Mishnah's system of purity, takes up cases involving thieves and robbers who have stolen leather hides from fellow Israelites. Here, the Mishnah poses the rather bizarre question of whether the intention of a thief or robber can define the classification of a leather hide which he has stolen. We recall from Chapter Three that the classification of an object depends upon the intention of the person who owns that object. If, for example, a person intends to put to use a leather hide which he owns, it automatically falls under the rubric of a useful thing and hence can absorb cultic impurity. By contrast, the intention to discard leather has the effect of placing it in the category of useless objects, with the result that it cannot become contaminated.

The case at hand takes up a related question. Here the Mishnah asks whether a person's intention can define the status of something which he does not own, but which he has in his possession. In turning to this rule, we shall see that the intention of a thief or robber, like the intention of a priest who has ignored his instructions, cannot determine the status of an object:

A. [As regards hides] in the possession of a thief, [which he secretly stole from a householder]--

B. [the thief's] intention (mahshabah) [to use them places them in the category of useful things and so] makes them susceptible to impurity. [Since the thief stole the hides in secret, the householder does not know who has them, and consequently, the householder reconciles himself to the loss. The thief ipso facto acquires ownership of the hides with the result that his intention now determines the status of the hide.]

C. But [as regards hides] in the possession of a robber, [which he took by force from a householder]--

D. [the robber's] intention (*mahshabah*) [does not place them into the classification of useful things and so] does not make them susceptible to impurity. [Since the householder knows who has stolen his hides, he will try to recover them through litigation. Because the owner has not given up hope of recovering his possessions, the robber never acquires ownership of the hides, with the result that the robber's intention cannot affect the status of the hide.]

E. Rabbi Simeon says, "Matters are [precisely] reversed. [The correct version is as follows:]

F. "As regards hides which] a robber [stole]--

G. "[his] intention (*mahshabah*) [to use them places them in the classification of useful things and hence, they become] susceptible to impurity. [According to Simeon, since the robber stole the goods by force, the householder knows for certain that they were stolen and not misplaced. The householder knows, moreover, that it is unlikely that he will recover stolen property. Since the householder has despaired of recovering his goods, the robber *ipso facto* acquires ownership of the hides and hence his intention has the power to determine the status of the hides.][22]

H. "[As regards hides which] a thief [stole]--

I. "[his] intention (*mahshabah*) [to use them does not place them in the classification of useful things and so] does not make them susceptible to impurity.

J. "[The reason that the intentions of the robber (G) can classify the hide is] because the owner has despaired [of recovering the object. But since the thief (H-I) stole the hides secretly, the householder does not know for certain that they were stolen. He will assume that he merely misplaced them or lent them to someone else, and therefore, he is certain that he will get them back. As the owner never despairs of recovering the hides, the thief never acquires ownership of them and hence his intention has no effect on the status of the hides.]

M. Kel. 26:8

The rule at hand takes up two situations: cases in which 1) the owner has despaired of recovering the property (A-B, F-G) and 2) in which he still hopes to recover the property (C-D, H-I). In the former cases, the thief 's (or robber's) intention determines the classification of the stolen goods. When the owner gives up hope of recovering the stolen objects, he has in effect renounced ownership of that object. By default, the thief or robber acquires ownership of it and thus gains the legal capacity to define that object's status. By contrast, in those cases in which the owner seeks to regain the stolen property, the thief's or robber's intention has no power to define the status of that object. This is for two reasons. First, he has that object without the owner's permission, and second, he never acquired ownership of that object.

It is this latter situation that most closely corresponds to the case of the priest and householder discussed above. A priest also has in his possession an animal which belongs to another person. To be sure, the householder has willingly turned over that animal to the priest. However, by performing an unnecessary sacrificial act and thus ignoring the instructions of the householder, the priest treats the animal as if it were his own, and not the householder's. In this respect, he ceases to act as the householder's agent and hence, the Mishnah equates him with a thief, whose intentions are powerless. In sum, we see that all principles governing agency in the other parts of the mishnaic system also explain the relationship between a priest and a householder. A priest's intentions can invalidate a rite because a householder has transferred those powers to him. Consequently, as long as the priest carries out the designated task, he can exercise those legal capacities.

Priests as Agents of Householders: The Underlying Significance

In claiming that the priests are merely agents of householders, the Mishnah substantially restricts the powers of the priesthood. To begin with, as demonstrated above, the Mishnah conceives of the priest's powers of intention as deriving from an Israelite householder. It is the householder who commissions the priest to perform the sacrifice. Consequently, a priest performs a valid sacrifice only by faithfully carrying out the wishes of the householder. In effect, therefore, the Mishnah has turned Scripture's theory of the priesthood on its head. In Leviticus, the priests play the definitive role in the sacrificial system. Leviticus knows of no constraints by householders on the exercise of the priestly duties. In this respect, the Mishnah has demoted the priest and given householders a more central role in the sacrificial system. It is the intentions of householders which define the classification of the animal. Once a householder has designated an animal for a particular kind of offering, God expects the priest to offer it with the same category in mind. If the priest ignores the householder's classification of the animal, God repudiates the sacrifice. As agents of householders, therefore, priests are merely cogs in a machine which a householder sets in motion and ultimately controls.

The limitations which the Mishnah places on the priesthood show that the Mishnah does not speak from the perspective of the priestly caste.[23] Indeed, the sages are more sympathetic to the interests of lay Israelites as is evident by their desire to circumscribe the powers of the priests in favor of Israelite householders. This fact correlates with findings from previous chapters which showed that the sages found the priestly conception of the world untenable in certain critical respects. We recall that the priestly writings conceive of the world as being organized into a rigid and static scheme of classification which was set in place at creation itself. In the priestly view, humans are merely passive recipients of a preexisting divine scheme of classification. The Mishnah modifies the priestly perspective, however, by granting humans a critical role in implementing the divine scheme of classification. We are thus led to a paradoxical conclusion. Of all the Scriptural writings, it is the priestly writings which most intrigued the Mishnah's sages. At the same time, however, critical aspects of the priestly perspective were problematic for the sages and required substantial revision. In the conclusion to this study, I will attempt to explain both of these tendencies, namely, why the sages found the priestly writings so compelling and why they modified them in the way they did.

The Role of A Priest's Intentions in the Sacrificial System: Mishnaic Innovation or Scriptural Inheritance?

Having examined the Mishnah's conception of intention in the sacrificial system on its own terms, we now consider the extent to which the Mishnah draws upon Scripture for its ideas. The Mishnah's stress on a priest's thoughts and plans, like other aspects of the Mishnah's theory of intention, derives from two streams of biblical thought, one which emphasizes the importance of the cult and sacrificial system, and the other which places stress on inward obedience to God and inward motivation to carry out God's will. The combination of these two steams of biblical thought in this case is particularly significant, because in the biblical corpus, these two streams of thought are often in tension with one another. On the one hand, those biblical passages which stress the importance of the cult and the role of the priest as the intermediary between Israelites and God ascribe little importance to the inward dimension of religious experience. In Leviticus, for example, the validity of the sacrifice depends entirely upon the priest's actions, not upon the intentions he has in mind. As long as he performs the sacrifice according to the prescribed procedure, the sacrifice is valid. He spoils the rite only if he does something improperly.[24]

On the other hand, those biblical passages which stress the importance of inward obedience to God and inner motivation to carry out God's law tend to denounce the cult and the sacrificial system. In the following passage, for example, Samuel accuses Saul of hypocrisy for sacrificing animals captured in war when in fact God commanded him to destroy all of the enemies' possessions. In this writer's view, sacrifices in and of themselves are meaningless without a commitment to obeying divine instructions.[25]

> Does the Lord delight in burnt-offerings and sacrifices
> As much as in obedience to the Lord's command?
> Surely, obedience is better than sacrifice,
> Compliance than the fat of rams (I Sam. 15:22)

For this writer sacrifices do not serve as a substitute for obedience to the divine will. By itself, sacrifice is an empty act which does not win God's approbation.

An even more pronounced dichotomy between sacrifices and obedience to God appears in the writings of several of the classical prophets.[26] Hosea, for example, claims that God desires "goodness not sacrifice, obedience to God, rather than burnt-offerings (Hosea 6:6). " According to Amos, God said, "I loath, I spurn your festivals, I am not appeased by your solemn assemblies. If you offer Me burnt-offerings-or your meal offerings-I will not accept them...But let justice well up like water, righteousness like an unfailing stream. Did you offer sacrifice and oblation to Me those forty years in the wilderness, O House of Israel?" (Amos 5:21-25).

Jeremiah, too, rejects the cult as empty formalism. "Thus said the Lord of Hosts, the God of Israel: add your burnt-offerings to your other sacrifices and eat the meat! For when I freed your fathers from the land of Egypt, I did not speak with them or command them concerning burnt-offerings or sacrifice (Jer. 7:21-24)." For Jeremiah, what is critical is that God's will be inscribed on peoples' hearts.

> Thus said the Lord: Cursed is he who trusts in man, who makes mere flesh his strength, and turns his thoughts from the Lord...Blessed is he who trusts in the Lord, whose trust is the Lord alone...Most devious is the heart; it is perverse - who can fathom it? I the Lord probe the heart, search the mind - to repay every man according to his ways, with the proper fruit of his deeds (Jer. 17:5,7,9-10).

Jeremiah claims that the sacrifical system deceives Israelites as to the nature of their obligation to God. They believe they can carry out divine will through the performance of sacrifices alone. In fact, however, true devotion to God requires obedience which springs from the heart.

One final passage drawn from Psalms will illustrate the tendency within one stream of biblical thought to conceive of the cult as undermining an understanding of the divine will.

> You gave me to understand that You do not desire sacrifice and meal offering; You do not ask for burnt-offering and sin offering...To do what pleases You, my God, is my desire; Your teaching is in my inmost parts (Psalm 40:7,9)

The Mishnah, as is now evident, rejects out of hand the biblical stream of thought which claims that the sacrificial system is somehow incompatible with inward obedience to God's will. On the contrary, in the Mishnah these two elements go hand in hand. Without the cult, one cannot properly worship God. At the same time, the priest's thoughts, intentions and plans play a central role in determining whether God accepts the offering at all. The following passage, perhaps more than any other, shows how devotion to God and the cult are compatible and, indeed, inseparable in the Mishnah.

A. [The fact that Scripture describes both expensive and inexpensive offerings as a "pleasing odor to God" (Lev. 1:9,17;2:2)],
B. indicates that [in God's view] there is no difference between a person who gives [a] more [valuable object] and a person who gives [a] less [valuable] object,
C. provided that the person directs his mind to heaven.

M. Men. 13:11

In rejecting the stream of thought which considered the cult and obedience to God incompatible, the Mishnah carries forward another strand of biblical thought, in which these two ideas peacefully coexist. The Deuteronomist and

Ezekiel, for example, incorporate both ideas into their respective systems. The Deuteronomist apparently saw no contradiction in charging the people to "love the Lord God with all your heart and soul," and at the same time emphasizing the importance of the sacrificial system (Deut. 12:4-19).[27] Likewise, in the writings of the prophet Ezekiel, both inner obedience to God and the cult form major preoccupations.[28] In Ezekiel's depiction of the redemption from exile, God both will give Israel a new heart (Ez. 11:16-20) and reestablish the sacrificial cult (Ez. 43:18-21, 45:18-25, 46:4-15). In one respect, therefore, Ezekiel and the Deuteronomist anticipate the Mishnah in that they detect no incompatiblity between the cult and inward obedience to God's will.

Yet, at the same time, the sages of the Mishnah go further than either Ezekiel or Deuteronomy in synthesizing these ideas. In both Ezekiel and Deuteronomy, the idea of inner obedience to God's will and the sacrificial system are two separate strands of the same system. That it to say, the two ideas coexist but do not intersect. The discussion of the cult does not prompt reflection upon the importance of inward devotion to God. In the Mishnah, as we have seen, discussion of the sacrificial cult inevitably turns to the place of the heart and mind in the divine-human relationship, for in the Mishnah, one element is inextricably bound up with the other. Once again, therefore, we discover that the Mishnah significantly modifies the priestly world view. Although the sages accept the importance of the cult, they stress another theme which in the biblical writings is in tension with the priestly world view.

Conclusion: When and Why Plans are Important in the Mishnaic System

Having analyzed the role of plans in the Mishnah's sacrificial system and laws of purity, we now need to formulate a general theory to explain why the Mishnah appeals to plans in the particular legal contexts in which it does. Thus far, we have isolated two factors which seem to account for the Mishnah's interest in plans. First and most importantly, the sages ask about a person's plans only in contexts in which the classification of objects is important. Second, the sages inquire about a person's plan only when they cannot predict an object's use from normal Israelite behavior.

We may state the above findings in terms of a hypothesis which can be tested by surveying the Mishnah's rules. The Mishnah will appeal to a person's plans only when two conditions obtain: 1) the classification of an object is important and 2) it is impossible to determine that object's classification by appealing to Israelite conventions. If one or both of these conditions does not obtain, we should find that the sages will ignore a person's plans. The obvious way to test this theory is by considering in what areas of mishnaic law the Hebrew term for plans (i.e., *mahshabah*) appears. If our hypothesis is correct, we should find that this term appears quite frequently in those areas of law which meet the two conditions specified above. By contrast, in those contexts in which one or both of the specified conditions is lacking, we should find that the term *mahshabhah* does not make its appearance. Let us now put our theory to the test.

The term *mahshabah* and its related verbal forms appear seventy-five times in the mishnaic corpus.[29] With the exception of two cases, which we shall examine below, the term appears only in the system of purity and the sacrificial system. The distribution of this term throughout the Mishnah, as we shall now see, accords fully with our theory. Its importance in the laws of purity and sacrifice is predictable, for these two areas of law satisfy both of the postulated conditions. By the same token, the absence of the term *mahshabah* in other areas of law also confirms our theory, because in these contexts we almost never find both of the stated conditions. One or the other is nearly always lacking. Either the classification of objects is not an issue, or the sages can predict the object's use by relying upon Israelite norms. Let me now spell this out in detail.

The importance of plans in the laws of cultic purity and Temple sacrifice follows from the Mishnah's overriding concern with the classification of objects in these contexts. In the laws of cultic purity, as we saw in Chapter Three, the principal issue is determining whether household objects fall into the category of useful or useless objects, food or waste. The classification of objects is critical because, in the sages' view, God has ordained a different set of rules for each category of object. Classification, as shown in this chapter, is also an important issue in the laws of sacrifice. In this context, the sages need to know whether a slaughtered animal belongs to the category of a sacred offering to God or a secular slaughter for food. This distinction is important because certain restrictions apply to sacred objects but not to secular ones. Both the laws of cultic purity and the laws of Temple sacrifice, therefore, satisfy the first condition: the classification of objects constitutes the fundamental issue which the sages wish to address.

Both areas of law satisfy the second condition as well. In these contexts, the sages often find it impossible to anticipate an object's classification by appealing to Israelite norms. This is because the objects to be classified (such as leather hides and dead cows) frequently serve more than one purpose in Israelite society. It is impossible, therefore, to predict what an individual will do with a given object, and hence, the only way to determine its classification is by taking account of his plan.

A similar problem arises in the laws of sacrifice. In the society presented by the Mishnah, slaughtered animals serve either as an offering to God or as food for an Israelite's household. On the basis of Israelite norms alone, therefore, one cannot determine whether a priest slaughtered the cow for holy or secular purposes. Again, to resolve such ambiguity, the framers take into account what the person plans to do. Our theory, therefore, readily accounts for the importance of plans in the laws of cultic purity and Temple sacrifice, for these laws satisfy both of the postulated conditions.

The Mishnah's indifference to plans (*mahshabah*) in the remaining areas of mishnaic law also conforms to our theory. These laws fail to satisfy at least one of the two conditions we specified. In the case of civil law and rules of appointed times, the classification of objects is not at issue. Rather, the recurring concern here is to determine whether someone has acted in violation of a law. Has the person at hand defrauded someone by selling overpriced goods? Has he or she, for example, violated the Sabbath laws? This is the kind of question which occupies the sages in this area of law. Since in this context the classification of objects is unimportant, the Mishnah almost never appeals to a person's plan.

One rule, however, proves to be an exception. This law, as we shall now see, reflects a theory inconsistent with what we have found elsewhere in the Mishnah. The case at hand involves an Israelite who asks another to guard one of his or her possessions. According to Scripture, the bailee (the one guarding the object) is forbidden to use or even handle the bailment (the property being guarded). If the bailee does so, a fine is incurred. In the rule at hand, however, the bailee merely formulates the plan of using bailment. The question is whether the bailee incurs liability for the mere intention to violate the law:

A. [If] one puts to use what had been left in his keeping [and it is subsequently damaged or stolen] --

B. The School of Shammai says, "He suffers whether its value increases or decreases. [That is, the bailee must pay the owner its original worth, if it has fallen in value, or he must pay the owner additional money if its value has increased.]"

C. The School of Hillel says, "[The bailee must compensate the owner the value it had] at the moment it was put to use."

D. [If] one plans to use what had been left in his keeping [and it is subsequently damaged or stolen]--

E. The School of Shammai says, "He is liable."

F. The School of Hillel says, "He is not liable, unless he actually handles the object,

G. "as it says [in Scripture, ' When a man gives money or goods to another for safekeeping, and they are stolen from the man's house-if the thief is caught, he shall pay double; if the thief is not caught, the owner of the house shall depose before God that] he has not laid hands on his neighbor's property (Ex. 22: 6-7).' "

M. B.M. 3:12

This is the only rule in the Mishnah which asks whether an Israelite incurs liability for merely planning to violate a law. Indeed, all the other passages considered in this study presumed the opposite, namely, that a person cannot incur liability for the mere intention to violate the law. There are two ways of accounting for the relationship between this rule and the Mishnah's larger theory of plans. The two views mentioned here are purported to represent authorities who lived prior to 70 A.D.. If this is the case, then the rest of the Mishnah's rules, which impose no liability for merely intending to violate the law, carry forward the view of the Hillelites. On the other hand, there is some evidence that the disputes attributed to the two schools are pseudepigraphic.[30] Later authorities may have projected their own views onto the earlier authorities, as a way of legitimizing their own positions. If this is the case, then the dispute at hand is intended to justify the Mishnah's general theory that a person incurs no liability for his or her plans. It does this by attributing this view to the school of Hillel, the school granted normative status within the tradition. In any case, this law is the single case in which the term *mahshabah* appears without the two postulated conditions.

In the laws of agriculture, the term plan (*mahshabah*) does not appear, because those rules fail to satisfy the second of the specified conditions. In this context, a person's plan is irrelevant, because it *is* possible to predict his or her behavior by reference to normal behavior. By appealing to Israelite conventions, the sages can determine the status of a farmer's produce (i.e., whether it belongs to the category of sacred, secular, or waste). Since most Israelites raise crops for subsistence, there is no question as to what an individual farmer will do. Presumably, he will use his produce for food, by eating it or selling it in the market. Unless an Israelite indicates otherwise by his actions, therefore, the crop falls into the category of secular food, not holy produce dedicated to the Temple.[31]

It turns out that the word plan (*mahshabah*) does appear once in the laws of agriculture (M. Sheb. 8:1). But this law, as we shall now see, is an exception which proves the rule, for it meets both of the specified conditions. The rule involves determining whether certain edible substances are subject to the restrictions of the Sabbatical year. During the Sabbatical year, Israelites must let their land lie fallow. But in order to ensure that people have enough to eat during the seventh year, the Mishnah makes a special provision. During the Sabbatical year, Israelites must use a given substance in the way that people normally use that substance during the other years of the Sabbatical cycle (i.e., the previous six years). This rule ensures that people maximize the usefulness of any produce they have stored away. They cannot waste good food on some other purpose. Accordingly, before using a product during the seventh year, an Israelite must first determine its status. If in the previous six years it normally falls under the rubric of food, then during the seventh year he must use it for that purpose. He cannot waste such substances, for example, by using them as animal fodder.

In turning to this rule, we see that the Mishnah invokes the Israelite's plan in order to classify certain types of wild spices. If one plans to use them for food, they belong in that category. But if one plans to use them as kindling wood, they fall into the category of waste.

A.   [The sages] stated a general principle regarding produce of the seventh year:

B. [Concerning] all [produce] that [during the preceding six years] is [normally] designated as food for humans--

C. [Israelites] cannot derive from it a salve for people, and needless to say, [they cannot use such produce to make a salve] for animals. [Since it normally serves as food, they cannot use it as salve, which is a less valuable function.]

D. And [concerning] all [produce] which [normally] is not designated [during the six years prior to the Sabbatical year] as food for people, [but is designated as fodder for cattle]--

E. [Israelites] may make a salve from it for man but not for cattle. [Since this produce generally is used as fodder, it may serve that purpose or its equivalent during the Sabbatical year. Hence, an Israelite can use such produce as a salve for people. However, by using it as a salve for animals, he does not maximize the usefulness of the produce and hence violates the law.]

F. And [concerning] all [produce] that is neither designated as food for people nor as fodder for cattle [for example, plants which are ordinarily not cultivated for any purpose]--

G. [If] one planned [to use] it as food for people and as fodder for animals, [Israelites must] subject [those plants] to the restrictions [that apply to the food of] people and to the restrictions [that apply to the fodder] of animals. [That is, since he has designated it as human food, he may not use it as a human salve. Furthermore, since he has also designated it as animal fodder, he cannot use it as a salve for his animal.]

H. [If, by contrast], one planned [to use] it as wood [that is as fuel], it [falls into the classification of] wood [and so is not subject to the restrictions governing food during the Sabbatical year].

I. [What are examples of plants that are neither designated for human or animal use as at F? Spices] like savory, marjoram and thyme.

M. Sheb. 8:1

The fact that the Mishnah appeals to an Israelite's plan in this case should not surprise us. To begin with, this rule deals with issues of classification. More importantly, this rule meets the second of our two postulated conditions. It is impossible to predict how an Israelite will use certain spices from normal Israelite behavior, because people do not consistently use these plants for a single purpose. Some Israelites use them as spices, whereas others use them for fodder or kindling wood. Therefore, to determine their status during the Sabbatical year the sages must appeal to an Israelite's intention. Thus, the one context in which the term "plan" appears in the laws of agriculture fully satisfies the two specified conditions.

It is more difficult to explain the absence of the term "plan" (*mahshabah*) in the Mishnah's discussion of family law (*Nashim*), for these rules do satisfy both of the postulated conditions. First, the problem of classification is central in these rules. The sages wish to determine the status of women and treat this problem as analogous to the classification of objects. Is a woman under the control of her father (i.e., in the category of daughter), under the control of her husband (i.e., in the category of wife), or under no man's control (i.e., in the category of divorcee or widow)? Second, the sages generally cannot determine a woman's status by appealing to norms, for women may fall into any of the above categories. We must ask, therefore, why a man's plan has no effect upon the classification of a woman. For example, a man's mere intention to marry a woman does not put her into the category of a wife. He must first perform some procedure in order to marry her. Similarly, a man's plan to divorce his wife does not place her in the category of a divorcee. Why not?

The answer emerges when we recall that plans have the power to classify only objects with an ambiguous status. But once an object has entered a given category, intention can have no further effect upon it (Chapter Three). The same principle applies to the classification of women. In the Mishnah's view, a woman has a defined status from birth. She is the daughter of a man and hence under his control. Since her status is already determined, another man's plan to marry her can have no effect upon her status. In order to marry her, he must perform an act of betrothal.

In summary, then, a survey of the Mishnah's rules verifies our hypothesis that two factors explain the Mishnah's interest in a person's plans. First, the Mishnah appeals to plans only when discussing the classification of objects. Second, plans serve as a criterion for classification only when it is impossible to determine an object's classification by appealing to Israelite norms.

Chapter Five

Conclusion

The Mishnah's Theory of Intention

The Mishnah employs the words for intention (i.e., *kavvanah* and *mahshabah*) in a variety of contexts, ranging from civil law to rules of purity. Throughout this study, I have claimed that a theory underlies the various statements in which intention is discussed. By a theory of intention, I mean a "systematically related set of statements"[1] about when and why intention matters. I shall now proceed to defend this claim. What constitutes evidence that the diverse rules involving intention add up to a theory rather than just a collection of unrelated statements about the same topic?

Let me clarify this question by drawing on an analogy. Imagine cutting every quotation that contains the word "peace" from a newspaper. Assembling these quotations, you would probably find little agreement about what peace means or how it can be attained. The term might refer to the cessation of war in one context and the peace of afterlife in another. Furthermore, even those people who use the term to refer to the cessation of war might disagree about how to realize that goal. One might argue that the only method for achieving a lasting peace is by declaring a freeze on the production of nuclear weapons. Another might insist we can achieve peace only by building up an arsenal of weapons which will serve as deterence to other countries. While all of these statements refer to the same subject matter, they obviously do not form a theory in the sense of sharing certain fundamental assumptions about the topic in question. They are merely a random collection of statements bearing on a similar theme. But now suppose that you cut out all the statements about peace from a journal which espouses a particular point of view. Although different people are represented by these statements, it is probable that the various statements will together present a theory, because they rest on certain shared assumptions about the nature of peace and the methods to attain it.

Our analysis of the mishnaic statements about intention has demonstrated that they coalesce to form a theory about when and why intention matters. By analysing rules involving intention in one part of the Mishnah, we discovered principles that also explained when and why the framers would appeal to intention in another part of the Mishnah. For example, in the first part of our study, we discovered that the Mishnah appeals to an actor's intention only when the action bears more than one interpretation against the background of behavioral conventions assumed to prevail in Israelite society. Precisely the same principle emerged when we analysed the mishnaic rules involving a person's plans. The sages appeal to plans only if, on the basis of normal Israelite behavior, they cannot predict what the individual in question will do. The fact that similar principles underlie the statements about intention in various parts of the mishnaic system proves that we have at hand not a random set of unrelated statements but a theory about when and why intention matters.

The Mishnah's theory of intention, like all theories, takes as its point of departure certain basic presuppositions about the nature of the world and the place of human beings in that world. The Mishnah's theory flows out of its own distinctive set of assumptions about the nature of God and the relation of God to humanity. We need now isolate those fundamental notions that give coherence and sense to the Mishnah's theory. The axioms underlying the Mishnah's theory are by definition those ideas which repeatedly make their appearance when we analyse any of the statements the sages make about intention. To discover these presuppositions, therefore, we need only identify the ideas which emerged in each of the various chapters of this study. These will be the founding assumptions upon which the sages have erected their theory.

Having framed the question to be addressed, the answer is not far to seek. It turns out that four basic assumptions underlie all the mishnaic rules concerning intention: 1) intention is the human counterpart of the divine will, 2) intention serves as a criterion for classifying things (whether actions or objects), 3) the stress on intention derives from the importance of teleological criteria in defining an object's classification, and 4) intention plays a subordinate role to social norms.

The First Axiom: The Correspondence between Human Intention and Divine Will

The capacity to think or, more specifically, the ability to formulate intentions and plans, makes human beings like God. This idea provides the point of departure for everything the Mishnah says about human intention. From the sages' standpoint, "being created in God's image" means being able to exercise one's mind in the same way that God exercises the divine will. The sages work out the correspondence between human intention and divine will in each of the various parts of their theory. Most significantly, they ascribe to human intention the same characteristics that the priestly writer attributes to God's will in the biblical story of creation (Gen 1:1-2:4).

This story serves as a paradigm for the Mishnah's theory of intention in two respects. To begin with, the sages ascribe the same sorts of power to human intention that the biblical writer imputes to God's will. In the biblical account God wills the world into existence. Likewise, in the mishnaic system, human beings have the power to transform the character of objects around them. Merely by formulating a plan to use an object for a particular purpose, an Israelite alters one of the most basic properties of that object, namely, its ability to absorb or withstand cultic contamination. For example, when a person plans to use a given object, the object can absorb impurity, whereas prior to the formulation of the intention, it could not become contaminated. By the same token, when a priest slaughters an animal, the plan he formulates has the power to desacralize the animal. In the system of the Mishnah, therefore, the thoughts and intentions of human beings have the effect of restructuring the very character of reality.

There is a second correspondence between God's will as portrayed in the biblical account of creation and the mishnaic understanding of human intention. In the biblical myth, God's principal task in creating the world involves mapping out lines that differentiate the world into its constituent categories. God creates an expanse which separates the waters above (sky) from the waters below (the seas). By the same token, God distinguishes the light from darkness, the day from night, the water from the land, the profane days from the Sabbath and so forth. According to the biblical writer, classifying the world was itself an essential part of the divine labor in creating the world. As part of classifying the world, God also gave each category a name. For example, "God called the light Day and the darkness He called Night."

In the system of Mishnah, human beings carry out a similar exercise. When they distinguish between useful and useless objects or between food and waste they parcel out reality between the human domain and the domain of nature. Moreover, when an Israelite distinguishes what is sacred from what is profane, he or she imitates the divine act of separating the profane days of the week from the Sabbath. From the Mishnah's standpoint, human beings are endowed with powers similar to God's, because they have the capacity to carry out the same intellectual operations as God, namely, the ability to classify the world.

The fundamental similarity which the sages perceive between human beings and God leads them to treat humanity as God's agent. The Mishnah apparently bases this idea on the Yahwist's account of creation, in which God asks Adam to name the animals (Gen. 2: 19-20). In the sages' view, by asking Adam to name the animals, God in effect assigned humanity the task of classifying the world into its constituent categories. Thus in the mishnaic system, as we have seen, Israelites are responsible for imposing order on the world around them. Just as Adam named the animals, Israelites give names to the objects around their homes and on their farms.

The connection between the Mishnah's theory of classification and the Yahwist account of creation is evident in the word the Mishnah adopts to speak about classification. In mishnaic Hebrew, the word for classification (sm) is the same word used in the biblical story of Adam's giving names (smwt) to the animals. In addition, the Mishnah refers to the act of classification as "calling something a name (*lqrwt sm*)." This expression is used by the Yahwist in speaking about Adam's acts of classification (Gen. 2:19-20).

The mishnaic idea that intention is the human counterpart to the divine will leads to its corollary: in evaluating a person's action, God takes into account the intention which accompanies that act. In so doing, God determines whether or not the act in question constitutes a repudiation of the divine will. An actor rejects God's will when he or she intentionally performs an act which constitutes a violation of the law. An intentional violation signifies that the actor has set human will against the divine will. The sages also believe that God takes account of the purpose with which the person acted. If the actor's purpose was licit, no liability is incurred. But if the purpose was forbidden, the actor has repudiated God's law and hence incurs punishment.

Following the same line of reasoning, the sages claim that an actor's purpose plays an important role in determining whether this person has fulfilled a religious duty. If the actor performs the requisite religious act but does not specifically form the intention of satisfying that religious duty, the act does not fulfill the obligation. Although the actor carried out God's law, he or she did not do so with the intention of fulfilling God's command. In the Mishnah, therefore, few actions are inherently a violation or a fulfillment of divine law. All depends upon the intention with which the person acts. In asserting that God takes account of an actor's intention, the sages carry forward their basic belief that human intention corresponds to the divine will. If the capacity to formulate intentions makes human beings like God, it follows that human beings are most like God when they bend their will to the divine will. Conversely, when they set their will against God's, they repudiate the resemblance between themselves and God.

The Second Axiom: The Role of Intention in Classification

In the mishnaic system, intention serves as an important criterion in classifying things. In assigning either objects or actions to their respective categories, the framers frequently appeal to a person's intention. We have already seen how an Israelite's intention categorizes household objects. The intention to use an object places that object in the category of useful things and hence makes it capable of absorbing impurity. Similarly, the intention to eat a given substance places it into the classification of food with the result that it becomes susceptible to impurity. Intention, as I said above, also serves as a criterion for assigning actions to their respective categories. A person's intention determines whether the action he or she performs falls under the rubric of a transgression or satisfies a religious obligation.

It turns out, therefore, that the Mishnah's interest in intention flows from a more general concern with taxonomy. This leads to the following striking conclusion: were the sages not interested in classification in the first place, intention would play only a minor role in their system. In other words, if the framers did not care about sorting things into categories, they also would take less interest in human intention.

Evidence internal to the Mishnah supports this claim. Our analysis of the terms for intention shows that, with a single exception, the sages never appeal to intention in a context that does not involve the classification of either an object or an action. For this reason, the Mishnah does not discuss cases involving a person who merely intends to violate God's law, for example, by committing murder, adultery, or any other crime.[2] Since in cases such as these the Israelite has performed no action (and therefore nothing requires classification), the Mishnah has no reason to discuss intention in these contexts.

Furthermore, even in those contexts in which the sages discuss the classification of either an object or an action, they appeal to intention only as a last resort. If they can assign an object or action to its category by appealing to some other criterion, they simply ignore human intention. For example, if an object has already served a purpose, the sages do not take account of how the owner intends to use it. They can classify it simply by appealing to its actual function. We find, therefore, an unmistakable correlation between the Mishnah's interest in intention and its propensity to classify things. The cases in which the Mishnah invokes intention will be the same cases in which they face a problem in determining the classification of an object or an action. Conversely, when classification is not an issue, the Mishnah will take no interest in intention at all.

The Third Axiom: The Importance of Teleological Criteria in the Mishnah's System of Classification

The importance of intention in classifying objects and actions derives not only from the sages' desire to classify things. It also stems from a more basic judgment on their part about the proper strategy for placing things into categories. In their system, they consistently appeal to teleological criteria in assigning objects and actions to their respective categories. By this I mean that the sages define an object or action in terms of its end or *telos*. We have seen that the status of objects also depends upon their function. The function of an object, by definition, is the end that that object serves. Thus, classifying objects according to their function reflects a teleological concern. Likewise, in evaluating an action in terms of its purpose, the sages are also appealing to a teleological criterion. In this case, they are classifying the action by making reference to the goal or end that the action is meant to achieve.

The Mishnah's insistence upon using teleological criteria ultimately makes it necessary to invoke a person's subjective intention. Since the sages classify objects according to their function, an ambiguity arises with respect to objects which are not yet put to use. For example, when a householder finds a dead cow in the field, it is not clear whether it falls under the rubric of food or waste, because he has so far done nothing with it. A logical way to determine the function of such objects is by appealing to the Israelite's intention. If he intends to use it, it falls under the rubric of a useful thing, whereas if he decides to discard it, it enters the category of waste. We see, therefore, that in a system which places emphasis on the function of objects, intention will also turn out to be important. Similarly, since the sages classify an action according to its purpose, they invariably need to know what an actor has in mind. This is because in many cases the action itself bears more than one interpretation. Consequently, without knowing what the actor at hand actually intended, it is impossible to determine the purpose of the action.

What we have discovered here in the Mishnah is also true elsewhere. Other systems that evaluate actions in terms of their purposes also take an interest in the actor's actual intention. This is true, for example, in recent discussions in analytic philosophy. Those thinkers who make the purpose of an action an important category in their system also need to know, under certain conditions, what the actor is thinking. We have already discussed the following passage from Anscombe's work in which she discusses a man whose job it is to pump a supply of water into a house. On one particular day, the man pumps a poisoned supply of water into the house. Now in this case, his action bears several interpretations. It is unclear whether he is pumping the water simply to earn his pay or whether he in fact intended to kill the owners of the house. Anscombe admits that in such a situation one needs to know what the actor has in mind:

> Up to a point, then, there is a check on his (the actor's) truthfulness in the account we are thinking he would perhaps give; but still, there is an area in which there is none. The difference between the cases in which he doesn't care whether the people are actually poisoned or not, and in which he is very glad on realising that they will be poisoned if he co-operates by going on doing his ordinary job, is not one that necessarily carries with it any difference in what he overtly does or how he looks. The difference in his thought on the subject *might* only be the difference between the meanings of the grunt he gives when he grasps that the water is poisoned. That is to say, when asked 'Why did you replenish the house supply with poisoned water?' he might either reply 'I couldn't care tuppence' or say 'I was glad to help to polish them off', and if capable of saying what had actually occurred in him at the time as the vehicle of either of these thoughts, he might have to say only that he grunted. This is the kind of truth there is in the statement *"only you can know if you had such-and such an intention or not". There is a point at which only what the man himself says is a sign* (emphasis supplied).[3]

Here, in a contemporary system of philosophy, we discover an interesting parallel to the Mishnah's system. Anscombe, like the sages of the Mishnah, believes the proper way to evaluate an action is by making reference to its purpose. Furthermore, Anscombe recognizes that in some cases it is impossible to determine the actor's purpose by observing his or her action. Consequently, she is forced to admit that in such cases one needs to take account of the actor's subjective intention. We discovered precisely the same principle in the Mishnah. Since the sages decided to evaluate an action in terms of its purpose, they sometimes needed to appeal to the intention the actor had in mind. In summary, therefore, we find that the emphasis the sages place on intention stems from the logically prior decision to classify things in terms of teleological criteria. Since they evaluate actions in terms of their purpose, and since they classify objects by appealing to their function, they often need to make reference to a person's intention.

It stands to reason, therefore, that had the Mishnah adopted non-teleological criteria by which to classify things, intention would play a relatively insignificant role in the system. Suppose that the sages had decided to classify objects according to their size, color, or shape. In this case, the framers would not have needed to know the owner's intention, because the classification of an object would be readily apparent from its phenomenal features. All objects of the same shape or of the same color would automatically fall into the same category.

Intention would also be unimportant had the framers decided to classify actions not according to their purpose but according to their observable characteristics. Indeed, we are already familiar with a system which ignores an actor's intention for precisely this reason, namely, the system of Leviticus. For example, Leviticus prohibits donning a garment made from linen and wool regardless of the purpose that the action was meant to serve. Because the writers of Leviticus do not evaluate this act in terms of its purpose, they never appeal to the intention that the actor had in mind. Whether he intended to use it as clothing or to model it for customers, he has committed a transgression.

Similarly, in Leviticus the rite of sacrificing an animal is valid as long as the priest follows the proper procedure. His purpose in offering the animal does not affect the validity of the rite. Again, since the authors of Leviticus do not judge the act in terms of its purpose, they do not care about the intention the priest had in mind. Had the framers of the Mishnah followed the example of Leviticus in considering the purpose of an action irrelevant, they also would have taken little interest in the intentions that actors actually formulate. We therefore conclude that the mishnaic stress on intention follows from the framers' initial assumption about how to classify the world.

The Fourth Axiom: Norms as a Criterion of Classification

Human intention is not the only criterion the Mishnah relies upon in classifying objects and actions. In fact, intention turns out to be less important than a second criterion: normal Israelite behavior. The Mishnah suggests that both the function of objects and the meaning of human actions are often self-evident against the background of norms which are presumed to operate in Israelite society. Israelites tend to use certain types of objects and discard others. By the same token, Israelites tend to eat certain types of substances and regard others as waste. In the sages' judgment, it is also possible to deduce the meaning of an individual's action from the normal meaning of that act in Israelite society.

If most people perform the act in question for a specific purpose, one may assume that the individual at hand also has that purpose in mind.

What is the precise relationship between norms and intention in the Mishnah's system of classification? It turns out that intention plays a subordinate role to norms in the sense that the sages prefer to base their classification of objects and actions on normal Israelite behavior rather than on an individual's actual intention. Consequently, if an individual performs an action which normally bears a specific meaning in the context of Israelite society, the sages will impute to the actor the normal meaning of the act, and ignore the actual purpose of the actor. To cite one example, the sages always ascribe to a person who takes a vow the standard meaning of his or her words, even though the votary may have had a different meaning in mind.

Intention is also subordinated to norms in the Mishnah's system of classifying objects. The Mishnah assigns objects to categories on the basis of their normal function, even if a person has formed an intention of using the object in question for some other purpose. The best example of this tendency was the case of a tanner who intends to use an untanned hide. Since tanners almost never consider such hides to be useful things, his intention has no power to place the leather in the category of useful objects (M. Kel. 26:8) When a clearly defined norm exists, therefore, it overrides the individual's intention.

In some cases, norms do not provide a definitive classification of an object but only narrow the range of possibilities. This is the case when people use objects like the one at hand in several specific ways. From normal Israelite behavior alone, it is impossible to determine the precise function that the object will serve. But at the same time, it is clear that Israelites put such objects to a limited range of uses. In cases such as these, norms determine the boundaries within which an individual's intention has the power to define the status of the object. As long as the individual intends to use the object for at least one of its normal functions, his or her intention determines that object's classification. But the intention to use the object in an idiosyncratic way has no effect whatsoever.

Why does the Mishnah subordinate intention to norms in its system of classification? At first blush, a relatively simple answer seems to present itself. It would appear that the sages consider norms to be more reliable than intentions in two respects. First, norms provide a more objective criterion for determining the meaning of a person's action than do intentions. This is because people have no access to one another's intentions. When an actor claims to have had a specific intention in mind, there is no way of determining whether he or she is telling the truth. The sages' propensity to rely on norms, therefore, may stem from the fact that intentions are unverifiable and hence problematic for a functioning legal system.

Second, intentions are also less reliable than norms for anticipating an Israelite's future behavior. If an Israelite intends to use an object in an idiosyncratic fashion, the sages assume that the person will ultimately change his or her mind and conform to the typical practice. In sum, the Mishnah's reliance on norms may stem from the fact that human intentions are unverifiable and unreliable for predicting a person's action.

According to the interpretation just given, the Mishnah is treated as essentially a legal code which is concerned with the proper functioning of the law. The concern with objectivity and reliability stem from the sages' attempt to create a working legal system. As in other legal systems, a person's subjective intentions play no role in determining the legal outcome.[4] On the surface, this interpretation is compelling. However, as I have argued previously, treating the Mishnah as merely a legal system fails to explain one important fact. If the sages were solely interested in developing a viable legal system, why would they ever take account of a person's actual intention?

The sages' frequent appeal to an individual's subjective intention can only be understood in light of certain theological presuppositions. The Mishnah relies on intention because it takes for granted that God holds actors accountable for their innermost thoughts. The sages, therefore, conceive of God as serving as an adjunct to the human court. When humans cannot determine an actor's intention, God steps in and makes certain that justice is done. The Mishnah makes this viewpoint explicit in specifying the penalties for certain transgressions. A person is only liable to the divine penalty of a premature death if the human court cannot convict the actor of the crime and impose punishment. But a person who is convicted and flogged is no longer subject to the divine punishment of premature death (M. Mak. 3:1-2, 15; M. Ker. 1:1). In essence, the Mishnah is claiming that God administers justice when the court does not have sufficient evidence to do so. In this way, the Mishnah sidesteps a problem that faces all legal systems, namely, the possibility that a person can be guilty of a crime yet be acquitted for lack of evidence. In the Mishnah, a person always gets the appropriate punishment, one way or another. The laws set down in the Mishnah, therefore, do not represent a legal system that is meant to be adjudicated exclusively by human beings. It also represents laws for which God holds a person accountable.

The Mishnah's stress on norms may also stem from certain theological convictions. This is suggested by the fact that the Mishnah appeals to normal Israelite practice even in cases which are not routinely adjudicated in a human court. The rules of purity and vows are cases in point. The Mishnah does not conceive of these types of cases as being routinely brought to a human court. A person who takes a vow must know from what he or she is expected to abstain. By the same token, a householder must determine for himself whether various objects around the home are susceptible to impurity. Such cases are not routinely adjudicated by a court. Rather, the Mishnah takes for granted that God holds a person responsible for fulfilling a vow and for obeying the rules of purity.

Significantly, norms play a critical role in both of these areas of law. In determining whether an object is susceptible to impurity, a householder must find out whether most Israelites consider it useful. If so, then it is automatically susceptible to impurity. Similarly, a person who wants to fulfill a vow must determine the normal meaning his or her words bear. In these instances, the emphasis on norms cannot be explained as deriving from the sages' concern with verifying the Israelite's intention, because these cases are not adjudicated by a court.

It is for this reason that I have offered an additional explanation for the Mishnah's interest in norms. The stress on norms suggests that the sages believe that God takes account of the norms in judging an Israelite's action. The Mishnah implies that God holds a person responsible for the normal meaning of a vow. Similarly, in the sages' conception, God takes account of normal Israelite behavior in determining what can and cannot absorb impurity. God treats as susceptible to impurity whatever most Israelites deem to be useful.

To be sure, the notion that God appeals to Israelite norms in judging human action seems counterintuitive. After all, according to the Mishnah, God knows an Israelite's actual intention. It seems, therefore, that the emphasis on norms derives from the conviction that Israelite society, in obeying divine law, comes to embody the divine will. Consequently, the norms produced by this community become normative in the sense that they serve as models of virtuous behavior. One carries out the divine will, therefore, by paying attention to the norms whenever deciding upon a course of action. This explanation accounts for the fact that the Mishnah actively encourages Israelites to take account of the behavioral and linguistic norms which operate in their society. As we have seen in case after case, an infraction of divine law often occurs when one fails to determine the norm or conform to it.

Explaining the Mishnah's Theory of Intention: A Sociological Perspective

At a certain point in analysing a theory, one discovers those basic assumptions upon which the theory as a whole rests. These assumptions or axioms admit no further analysis, for they constitute the points of departure for the entire theory under discussion. In my judgment, the four axioms discussed above provide the foundation upon which the Mishnah's theory of intention rests. Having isolated these axioms, we can penetrate no deeper into the framers' thought, because these ideas are the unquestioned premises of their theory of intention.

The question therefore arises as to how to account for the Mishnah's preoccupation with the constellation of themes represented by the four axioms spelled out above. This question is complicated by the fact that none of the ideas taken by itself is entirely new. Each is a common place notion in the biblical writings. At the same time, these ideas were unrelated to one another in the biblical corpus. Although each of them may be found in the Bible, they tend to represent different streams of thought. In combining what were unrelated biblical ideas, therefore, the Mishnah has produced a theory totally unlike anything found in the literature of ancient Israel. In the same way that the combination of two colors may produce a third, the Mishnah created a new theory by bringing together what previously were independent themes.

In trying to account for the Mishnah's theory of intention, it is important to consider the nature of the group that produced the Mishnah and their purpose in writing it. Unfortunately, the sages of the Mishnah tell us little about themselves and their purpose in creating the Mishnah. However, from the traits of the document itself, we can speculate as to the nature of their activity.

At the simplest level, the Mishnah appears to be the work of intellectuals reflecting upon the inherited religious tradition as represented in the literature of ancient Israel. By Weber's account, intellectuals systematize the religious tradition which, because it has developed over time, is necessarily disorganized and full of contradictions.[5] Systematization involves imposing logical organization on accumulated knowledge, working out contradictions, and filling in lacunae. Much of the Mishnah, including its theory of intention, is understandable as an attempt by intellectuals to systematize the biblical legal traditions.[6]

The sages' desire to systematize the biblical rules is evident in the attention the Mishnah devotes to the potential conflict among Scriptural laws. The Mishnah examines hundreds of situations in which two or more biblical rules conflict with one another.[7] For example, the Mishnah takes great interest in the potential conflict between the Sabbath laws and other biblical laws, such as circumcision. According to Scripture, one must cease one's labors on the Sabbath day which, in the Mishnah's understanding, means that one must forgo all creative or destructive acts. This law may come in conflict with the duty to circumcise a male Israelite child on the eighth day after his birth. This conflict occurs if the eighth day after the birth of a male child is a Sabbath. Does the command to cut the child's foreskin override the prohibition on performing destructive acts on the Sabbath day (M. Shab. 19:2)? Cases such as this one represent the sages' desire to anticipate and resolve all possible conflicts between various biblical laws.

The same effort towards systematization is evident in the sages' concern with ambiguity. The Mishnah takes up hundreds of situations in which an object or situation fall between two established classifications of biblical law.[8] We have seen countless examples of this tendency in the study at hand. To cite one example, the Mishnah takes up the statement in Leviticus that food can absorb impurity if it becomes wet. Now it is clear that grain constitutes food and that wood does not. But what about other substances such as wild spices? Because they are wild, some people treat them as weeds. But because they are spices, others use them for seasoning (M. Sheb. 8:1, M. Uqs. 3:2). The attention to ambiguous cases, like the interest in the potential conflict of rules, derives from the sages' attempt to create a system out of the biblical laws.

Many of the mishnaic cases which strike the contemporary reader as bizarre or farfetched merely represent the sages' desire to rationalize their system, in the sense of carrying their legal principles to their logical conclusions, and imagining all possible permutations of a given situation. Consider, for example, the way in which the Mishnah discusses the biblical rule that a man must marry his deceased brother's wife. The Mishnah takes up a series of hypothetical cases in which a husband had died. The simplest case is where the man who dies has only one brother. Here the brother is obligated to marry the widow of his deceased brother. But as the Mishnah progresses from case to case, other permutations of the situation are considered, which introduce complications in the law. The Mishnah varies the total number of brothers involved, the number of brothers who are married, the number of brothers who die, and the relationship of the brothers' wives to one another (in some cases the wives are sisters which complicates the problem, as marriage to one's sister-in-law is considered incest) (M. Yeb. 3:1-7). This series of cases, then, represents an attempt to carry one legal principle to its logical conclusion by testing it in all possible situations. There are many other instances of this tendency in the mishnaic corpus. [9] As a literary work, therefore, the Mishnah represents an attempt to turn the biblical rules into a fully exposed and coherent system.

We are now in a position to understand why the Mishnah owes such a substantial debt to the mode of thought and ideas of the priestly writers of Scripture. We have seen, for example, that the Mishnah takes great interest in the laws of sacrifice and purity, both of which are concerns of the priestly writings. Moreover, the interest in classification which dominates the priestly writings is also absorbed into the mishnaic system. I would suggest that the Mishnah's sages found the priestly writings more compelling than other strands of Scripture because they represented the most systematic part of the biblical corpus. Like the sages of the Mishnah, the priests were interested in presenting a fully exposed system of Judaism. The priestly writings spell out in extraordinary detail the laws of sacrifice, laws of purity, genealogies, the specifications for building the Temple. Their concern was to provide a systematic and comprehensive account of the tradition as they understood it. The sages of the Mishnah had precisely the same concerns. As a group of intellectuals, they wished to work out a coherent and systematic account of God's will. For this reason, the priestly strand of Scripture drew their attention. To borrow a phrase from Lévi-Strauss, the sages of the Mishnah turned to the priestly writings because they were "good to think." In these writings, the sages found a system that displayed all the characteristics which as intellectuals they considered important.[10]

To return to the main point of this inquiry, the Mishnah's theory of intention can also be understood as part of the sages' general interest in systematizing and harmonizing biblical laws and ideas. This is most clearly evident in the mishnaic conception that human intention has the power to classify things. This idea represents a combination of two separate themes in the literature of ancient Israel, 1) the notion that God takes an interest in human thoughts and intentions, and 2) that the classification of objects is important in carrying out God's will. The former idea is a frequent theme in some of the biblical works, especially the prophetic writings, Deuteronomy, and Psalms. However, in biblical literature this theme is not integrated with an interest in classification, which is the hallmark of the priestly writer. The Mishnah, therefore, has joined these two streams of thought by introducing the category of human intention into the priestly world view. Whereas according to the priestly writer, the classification of all objects is determined by God (Genesis 1, Leviticus), in the Mishnah the classification of objects depends to a great extent on how people use or intend to use them.

In the course of this study, we have also discovered a second way in which the Mishnah brings together two biblical traditions. The Mishnah creates a synthesis of the two biblical stories of creation (Gen. 1 and 2). In many respects, the priestly account of creation (Gen. 1) is at the heart of mishnaic theology. This story says that as part of the work of creation, God classified the world into its constituent categories. The Mishnah explicitly links its system of purity to God's act of classification. It claims, for example, that things which are susceptible to impurity were created on alternate days of creation (M. Kel. 17:14). In making this claim, the Mishnah is suggesting that God's act of ordering the world is directly related to the classification scheme which governs the system of purity.

The Mishnah also refers to Genesis 1 when determining whether the seas can serve as a immersion pool (*mikveh*) for cleansing a person of ritual impurity (M. Par. 8:8, Miq. 5:4). The fact that God called the gatherings (*mikveh*) of water "seas" (Gen. 1:10) is used to prove that the sea can serve as an immersion pool (*mikveh*) for the purposes of ritual purity. Here, too, we see that the priestly account of creation functions for the Mishnah's framers as a paradigm for their system of purity.

But the Mishnah undermines the priestly theory of creation by combining it with the theology represented in the Yahwist story of creation (Gen. 2). One significant difference between this account of creation and the priestly version is the central part played by humanity. Whereas in the priestly story, Adam has a passive role in creation, in the Yahwist's version, Adam not only is created to till the garden but actually participates in ordering the world by giving names to the animals (Gen. 2:15, 19-20). As I have argued in Chapter Three, the Yahwist's idea that humanity plays an active role in classifying the world is at the center of the Mishnah's theology. In the Mishnah, humans carry forward the work of creation by determining which objects absorb impurity.

As is now evident, the Mishnah's theory of intention reflects in part the work of intellectuals interested in systematizing and harmonizing various strands of the tradition. At the same time, we can detect a polemic underlying the Mishnah's treatment of the biblical ideas. The Mishnah is clearly committed to the priestly framework and its overriding concern with issues of classification and ontology. Yet at the same time, the Mishnah dramatically relativizes the priestly world view by making the classification of objects dependent upon how humans think and act. The priestly writers, we recall, envisioned the world as divided into a set of fixed categories which had been established by God at the very creation of the world. In this view, everything has its clearly defined and unalterable place. The Mishnah retains the basic set of distinctions which occupy the priestly writers, such as the distinction between pure and impure, sacred and profane. But the Mishnah argues that people play a significant role in determining which objects fall into the various categories. A given object, therefore, no longer has a preexistent classification. Its status ultimately is determined by how Israelites use that sort of thing.

Accounting for this shift in perspective raises a complicated question in the interpretation of the Mishnah, because the Mishnah itself provides no explanation for its position. One school of thought relates this new stance to the despair among Jews over the destruction of the Temple by the Romans in 70 C.E. and the loss of a second war to Rome in 135 C.E.. According to this argument, the sages of the Mishnah responded to the chaos and disorder following the destruction of the Temple by asserting that Israel does have the power to control her destiny. The sages expressed this conviction by granting human intentions and perceptions a definitive role in ordering the world. In a world in which they lacked all social and political control, the sages of the Mishnah claimed that what humans do and say actually makes a difference. By this account, the Mishnah's theory of intention testifies to a group which has triumphed over its subjugation and humiliation.[11] This explanation is suggestive in that it makes sense of why human intention and perception become so important in the mishnaic corpus. However, in my judgment we lack sufficient evidence to support such an interpretation. Apart from a few isolated references in the Mishnah, there is little indication that the sages despaired over their military defeat and the destruction of the Temple, let alone created their theory of intention as a response to those experiences. Therefore, while this argument is plausible, it is not very convincing.

In what follows, I will provide an alternative account of the same set of facts. Specifically, I will attempt to relate the Mishnah's conception of intention to the social characteristics of the group which produced the Mishnah. Simply stated, the sages of the Mishnah belonged to a social group which differed from that of the priestly caste. Consequently, they altered the priestly view of the world to conform to the characteristics of their own social group. In making this claim, I am basing myself on a modified version of Durkheim's theory that a people's system of classification is directly related to the organization of its society.

Durkheim argued that it was the structure of society which originally gave human beings the idea of classifying their world. By Durkheim's account, the tendency to classify is not an inherent property of the human mind, as Kant had suggested and as Lévi-Strauss would later argue, but arose as people reflected upon the organization of their societies. Consequently, Durkheim suggested that the type of classification scheme which a group of people devised corresponded directly to the organization of their social group. If a society was divided into two clans, then people in that society would divide the world into pairs of opposites. One set of things would correspond to one clan (eg. the moon, the black cockatoo), while their opposites would correspond to the other clan (eg. the sun, white cockatoo).[12]

Durkheim's theory has been challenged from a number of quarters as being overly simplistic. In most societies, there is no simple correspondence between the classification system and social organization.[13] Nonetheless, a modified version of Durkheim's theory is still persuasive. It would appear that a group's social characteristics and location in the social system influences how that group perceives the world and consequently goes about classifying things.[14] In other words, although there is no one to one correspondence between social organization and schemes of classification, the social characteristics of a given group will shape its theory of taxonomy. Extending this argument to the Mishnah, it seems that the sages' desire to alter the priestly scheme of classification stemmed from the fact that they constituted a different sort of group than the priests, and hence found the priestly system of classification problematic.

There are a number of significant differences between the social characteristics of the priests and those of the Mishnah's sages. First, and perhaps most important, is the fact that the priesthood was a hereditary office. One was born a priest and retained that status for life. Consequently, a priest could not "drop out" of the priesthood, nor could a non-priest join the priesthood. Because the priestly status was fixed by birth, it was understood as being conferred on a person by God, for God had designated all Aaron's descendants as priests (Ex. 28-29, Lev. 8-10). In this respect, the priests constituted a caste that had a fixed relationship to all other groupings within Israelite society.[15]

In addition to constituting a caste, the priests also shared a single occupation and hence belonged to a single class within Israelite society. The priest's calling was to oversee the proper functioning of the Temple cult. Consequently, the priests could not own land or head farming establishments like the majority of Israelites (Deut. 18:1-6). As a landless class, the priests were supported from taxes on livestock and produce of Israelite farmers. In addition, the priests were entitled to eat parts of the animals which Israelites sacrificed in the Temple. We see, therefore, that the priests constituted a homogeneous group in the sense that all those persons who shared the title priest also belonged to the same class of society and engaged in the same calling.

It is now obvious that the social characteristics of the priestly caste correspond in fundamental respects to the priestly world view as represented in Genesis 1 and Leviticus. The priestly writers envisioned the world as divided into a set of fixed and unalterable relationships. In their scheme, everything had a clearly defined place which God had determined at creation itself. This view speaks to and for a group that occupies a specified position within a rigid and highly stratified social system. Just as the status of priest was a clearly defined and unalterable status within the social system, objects in the priests' scheme also have definite and fixed classifications.

There is also a significant correspondence between the priestly theory of classification and the social fact that the status of a priest is fixed by birth. In this community, status is determined by God at conception and hence a priest has no power to alter his own status. The same conception of status is found in the priestly world view, where humans are given no significant role in determining the classification of things. In the story of creation, for example, the classification scheme was determined by God and thus existed prior to the creation of Adam. For this reason, Adam had no active role in organizing the world. He was but another element to be fit into the preexisting divine scheme. In Leviticus, too, the classifications appear rigid and predetermined. People play no role in determining an object's classification. Just as a priest has no power to define or alter his own status, in the priestly view of reality, one has no power to change the classification of a given object.

Because the sages of the Mishnah formed a very different type of social grouping than the priests, they felt compelled to introduce changes into the priestly theory of classification. In particular, status and prestige were determined very differently in the sages' community. The title of sage was not hereditary but based on an individual's mastery of Scripture and its interpretive tradition.[16] In addition, the status of "colleague" (hbr) was based on one's way of life. One acquired this status by choosing to obey the rules of tithing and by keeping the laws of purity in one's home (M. Demai 2:2-3). In this community, therefore, one's status depended upon the choices and decisions one had made. Each individual had the power to alter his social location through discipleship and learning. For the sages, therefore, Israelite society was not a fixed set of relationships as it is was for the priests. Although a person could never decide to be a priest, an individual could choose to be a colleague and could aspire to be a sage.

The nature of status and prestige in the sages' community influenced their conceptions of classification. Since status in this group was linked to one's decisions and actions, the sages also granted humans an important role in determining the classification of things. In the sages' conception, the status of objects is not predetermined and unalterable, but depends to a great extent on how people think and act.

The sages' unwillingness to accept a rigid system of classification may also have stemmed from the fact that they did not form a homogeneous grouping in the same way as the priests. Evidence suggests that the sages did not receive renumeration for their scholarly activity as sage and so had various occupations, including scribe, householder, baker, tanner, etc.[17] Consequently, the sages constituted a status-grouping rather than a distinctive economic class. When a group is not homogeneous, it is much more difficult to agree upon a single, all-encompassing definition of reality. This would explain why social norms play such a definitive role in the Mishnah. The Mishnah clearly recognizes the fact that people of differing occupations and in different geographical locations act and think differently from one another. Indeed, the Mishnah claims that no single group's vision of reality is definitive for everyone else. Instead, the norms of a given group are normative only for members of that group. Consequently, the classification of a given object may differ depending upon the geographical location of its owner, or his occupation.

The Mishnah, therefore, represents the attempt by a new social group to appropriate the priestly world view, and make it into a meaningful system for all sectors of Israelite society. This tendency is evident in the Mishnah's concern with how the levitical laws apply to all the various classes of Israelite society, including the householder, merchant, tanner, baker, and others. Moreover, even those tractates that deal explicitly with the Temple and cult discuss it very much from the perspective of non-priests.[18] In this study, for example, we have seen that the sages devote a great deal of attention to discussing the intentions of priests when sacrificing an animal. But as I have shown, the underlying concern is whether the priest's intentions correspond to the original intentions of the householder who brought the animal for sacrifice. So even when discussing the sacrificial cult, it is the householder and his concerns which trigger the framers' interest.

The same tendency is evident in the Mishnah's discussion of the various donations which Scripture requires the Israelite farmer to give to the priests and levites. But in discussing these topics, the Mishnah departs from Scripture by taking the perspective of the farmer. Whereas Scripture speaks from the perspective of those who receive the various offerings, the Mishnah reflects the concerns of the persons who have to dedicate such offerings, namely, the Israelite farmer. The Mishnah focuses, therefore, on the question of when and how one removes the tax from one's produce.[19]

The Mishnah thus forms a kind of palimpsest , where one view of reality is superimposed upon another. At the foundation lies the priestly world view which was appropriated from Scripture. Superimposed upon this base is another system which is the sages' own contribution and speaks for and to their own social group. The dual character of the Mishnah is particularly evident when the

Mishnah discusses the ranking of Israelites according to status. The Mishnah recognizes that with respect to the Temple cult, a priest takes priority over other types of Israelites, because only a priest can perform certain Temple functions. On this scale, therefore, the priest stands at the top rung. Next stand other Israelites who can perform some but not all of the cultic functions. On the bottom rung stands the bastard (*mamzer*), who is not even permitted to enter the Temple. This system of ranking obviously derives from Scripture and represents the priestly caste.

At the same time, the Mishnah recognizes a second scale of ranking based on another criterion, namely, the extent of one's learning. On this scale, the sage stands on the highest rung, followed by the disciple of a sage. On the bottom rung stand non-educated Israelites. This scale obviously speaks for the sages and their social group. Significantly, the sages explicitly claim that this second scale, which is based on learning and discipleship, takes priority over the first scale which is based on one's status in the caste system. Thus a bastard who is a disciple of a sage takes precedence [in matters of honor] over a priest who is ignorant (M. Hor. 3:8). In summary, I have argued that the Mishnah's revision of the priestly world view derives from the nature of the social group which produced the Mishnah. Because membership in this group did not depend upon heredity, and because the group itself was not homogeneous, it was unwilling to embrace a rigid and static system of classification.

Although we have no way to empirically test the theory set out above, the Temple Scroll found at Qumran lends support to the thesis at hand. This scroll written some time in the second century B.C.E. takes up many of the issues addressed in Leviticus, including the rules governing the functioning of the cult, and sources of impurity.[20] Evidence suggests that this document was produced in the community at Qumran,[21] a group in which status was determined in accordance with heredity. One priestly line, the descendants of Zadoq, functioned as leaders of the community. The presence of a priest was required at all social functions at which ten or more members were present.[22] In addition, the structure of the community was strict and formal. Each member had a definite place in a hierarchical ranking.

The Temple Scroll, therefore, can serve as a test case for our theory. Since the group that produced it defined status in terms of heredity, our theory predicts that we would find no sign of the relativizing tendency which was so evident in the Mishnah. In particular, we would expect to find that in this system human intention would play no role in determining the classification of objects. Examination of the Temple Scroll confirms our expectations. The scroll exhibits none of the tendencies which are so prominent in the Mishnah. The Temple scroll considers the classification of objects to be self-evident and unproblematic, and consequently, no attention is given to determining the categories into which various objects fall. More significantly, the two crucial words in the Mishnah which stand for intention, namely, *mahshabah* and *kavvanah*, do not appear even once in the Temple scroll.[23] The Temple Scroll, therefore, lends support to the theory set out above: the Mishnah's tendency to base the classification of objects on human activity and intention derives from the growth of a social group which does not determine status on the basis of lineage.

The theory at hand also fits well with what we know about larger trends in the period at hand. Between the second century B.C.E. and the first century C.E., there is a growing shift away from a Temple-centered Judaism, and consequently away from a priestly definition of Judaism. Three developments during this period attest to this trend. First, the development of the synagogue signals a new attitude toward worship and the cult. The synagogue represented the possibility of worshipping God outside the confines of Jerusalem and without recourse to the Temple cult or the priestly class. Archeological and literary evidence now places the origin of the synagogue in the second century B.C.E.[24]

Second, the same period witnessed the emergence of the Pharisees, the predecessors of the sages who actually wrote the Mishnah. Literary evidence suggests that the Pharisees observed levitical rules of purity in their homes.[25] The fact that this group was keeping levitical rules outside the Temple also supports the view that new modes of piety were emerging that were not entirely centered on the Temple and the priests.

Third, it is well known that the Temple ceased to play a central role in earliest Christianity. Paul, for example, conceives of the Christian community as replacing the Temple and explicitly refers to the community as the "Temple of God" (I Corin. 3:16-17). Similarly, The Gospel of Mark speaks of Jesus as the replacement of the Temple (15: 29,37-38). In both instances, we see that the Temple had merely a symbolic value. As a functioning institution it was unimportant.

What we find, therefore, is that among those who claimed to put forward a definitive theory of God's will and the holy life, the Temple no longer served as the center, and the priests no longer held a preeminent status. Perhaps this trend was given greater impetus with the destruction of the Temple in 70 C.E.. But all indications suggest that this process was well under way before the Temple was destroyed. As Jonathan Smith puts it, "if the Temple had not been destroyed, it would have had to be neglected."[26] The Mishnah's attempt to articulate a form of Judaism that speaks for a non-priestly group, therefore, fully accords with other developments during the period in question.

In conclusion, we now know why intention plays such a key role in the mishnaic system as a whole. The idea that human intention is able to change the status of things expresses the distinctive perspective of the social group which produced the Mishnah. In this group, one's status depended upon what one thought and did, and so, in its understanding of the world, humans could also alter the character of reality itself. For this reason intention provided the point of departure for the sages' revision of the priestly world view which they had inherited from Scripture. Since the priestly vision of reality corresponded to the characteristics of the priestly caste it could not speak for the new carriers of the tradition, namely, the sages. By introducing the concept of intention into the priestly system, however, the sages relativized the priestly world view and thus made this vision of reality their own. In sum, the Mishnah's theory of intention represents at the cognitive level what had already occurred in the social realm, namely, the emergence of a distinctive group, with characteristics that differed from those groups which previously played a dominant role in defining Judaism.

Notes

Notes to the Introduction

[1] Philosophers have devoted a great deal of attention to the problem of defining intention, e.g. Anscombe, *Intention*; Meiland, *Intention*; Searle, *Intentionality*. The problem of defining intention or intentional action raises a broad range of philosophical issues about the nature of human action, the proper ways of describing action, and the nature of the human mind. For a particularly useful account of the debate, see Bernstein, *Praxis*, pp. 230-304, and Wright, *Explanation*. These issues, however, lie outside the scope of the present inquiry. For the purposes of this study, we want to arrive at an understanding of how the Mishnah's framers define and use the idea of intention. At the outset, therefore, we begin with only a provisional definition of intention, which we will modify as we proceed to investigate the Mishnah's rules.

[2] Anscombe argues that one of the central features of an intentional action is that the question "Why?" may be asked of it. That is, if the action was performed intentionally, one can give an answer to the question, "Why did you do that?" Anscombe notes, however, that this characteristic by itself is not sufficient to distinguish intentional from unintentional actions. For example, a person who jumps in fright can answer the question, "Why did you do that?," even though this is not an intentional action. In addition, therefore, Anscombe distinguishes an intentional action from other actions, by how the question "Why?" is answered (Anscombe, *Intention*, pp. 9-24). Also helpful is Taylor's view that to "speak of an 'intentional description' of something is to speak not just of any description which this thing bears, but of the description which it bears for a certain person, the description under which it is subsumed by him" (Wright, *Explanation*, p. 58, quoted in Bernstein, *Praxis*, p. 271-272).

[3] The importance of intention in rabbinic literature in general and the Mishnah (or tannaitic stratum of rabbinic literature) in particular has been recognized by a number of scholars, such as Enelow, *Kawwana*; Gilath, "Intention"; Goldenberg, "Consciousness"; Higger, *Intention*; Jaffee, *Tithing*, pp. 3-5; Kadushin, *Worship*, pp. 185-198; Neusner, *Judaism*, pp. 270-283, *Form-Analysis*, pp. 186-193, *Ancient Israel*, pp. 72-77; [Avery-] Peck, *Priestly Gift*, p. 3; Sarason, "Mishnah," pp. 87-89; Zeitlin, *Studies*, vol. 4.

[4] According to M. Ker. 1:1, a person who intentionally violates the Sabbath law incurs the divine punishment of extirpation (*krt*). The mishnaic term extirpation (*krt*) refers to the divine penalty of a premature death. Two pieces of evidence support this view. First, the mishnah contrasts "extirpation" with death at the hand of the court (M. Ket. 3:1, M. Meg. 1:5). In these pericopae, the Mishnah says that although the court will not put the person to death, extirpation is invoked, suggesting that God will shorten his or her life. This interpretation of the term extirpation gains further support from M. Yeb. 4:13, where the expression "extirpation at the hands of heaven" occurs explicitly. It should be

noted, however, that according to M. Meg. 1:5 a person who intentionally transgresses the Sabbath law incurs the death penalty at the hands of the court.

5 The language of this passage is obscure. The Hebrew text states only that the person is exempt from punishment, without clarifying whether he is exempt from the divine punishment of a premature death or also from bringing a sin-offering. Presumably the text means that the actor is exempt from divine punishment, but must bring a sin-offering for having committed an unintentional violation (cf. M. Ker. 1:1-2).

6 Neither Gilath, Higger, nor Zeitlin pay any attention to the theological dimensions underlying rabbinic theories of intention. Kadushin deserves credit for being the first to recognize the interplay between the conception of intention and theology (Kadushin, *Worship*, pp. 185-195). Neusner also discusses the theological significance of the conception of intention (Neusner, *Judaism*, pp. 270-283).

7 Scholars have tended to treat the concept of intention in rabbinic literature as exclusively a problem in jurisprudence, rather than as a problem in theology. For this reason, the work on intention has been mostly descriptive, rather than analytic. Zeitlin, Higger, and Gilath, for example, emphasize the importance of the concept of intention in rabbinic texts. But they do not advance a theory as to why intention plays such a critical role. The tendency to treat intention strictly as a problem in jurisprudence stems from the view that the Mishnah and the Talmud are essentially legal documents. While it is true that the Mishnah speaks in a legal idiom, the Mishnah is also a religious document, which makes certain theological claims about the divine will, and the nature of the divine-human relationship, etc. Consequently, mishnaic law and theology must be treated as integrally related to one another. This study also departs from previous studies in another important respect. It accepts as its point of departure Neusner's insight, adopted from New Testament studies, that rabbinic documents can be studied as systems of thought independent of other rabbinic works (Neusner, "New Solutions"). For this reason, this inquiry focuses on the idea of intention in a single rabbinic document, the Mishnah. Other studies of intention, by contrast, tend to homogenize the rabbinic sources, ignoring the fact that they were written over a period of 500 years. While other rabbinic works are useful in helping to elucidate the meaning of particular passages in other works, it is important in my judgment to first treat each document on its own terms, and only then compare that work with another.

8 A particularly helpful account of this development is found in Bernstein, *Praxis*, pp. 230-304. The following account depends a great deal on Bernstein's presentation of this issue.

9 Analytic philosophy's interest in intention stems from a debate about the proper language to use in describing human action. The question is whether human action can be legitimately described in the same terms as those used in the physical sciences. Some thinkers believe that human action can be described in such terms, while others claim that human action is a distinctive phenomenon and thus requires its own language and concepts. In the view of these thinkers, action must be described in teleological terms, that is, in terms of the purpose, goal, or intention of the actor (Bernstein, *Praxis*, pp. 230-238). This debate does not bear on the present study. For the framers of the Mishnah it was a fundamental axiom that people are purposive beings. What we wish to know, then, is how this assumption shapes the mishnaic document.

10 See Bernstein, *Praxis*, p. 255.

11 See Bernstein, *Praxis*, pp. 255-257.

12 This study does not examine two other mishnaic words which relate to intention, namely, the words *zdwn* and *sggh*. This is due partly to the constraints of space but also because these terms tell us less about the Mishnah's theory of intention than the terms analyzed in this study. When the framers of the Mishnah use the terms *zdwn* and *sggh*, they generally do not spell out the nature of the case. For example, they say if a person intentionally purifies vessels on the Sabbath by washing them, he may use them. But if he does so unintentionally, he may not use them (M. Ter. 2:3). In this case, the Mishnah does not explain what counts as washing dishes intentionally. Since in cases such as these the Mishnah does not explain what it means by an intentional or unintentional violation, we cannot infer very much about the Mishnah's theory of intention from these rules. Consequently, the rules in which the terms *zdwn* and *sggh* appear are less valuable for our study than the cases in which the terms *kavvanah* and *mahshabah* appear.

13 As I will spell out in Chapter Two, *kavvanah* actually designates two aspects of intention. The Mishnah uses this term when determining whether the person acted intentionally, and when speaking about the purpose with which the action was performed. I will spell out the difference between these aspects of intention in Chapter Two. See also Higger, *Intention*, p. 247.

14 Higger (*Intention*, p. 247) defines *mahshabah* somewhat differently. In his view, *mahshabah* signifies "the planning or premeditation with reference to the effect of a general, future act, without any special act in mind." While Higger's definition applies to some cases in the Mishnah, in other cases *mahshabah* designates an intention where the specific act is anticipated (M. Toh. 8:6).

15 The translation and understanding of this passage are based on Newman, *Shebiit*, pp. 85-86.

16 Tractate *Makhshirin* may be the single exception. Neusner, for example, argues that this tractate is an unfolding essay on the nature of human intention (Neusner, *Form-Analysis*, pp. 186-193). In my view, as I will explain in Chapter One, this tractate takes up a specific problem within the Mishnah's larger conception of intention. Specifically, it examines the problem of determining the causes of a given occurrence. That is, how does one know whether what has occurred is the result of human action, divine intervention, or natural processes. It is in answering this question that the Mishnah turns to human intention. The Mishnah says a person has caused the result in question only if that result was intended. If the results were unintended, they are ascribed to divine action.

Notes to Chapter One

1 In jurisprudence, theorists refer to a theory that takes account of intention as a "doctrine of *mens rea*," which means literally a doctrine of a "guilty mind" (Hart, *Punishment*, p. 31). Since this term has a pejorative connotation, it does not satisfactorily describe the role of intention in the mishnaic system. In the Mishnah, intention often plays a positive role. For example, a person does not fulfill a religious duty unless he or she performs the required act with the specific intention of carrying out God's law. To capture the role of intention in the mishnaic system, therefore, I have decided to describe theories that take account of intention as "teleological." This term is drawn from current discussions in philosophy of human action. As I explained, a teleological perspective is one that makes the actor's intention a critical criterion in the understanding and evaluation of his or her action (Wright, *Explanation*, 83-131, Bernstein, *Praxis*, 235-238).

² See Hart, *Punishment*, p. 139, Fitzgerald, *Criminal Law*, pp. 113-118, Edwards, *Mens Rea* , pp. 31-46, 244-251.

³ As we shall see, intention is relevant in two kinds of civil cases, namely, those involving humiliation or homicide. Below, I will explain why intention plays a critical role in these instances.

⁴ If two witnesses warned the person not to perform the act in question and the person nonetheless did so anyway, the actor is flogged rather than being subject to the divine punishment of death (M. Mak. 1-2).

⁵ In some instances, a fine is imposed rather than a sin-offering (M. Ter. 6:1).

⁶ A number of writers have already noted the fact that intention is irrelevant in the law of torts. See Higger, *Intention*, pp. 252-253, and B. Lieberman, *Torts*, p. 232. None of these writers ask, however, why intention is unimportant in torts yet so central in the religious and cultic law.

⁷ God obviously cannot suffer bodily harm. However, damage can be done to divine (i.e., Temple) property. As we shall see below, even in such cases, the Mishnah invokes the actor's intention.

⁸ The word transgression (ᶜbrh) generally refers to transgression of divine law, although in one instance it does refer to an offense committed against a fellow human being (M. Yom. 8:9). The word sin (ht') and its related verbal forms refer exclusively to sins against God. This is why the term does not appear at all in the Mishnah's civil law.

⁹ I did not include the last part of this passage in which Judah says that the intention of the person who broke the pitcher is relevant in assigning liability. In mentioning intention, Judah seems to break with the Mishnah's theory of strict liability. Below, I will argue that Judah in fact only qualifies the theory of strict liability but does not reject it entirely.

¹⁰ Following the Talmud's interpretation (B. B.Q. 31a), several interpreters seek to explain away the Mishnah's ruling in this case. They claim that the case involves a situation where the first potter had the opportunity of preventing the damage by rolling out of the way or warning the second potter that he had fallen. According to this view, the Mishnah holds him responsible for failing to avert the damages (cf. Maimonides, Bertinoro, and Albeck). This explanation, however, is an example of the tendency to interpret the Mishnah in light of later notions of responsibility. It strikes these commentators as unfair that a person should be responsible for unintentional damage. However, the Mishnah is completely consistent in espousing this perspective. To begin with, we have seen that the Mishnah states explicitly that even if a person causes damage when asleep he must pay compensation for those damages (M. B.Q. 3:1). The case of the potter is perfectly in keeping with this principle. Just as a sleeping person has no control over any damage he or she causes, a person who falls also has no control. Nonetheless, the Mishnah imposes liability.

¹¹ I follow Albeck who interprets Judah's statement to mean that if the person intended to break the jar, he is liable for paying the damages. Maimonides, by contrast, understands Judah's statement in the following way: "If he intended [to take possession of the shards of the jar], he is liable, but if he did not intend [to take the shards of the jar], he is not liable." By Maimonides' account, the person is liable only if he has taken possession of the broken pieces of pottery. But if he does not intend to keep them, then he is not responsible for subsequent damage, because they are not his property. In my judgment, Albeck's reading is preferable, because in general the Mishnah uses the expression "if so and so

intended" to mean if the actor intended to do what was mentioned above. In this case, what was previously mentioned was breaking the jar. In any case, the meaning of Judah's statement does not affect our interpretation of this passage. According to either interpretation, Judah is espousing only a modified version of strict liability.

[12] In Chapter Two, I will distinguish between "intentionally doing something" and doing something "with a particular intention." For example, when a man breaks a jar, we can ask whether he broke the jar intentionally. That is, did he intend to break the jar or was this an accident? We can also ask a further question: What was his intention or purpose in breaking the jar? Did he wish to cause someone harm or merely to remove something stuck inside? In the case at hand, Judah takes account of whether the actor had an intention of breaking the jar. But Judah takes no interest in the actor's purpose in breaking it. The fact that Judah ignores this aspect of the actor's intention indicates that he does not dispense entirely with a theory of strict liability.

[13] Although the sages do impose a monetary fine on a person who intentionally causes humiliation, it is clear that in their view, the money does not adequately compensate the injured party. This is why in addition to the monetary fine, the sages require the actor to implore the victim's forgiveness (M. B.Q. 8:7).

[14] I follow Albeck, TYT, TYY, and Maimonides in understanding M. B.Q. 8:7 to be referring to a case where one person has shamed another. Two pieces of evidence support this conclusion. First, the Mishnah passage directly preceding this one deals with such a case. Thus, in context, this rule seems to carry forward that theme. Second, the rule at hand quotes a verse from Scripture to support its view that the guilty party must implore forgiveness. This verse refers to the case where Abimelech has shamed Abraham by sleeping with Sarah (Gen. 20:7). It is clear, therefore, that the passage at hand speaks of a case of one person who has shamed another.

[15] Higger advances two alternative explanations for why a person is liable only for an intentional act of humiliation (Higger, *Intention*, p. 255). First, Higger claims that there is no humiliation involved by definition if the actor had no intention of causing humiliation. It seems to me that this explanation is tautological. Higger is saying that the reason intention matters in cases involving humiliation is because intention is by definition part of the concept of humiliation. But the real issue is why, within a given system like the Mishnah, humiliation by definition means an intentional act of shaming someone? The answer, from the Mishnah's standpoint, is that cases involving humiliation cannot be measured solely in pecuniary terms. Consequently, another criterion is necessary for determining the seriousness of the offense. Intention serves that purpose. Second, Higger suggests that intention is important in cases involving humiliation because it is treated as analogous to blood shedding, "where the intent of the act is sufficient to constitute a crime." This explanation, however, does not make sense within the system of the Mishnah. As I point out in Chapter Four, the Mishnah, with only one exception, nowhere imposes liability on an actor for the mere intention to violate the law.

[16] M. San. 9:2, among others, demonstrates that the Mishnah does not consider a non-viable fetus to be a full human being. This pericope states that if a person intended to kill a non-viable fetus and accidentally struck a viable fetus, he is exempt from the death penalty. This is because he did not intend to kill a full human being. Therefore the Mishnah does not treat this act as an instance of murder.

[17] As we shall see below, in cases involving damage to divine property, an actor must pay compensation for the damage, even if it was produced unintentionally. But even here, the actor's intention is important in determining whether he or she incurs a minor penalty of a fine or the severe punishment of death.

[18] See note 4.

[19] "Refuse" is the term given to a consecrated animal which a priest has intended to eat after the span of time specified by Leviticus for its consumption. As I will explain in Chapter Four, the intention of eating a consecrated animal at the wrong time has the effect of desacralizing it and placing it in a special category called "refuse."

[20] In English, the words "intentional transgression" can have at least three meanings. First, we use this expression when referring to cases in which a person intentionally performs an act which constitutes a violation, without knowing or remembering that the act is forbidden. Second, this expression also designates cases in which a person performs an act even though he knows the act to be a violation. Third, we use the words intentional transgression when referring to cases in which the person not only knows that the act is a violation but specifically performs the act with the intention of violating the law. This meaning differs from the previous one in an important respect. In the previous definition, the actor performed the act knowing full well that it was a violation. But he did not perform the act with the specific intention of transgressing the law. In the latter definition, by contrast, part of his intention was to violate or flout the law. It is clear that the Mishnah does not conceive of the first type of case mentioned above as an instance of an intentional transgression. When a person transgresses because he has forgotten the law, the Mishnah invokes the penalty of a sin-offering which is the punishment for an unintentional violation (M. Shab. 7:1). Thus, the Mishnah conceives of a violation that results from a mistake of law as being an unintentional violation. As far as I know, there are no mishnaic cases in which the Mishnah distinguishes between the second and third types of violations mentioned above. Consequently, I assume that the Mishnah's framers conceive of these cases as instances of intentional transgressions.

[21] Brooks has advanced a similar argument to explain the mishnaic ruling that any produce which falls unintentionally during the harvest process must be left for the poor. By his account, the Mishnah implicitly equates the accidental dropping of produce with divine intervention. God has caused the person to drop the food so that it be left for the poor (Brooks, *Support*, p. 18). Greenstein makes a similar interpretation of various laws in Leviticus (Greenstein, "Biblical Law," p. 94). The same idea-that chance occurrences are ascribed to superhuman causes-is also found in other societies. The Azande for example attribute all misfortunes to witchcraft (Evans-Pritchard, *Witchcraft*, pp. 18-32). In this connection it is worth quoting Evans-Pritchard at length:

"In Zandeland sometimes an old granary collapses. There is nothing remarkable in this. Every Zande knows that termites eat the supports in course of time and that even the hardest woods decay after years of service. Now a granary is the summer house...Consequently it may happen that there are people sitting beneath the granary when it collapses and they are injured...Now why should these particular people have been sitting under this particular granary at the particular moment when it collapsed?...We say that the granary collapsed because its supports were eaten away by termites; that is the cause that explains the collapse of the granary. We also say that people were sitting under it at the time because it was the heat of the day and they thought it would be a comfortable place to talk and work. This is the cause of people being under the granary at the time it collapsed. To our minds the only relationship between these two independently caused facts is their coincidence in time and space. We have no explanation of why the two chains of causation intersected at a certain time and in a certain place, for there is no interdependence between them. Zande philosophy can supply the missing link. The Zande knows that the supports were undermined by termites and that people were sitting beneath the granary in order to escape the heat and glare of the sun. But he knows besides why these two events occurred at a precisely similar moment in time and space. It was due to the action of witchcraft...Witchcraft explains the coincidence of these two happenings (Evans-Pritchard, *Witchcraft*, pp. 22-33). For an alternative account of why some people equate chance events with super-human causes, see Hallpike, *Primitive Thought*, pp. 451-465.

22 The Mishnah says only that the actor is exempt. It is unclear, however, whether this means that the actor is exempt from the divine penalty of a premature death or from the penalty of a sin-offering. Since this is an unintentional violation, it would seem that the Mishnah means that the actor is exempt from the divine punishment of a premature death, but that he is liable for a sin-offering.

23 I here follow Albeck who substitutes the word $^c smh$ (its) for the word $^c smn$ (theirs).

24 I have argued elsewhere that the Mishnah distinguishes body fluids which are uncontrollable (menstrual blood, non-seminal discharge, semen) from those which may be removed from the body at a person's discretion (tears, ear wax, mucous, saliva, urine, milk). In the mishnaic system, those fluids which are uncontrollable make the human body impure. By contrast, those fluids which are released from a person's body at his or her discretion do not make the person impure, but they do have the power of making food capable of absorbing impurity. The Mishnah further subdivides controllable fluids into two groups: those which leave the body through an orifice (tears, ear wax, mucous, saliva, urine, milk) and those which do not (sweat, pus, and blood from a medicinal bloodletting). The latter play no part in the system of purity. They neither make the body impure nor do they have the power to make food absorb impurity. This is because the body orifices play a symbolic role in the Mishnah. The orifices are mostly muscular, and therefore, represent the ability to control. Fluids which leave the body through an orifice and are governed by human intention are fluids which are catalysts in the mishnaic system. Since the Mishnah concerns itself with that which comes under the control of human beings, those liquids which do not leave the body via an orifice, and by definition are uncontrollable, are not vested with any powers. They are simply uninteresting to the Mishnah. For a fuller account of this theory, see Eilberg-Schwartz, "Language of Jewish Ritual."

25 I here follow Maimonides, who argues that when a person drinks liquid, the water does not immediately appear on his body. Consequently, one cannot ascribe the appearance of sweat to his having taken a drink.

26 In this case, I adopt the position of Albeck, who argues that the Mishnah is seeking to distinguish between bodily moisture resulting from sweating and moisture that results from swimming. In addition, Maimonides notes that the person swam in water that had previously been drawn from a well or stream. Since that water had previously been drawn it has the power to make food susceptible to impurity. By implication, had the person dipped in water that had not been drawn

for human purposes, the water that subsequently appeared on his body would not have the power to make food susceptible to impurity.

[27] The Mishnah is somewhat ambiguous. It states only that the Israelite takes the produce to the roof because of infestation. My interpretation follows Albeck who understands the Israelite's intention to be to force the insects out of the food by drying the produce in the sun.

[28] Analytic philosophers would resist using the term "resulting action." In their view, since the person did not do what he or she had intended, we cannot refer to what happened as an action at all. Instead, they would refer to what occurred as the results. However, I have adopted these terms because they seem to make the most sense of the distinctions which the Mishnah is seeking to develop. In my judgment, were we to refer to what happens as "the results," we would fail to understand how the Mishnah goes about determining whether a given action is intentional.

[29] As we shall see below, the Mishnah takes for granted that an actor's intention is the cause of the action. If a person intended a result and it occurred, then that person is the cause of it. If what happened differs from the actor's intention, other factors must have intervened in the execution of the act. In analytic philosophy, a complex literature has emerged which examines the question of whether it is correct to conceive of a person's intention as the cause of his action. See the lucid summary of this issue in Wright, *Explanation*, pp. 22-33, 93-131.

[30] See M. Qin. 1:3-4; M. Eduy. 3:1, and my discussion below of M. Ker. 4:3.

[31] The Mishnah does not explicitly say that writing two letters is forbidden because it constitutes producing a meaningful idea. This interpretation gains support, however, from the latter part of M. Shab. 12:5, which says if a person wrote an acrostic, he is liable. That is, whenever he writes a meaningful word, he incurs liability.

[32] It may appear that this law deals with a case where someone has produced an unavoidable result, namely, in writing an H one inevitably produces two I's. But this is not so. In Hebrew, one can write the letter *het* in a single stroke, without producing two *zayins* . This appears to be what Maimonides has in mind when he says that the actor's pen slipped as he was drawing the top part of the *het* . The fact that the person produced two *zayins* was not a necessary consequence of making a *het*.

[33] Maimonides understands this rule to be referring to the case of an actor who intended to collect both figs and grapes, but he collected them in a different order from what he had intended. The language of the Mishnah does not support this interpretation. The Mishnah states only that the person intended to collect figs but collected grapes. If the Mishnah was concerned with the order in which the man carried out his action, it would have said so explicitly, as it does in other cases (cf. M. Tem. 5:3).

[34] Felik suggests that the Mishnah is talking about the color of the fig's stem, rather than the color of the fig itself (Felik, *Plant World*, p. 37).

[35] Gilath argues that Eliezer ignores the actor's intention and stresses only the deed. But this interpretation does not make sense. If Eliezer ignores intention completely, why does he only impose a sin-offering. According to Gilath's account, he should impose the divine punishment of a premature death.

[36] Higger discusses at length the meaning of "a person who is engaged (*hmt^c sq*)" (Higger, *Intention*, pp. 277-279). Although he does not deal with the

case at hand, he develops a similar interpretation of a parallel dispute in the Talmud. My interpretation also agrees in most respects with Green's (Green, *Joshua*, p. 235).

37 The stichs G-I appear to be an anonymous statement appended to the Mishnah. See Bertinoro , TYT, TYY, and Green, *Joshua*, p. 235.

38 My interpretation follows MS and Albeck, who understand the expression "he may (or need) not repeat (*l' ysnh*)" to mean "the actor may not repeat the sprinkling." Maimonides, TYT, Bertinoro, and Neusner (Purities, vol. ix, pp. 201-202), by contrast, understand this expression to mean that the actor *need* not repeat the dipping of the hyssop into the solution, because the solution which remains on the hyssop is still valid.

By Maimonides' account, what the person intends determines the status of the liquid. If from the outset he intends to sprinkle the correct type of object, he does not invalidate the solution. But if he intends to sprinkle the wrong type of object, he invalidates the solution. In my view, Maimonides' interpretation is problematic. If the intention alone disqualifies the solution, why would the Mishnah bother to speak about the sprinkling of the solution at all? If the solution is invalidated before the person begins to sprinkle, it is obvious that the sprinkling will have no effect on the object on which it lands.

For this reason I follow Albeck, who argues that the legal consequences depend on the type of object on which the solution falls. If it lands on the wrong type of object the entire solution is invalidated, including even the solution on the hyssop. Neusner, however, rejects Albeck's explanation. He claims that by Albeck's account, the Mishnah would have no reason to mention intention at all. For if, as Albeck claims, the object (and not the intention) determines whether the solution is invalidated, why would the Mishnah need to mention the actor's intention? However, Neusner overlooks the fact that intention does play a role, even according to Albeck's account. Since the resulting action does not correspond to the intention, the solution fails to purify the object upon which it lands, even if it lands on the correct kind of object, namely, one which requires purification.

39 It is true that in two of these cases the solution on the hyssop is invalidated (C,I). But this legal consequence has nothing to do with whether the action at hand is intentional. Rather, it stems from the fact that a person sprinkled the solution on an object which cannot absorb impurity. In doing so, the solution has been put to a use for which it was not designated, and hence the entire solution, including even the liquid remaining on the hyssop, is spoiled. The reason the remaining liquid is considered invalidated is because it was originally part of the liquid which fell on the wrong type of object. In many mishnaic rules, if the status of one item changes, the status of the other items which belong to the same group or batch of things also undergoes a change in status. For example, if one intends to eat a loaf of bread from the meal offering at the wrong time, that loaf of bread becomes refuse. But in addition the other loaves of bread become refuse as well. Since they comprise part of a whole (namely, the meal-offering) the status of one item affects the status of the others (M. Men. 2:2). Similarly, when in the case at hand part of the solution falls on the wrong type of object, the solution on the hyssop is also invalidated because it belongs to the same batch of solution.

40 Although the framers do not say explicitly that the actor strikes the victim with the intention of killing him, it is obvious that this is what they mean. The beginning of this law, which we have examined at the beginning of the chapter, states, "If a person intended to kill x but killed y." Furthermore, the rule ends with

a similar statement by Simeon. The entire rule, therefore, is framed by two statements which explicitly say that the intention of the actor is to murder the victim. The only reason the sages do not say this explicitly in the part of the rule under discussion is because they want to introduce two additional issues: the force of the blow and the place on the body where the blow falls. In order to speak about these matters, they must introduce the issue of the actor striking the victim. Therefore, rather than say that the actor intended to kill a victim, they say "he intended to strike another, and that blow had sufficient force, etc."

Notes To Chapter Two

[1] See Hart, *Punishment*, pp. 115, 117-118. Anscombe uses slightly different terminology to convey a similar idea. She distinguishes between an intention *of* doing something and an intention *in* doing it. For example we can ask whether a person had an intention of breaking a bottle. That is, was breaking the bottle something the actor meant to do or something that occurred by accident? We can also ask about the actor's intention in breaking it. In performing the act, did the actor intend to produce a weapon or merely to remove something stuck inside?

[2] In English, the term "purpose" generally refers to the intention with which a person acted. That is, when we speak about an actor's purpose, we are attempting to answer the question why a person performed the act in question. We do not use the term purpose, however, when determining whether the person acted intentionally. Thus we do not say that a person "purposes" to break a bottle. Adopting the term purpose also enables us to distinguish this kind of intention from the intention a person formulates prior to acting. In English, we generally use the term purpose in referring to a person's intention in performing an action, not to describe a person's intention prior to acting. Therefore, we do not say that one purposes to go home, but that one plans to go home. Mishnaic Hebrew makes the same distinction. The Mishnah uses the term *kavvanah* to describe the intention of an actor. But *kavvanah* almost never describes the intention of a person when no action has taken place. The Mishnah reserves a different word to describe this type of intention, namely, the word *mahshabah* , which will be the focus of Part Two of this study.

[3] See, for example, Meiland, *Intention*, p. 8, and Searle, *Intentionality*, pp. 79-110.

[4] It is difficult to understand precisely what the framers mean in this case. In a Torah scroll, the passages of the Shema do not appear in juxtaposition. Consequently, when a person reads from the scroll, it is impossible that he is simultaneously reading all the passages comprising the Shema when the time arrives for the recitation of that prayer. The framers, therefore, probably mean that he is reciting the first passage of the prayer, which is the most important.

[5] My interpretation of the expression *kwwn lbw* follows TYT, TYY and Albeck who understand this expression to mean that the actor intends his action to fulfill the religious obligation in question.

[6] See Douglas, *Purity and Danger*, pp. 53-57, and Soler, "Dietary Prohibitions," pp. 24-30.

[7] The Mishnah apparently relies upon Deuteronomy's formulation of the rule which states that one must not "wear" garments of mixed weave (Deut. 22:11). By contrast, it ignores the formulation of the Holiness Code, which claims that a person should not permit a garment of mixed weave "to come upon" the body (Lev. 19:19). See the comments of TYT and Albeck to M. Kil. 9:2, and

Mandelbaum, *Law of Agriculture*, p. 283. It is doubtful that the Deuteronomist actually meant to distinguish between cases in which a person "wears" a garment and cases in which a person dons it for some other purpose. The difference in language between the levitical formulation of the law and its formulation in Deuteronomy is insignificant. But the fact that the Mishnah seizes on this difference in language is important. It points to the Mishnah's tendency to make intention decisive whenever possible. The Mishnah uses the Deuteronomic formulation as an excuse to make the actor's intention decisive in determining whether he or she has violated the law.

8 Higger also draws attention to the distinction in rabbinic literature between doing something intentionally and doing something with a specific purpose. In his words, "When the intention of an act exists, purpose is the deciding factor (Higger, *Intention*, p. 263)."

9 See Hart, *Punishment*, pp. 114-115.

10 In general, Scriptural law only takes account of whether the person intentionally performed the act in question. Biblical law rarely invokes the actor's purpose in performing the act. This is true in the levitical law, for example, which only takes account of whether the actor did what he intended to do (Lev. 4:22, 5:17). The difference between the Mishnah and Scripture is also evident in the laws regarding homicide. In biblical law, a person is guilty of murder for intentionally doing the act which kills a person. For example, if a person intentionally throws something at a person and kills him, he is liable even if his purpose in throwing the rock was not to kill the victim but merely to hurt him (Num. 35:20-22). In the Mishnah, as we have seen, in order to incur liability, a person must have intended not only to strike the victim, but to kill him. To be sure, in the narrative sections of the Pentateuch, the biblical writers often invoke the actor's purpose. However, we find no evidence in the Mishnah, that the sages were deriving their emphasis on an actor's purpose from the narrative material.

11 See note 7.

12 These idioms appear in the following contexts among others: I Sam. 7:3, Ps. 78:8, Ez. 7:10, I Chron. 29:18, 2 Chron. 12:14; 19:3; 20:33, 30:19, Job 11:13. See also Higger, *Intention*, p. 15; Greenberg, *Prayer*, p. 64, note 2; and Kadushin, *Worship*, pp. 198.

13 See Eissfeldt, *Old Testament*, p. 243, and Speiser, *Genesis*, Introduction.

14 See BDB, p. 523.

15 When the Mishnah uses the word *kavvanah* it is almost always referring to the subjective intention of the actor. Only in a few cases does the term *kavvanah* designate the purpose which is ascribed to an actor (see my discussion of M. Ned. 3:9). The fact that the word *kavvanah* refers only to an actor's subjective point of view emerges after consideration of the laws under study. In many instances, however, the Mishnah takes account of an actor's intention despite the fact that the word *kavvanah* is not employed. By my account, these cases are speaking about a different type of intention, namely, an intention that is ascribed to the actor on the basis of his or her behavior. Many commentators to the Mishnah, however, fail to realize that the Mishnah distinguishes between the actor's subjective purpose and the purpose a spectator would ascribe to actor. They conclude, therefore, that when the term *kavvanah* does not appear in a rule, it means that the Mishnah does not care about the actor's intention at all. Consequently, these commentators assume that the Mishnah presents contradictory views about intention. In some cases, the sages care about intention and in other

cases they do not. But by understanding the term *kavvanah* to mean an actor's subjective intention, the contradiction disappears. When the Mishnah does not use the term *kavvanah*, it means that the sages ignore the actor's own interpretation of the act, because they deduce his intention from other evidence, namely, the normal meaning of the act in Israelite society. I discuss this point in more detail in the notes to M. Kil. 9:2, 5-6. Further evidence that *kavvanah* refers to an actor's subjective point of view derives from M. Erub. 4:4, 4:5, and 4:7. In the first two pericopae, the sages refer to a man's *kavvanah*. In the third case, although the same issue is under discussion, the sages replace the word intention with the word "says." This indicates that they equate *kavvanah* with what an actor would say he intends to do.

16 The Mishnah claims that actions often bear alternative interpretations. In one respect, this idea anticipates the insight of contemporary philosophers such as Anscombe who argue that actions can have more than one description. According to Anscombe, "Since a single action can have many different descriptions, e.g. 'sawing a plank', 'sawing oak', 'sawing one of Smith's planks', 'making a squeaky noise with the saw', 'making a great deal of sawdust' and so on and so on, it is important to notice that a man may know that he is doing a thing under one description, and not under another" (Anscombe, *Intention*, pp. 11-12). There is, however, one important difference between the Mishnah's idea that actions are ambiguous and the contemporary philosophical notion that actions bear more than one description. In philosophical discussions, all actions are considered to be inherently ambiguous because they can always be described in a variety of ways. The Mishnah, by contrast, only treats an action as ambiguous if in the sages' opinion that act normally serves more than one purpose in Israelite society. The Mishnah is not interested in the theoretical possibility that all acts can bear alternative interpretations. In fact, when a given act normally serves a distinctive purpose in society, the Mishnah claims that its meaning is unequivocal.

17 I here follow Bertinoro and Albeck who understand M. Shab. 13:3 to mean that destructive acts are permitted on the Sabbath day. TYT, however, understands M. Shab. 13:3 to mean that although a person is not culpable for performing destructive acts, such acts are nonetheless forbidden by law.

18 Maimonides and Bertinoro offer an alternative interpretation. They argue that a man fulfills his duty to hear the ram's horn only if the man who blows the horn intends his act to satisfy the obligation of the person who heard the blast. In the case at hand, the person blowing the ram's horn did not intend to fulfill the obligation of the actor, because the actor was not inside the synagogue. According to Maimonides, it is for this reason that the intention of the Israelite who hears the horn becomes paramount. In my judgment, this explanation introduces an extraneous issue, namely, the intention of the person blowing the ram's horn. In any case, this alternative explanation does not undermine the general theory being advanced. Even according to Maimonides' explanation, the intention of the actor becomes important precisely because of the ambiguity in the situation, namely, because he is outside the synagogue.

19 On the surface it might seem that my interpretation contradicts another statement of the Mishnah. In the same rule (M. R.H. 3:7), the Mishnah states that if a man blows a ram's horn while in a cave, he fulfills his obligation of hearing the horn blown. Although he performed the act in an unusual place, the Mishnah does not take into account this man's subjective intention. A closer inspection, however, indicates that my theory makes sense of this rule as well. In this case,

the man's action is unambiguous because he is the one blowing the horn. If a person blows a ram's horn in a cave, he obviously intends to fulfill his religious duty. What other explanation could account for his behavior? In the case at hand, by contrast, the man who is walking by the synagogue is not blowing the ram's horn. For this reason his action is ambiguous. Is he merely taking a stroll or does he have the intention of fulfilling his religious duty?

20 The Talmud recognizes that in the law of vows, the Mishnah places stress on the normal interpretation of the vow. In the Talmud's language, "The [interpretation of a vow] follows the [normal] language of human beings" (B. Ned. 30b, 49a, 51a). See also Maimonides' commentary to M. Ned. 3:6.

21 It is important to note that in this rule, as in the rules to follow, the term *kavvanah* does not convey its normal meaning. We recall that *kavvanah* usually refers to an Israelite's subjective intention. That is, the term designates the answer an Israelite would give to the question, "What are you doing?" But here, *kavvanah* clearly refers to the speaker's intention as deduced from the norms of society. The change in the meaning of the term *kavvanah* is reflected in the fact that the Mishnah employs the term in a different linguistic formula. When the Mishnah is referring to an actor's subjective intention (as at M. Ber. 2:1) it says "if he intends x...but if he intends y then ..." The fact that the sages specify two possibilities means that they cannot deduce the actor's intention from the action. Similarly, when they say a person may do x or y "provided that he does not intend ..." (see M. Shab. 22:3), they indicate that the actor may have in mind one of two intentions. But in the laws concerning vows, the sages merely assert that "he intended so and so", because in this case, they claim to know his intention from the words that he uses.

22 See Wimsatt, *Verbal Icon*, p. 5.

23 The Hebrew expression *hnwldym* is a participle that refers to a future event or result, see Jastrow, *Dictionary*, p. 577, and Maimonides' comments to M. Ned. 4:7.

24 I follow Albeck who understands the word *lhwlyd* to be in the Niphal, rather than in the Hiphil. Therefore, the meaning of the verb is "to be born," rather than "to give birth." See also Maimonides' comments on M. Ned. 4:7.

25 The word *konam* is another way of saying *korban* which means holy sacrifice, (see Albeck's introductory remarks to Tractate *Nedarim* , p. 138, and Jastrow, *Dictionary*, p. 135). A person often takes a vow to abstain from a substance like bread or wine by comparing it to a holy sacrifice. The expression *konam* is a short hand way of saying that one vows to treat a given substance like a holy sacrifice. In order to convey the sense of the vow, I have translated *konam* by the words "God forbid that."

26 This is one of the few cases in civil law in which the Mishnah takes account of the actor's purpose. This case, however, more closely resembles transgressions of religious law than tort cases, because here no monetary loss has occurred. The trader or householder has merely mixed produce of various grades, but he has not yet cheated another person. Since no pecuniary loss has occurred, the Mishnah treats this case like cases involving humiliation. The actor's intention becomes the decisive factor. See my discussion of M. B.Q. 8:1.

27 Rashi (B. B.M. 43b) and Bertinoro interpret this law as referring to a case in which a householder made a deal with a fellow Israelite to sell him produce from a particular field. After the deal was made, the householder mixes another type of produce with the produce he promised to sell. There is no indication in the

pericope itself, however, that an agreement has already been reached with another person. By my account, the Mishnah deals with a case in which the householder has not yet made a promise to sell his goods to another person. The question the Mishnah addresses is whether in preparing goods for sale, the householder is permitted to mix produce of differing qualities. This interpretation gains support from the following pericope, which specifically deals with cases in which a person is preparing goods for sale. At the end of M. 4:12, for example, the Mishnah says explicitly that a person selling goods cannot "deceive [his customer's] eye," by changing the appearance of the goods he is selling. That is, in preparing the goods for sale, he cannot alter the appearance of the merchandise so that it will appear to be worth more than its actual value.

[28] Rashi, Bertinoro, and TYT argue that the trader is permitted to mix grains of different types because other Israelites know that traders buy from numerous individuals and hence mix produce of different qualities. Since the customer knows that the trader mixes produce of varying qualities, he will not be deceived. If this interpretation were correct, however, the Mishnah should permit the merchant to mix grains no matter what his intention. Since the customers know that a trader combines produce, they will not be deceived by him even if he intends to defraud. To answer this problem, the above commentators assume that the second part of the Mishnah (I C) is dealing with a specific case of a merchant who tells his customers that the produce is from one field and therefore of one quality. This interpretation, however, is problematic because it claims that the beginning (I A-B) and end of the law (I C) deal with different situations. In my view, both parts of the pericope deal with a single situation, namely, a trader who is collecting produce for sale. The reason his intention matters is because his action bears alternative interpretations: does he intend to defraud his customers or only to collect enough for a bulk sale?

[29] It may appear from this law that the Mishnah discounts the householder's intention in deciding culpability. But this is not so. It is only because the Mishnah assumes the householder's intention is fraudulent that it regards his action as a violation. The term kavvanah is absent not because the Mishnah discounts the actor's intention altogether, but because it ignores his subjective intention.

[30] Mandelbaum, *Law of Agriculture*, pp. 290, 302, following Bertinoro and Sens, argues that in the case of the householder the Mishnah does not care about intention at all. But this is not true. The framers discount only the householder's subjective intention. But they do infer his intention in another way. As I have said, they deduce his intention from the norms of his social class. Since householders generally don garments for protection, the sages assume that the householder in the case at hand also puts on the garments for that reason. They declare him guilty, therefore, because they impute to him an illicit purpose.

[31] TYT following Maimonides explains the two cases differently. He argues that the householder is guilty because he actually "wore" the garment thus violating the injunction of Deut. 22:11 against "wearing a garment of mixed weave." The merchants, however, do not violate the law because they only drape the garment on their bodies without actually "wearing them" (see TYT on M. Kil. 9:2). This interpretation is problematic for the following reason. We know from M. Kil. 9:4 that in some cases a householder is guilty of transgressing merely for draping a garment on his shoulder. Draping the garment on the body constitutes a violation, therefore, if a person intends for it to serve as protection (i.e., as clothing). In

the case at hand, therefore, the merchants incur no liability, because in draping the garments they have no intention of using them for clothing.

[32] Hart, *Punishment*, p. 33.

[33] Rist, *Stoic Philosophy*, pp. 54-63.

[34] See Anscombe, *Intention*, p. 43.

[35] See Searle, *Intentionality*, p. 144.

Notes to Chapter Three

[1] Intending and planning to perform an action are not precisely the same thing, even though the two terms are sometimes interchangeable. For example, consider the following sentence: "I am planning a strategy." Here, we could not replace the term "planning" with the word "intending" because planning carries with it the connotation of deciding upon specific steps to achieve a result. However, in some sentences the words "intention" and "plan" can easily replace one another. For example, one could easily convert the sentence, "I plan to go home," to "I intend to go home," without significantly altering its meaning. For the present study, we shall use the term plan to designate those intentions that involve acting in the future. This will help us to distinguish this kind of intention from an actor's intention.

[2] Higger, *Intention*, pp. 247-248 also translates *mahshabah* as "plans." In addition, Higger claims that the term *mahshabah*, in contrast to the term *kavvanah*, generally does not refer to a specific course of action. According to Higger, "we have sufficient data to prove that there is a marked distinction between "*kawwanah*" and "*mahshabahah* "--the former signifying the intent of a particular act, with or without reference to the effect of that act; the latter, on the other hand, signifying the planning or premeditation with reference to the effect of a general, future act, without any special act in mind." Some mishnaic rules support Higger's distinction. But in other cases, the term *mahshabah* clearly refers to a plan to carry out a specific course of action. For example, M. Toh. 8:6 involves an Israelite who plans to remove a dead bird from a vat of wine in order to sell it to a gentile.

[3] According to the Mishnah edible substances can become impure only if the following two conditions are satisfied. First, they must fall under the rubric of food. Second, water must have been intentionally placed on the substance. See my discussion in Chapter Two of the rules from M. *Makhshirin*. Throughout my discussion, when I say that food can absorb impurity, I mean that it can do so only if both of these conditions are satisfied.

[4] I have not quoted this passage in its entirety. At the end of this rule, Yose takes the position that once the table loses all of its legs, it automatically becomes susceptible to impurity, whether or not the householder intends to use it. I will explain Yose's view in a subsequent discussion of this pericope.

[5] Since the pigeon at hand was not slaughtered according to the prescribed ritual, it falls into the category of carrion. In the mishnaic system, the carrion of fowl imparts impurity to a person if he eats it. It cannot make him or any object impure merely by coming in contact with them (see M. Zeb. 7:6). Although it is already in the category of carrion, once it falls into the category of food it becomes subject to additional restrictions. Food, we recall, can absorb impurity from other things. Hence, once the bird enters the category of food, it in effect renders itself unclean. That is, since in one respect it was already impure to begin

with, once it enters the category of food, it is as if it has come in contact with a source of impurity. For this reason, the sages now treat it as an impure food substance. Like other food substances that have become contaminated it can now impart impurity to other foods. So while previously, when it was only considered carrion, it had no power to contaminate other food products, once it enters the category of food it becomes an impure food product and thus can make other food substances unclean. See M. Toh. 1:1 and Maimonides' comments to that rule.

[6] See note 5.

[7] Since in this case the pigeon does not enter the category of food, it cannot contaminate other food products.

[8] The Hebrew word *mahshabah* does appear in Leviticus in the niphal and piel forms (Lev. 7:18; 17:4; 25:27, 37. However, in these contexts the word means count or reckon rather than plans.

[9] Leviticus is somewhat ambiguous about what sorts of substances can absorb impurity. Leviticus says "from among food that may be eaten". In my judgment, in context this expression means those substances which Israelites are permitted to eat can become impure. The fact that this refers to foods which Israelites can eat and not to all substances which human beings in general eat is evident by the parallel in Lev. 17:13. The same expression is used there in referring to a case where an Israelite is hunting a kind of animal that Israelites are permitted to eat. See Rashi's comment to Lev. 17:13, Porter, *Leviticus*, pp. 141-142, and Hoffman, *Leviticus*, p. 327. Moreover, in this chapter of Leviticus, the expression "from among....that... (mkl...'sr)" serves as a refrain (see Lev. 11:10, 21-22). In each of these verses, the expression is meant to exclude certain elements from the category which is being referred to. For example, in Lev. 11:2 the same expression is used to mean "these are the creatures that you may eat from among all the land animals." Here the expression "from among" indicates that Scripture is referring to a subset of all animals. The same is true of Lev. 11:10, 21-22. It would appear, therefore, that Lev. 11:34 means that of all the foods that exist only the ones that Israelites may eat can become susceptible to impurity. In any case, the force of my argument does not rest on this exegesis. It is clear that the priestly writers conceive of God as being the one who determined what counts as food (see Gen. 1:29; 9:3), whereas the framers of the Mishnah conceive of human beings as determining what constitutes food.

[10] Dihle, *Will*, p. 79 also notes that the term *mahshabah* has negative connotations in biblical literature.

[11] To convey the nuances of the term *mahshabah* in this passage, I have quoted the more literal translation of the *RSV* rather than the *JPS* translation on which I generally rely.

[12] There is a general consensus among biblical scholars that Genesis 2:5-24 is the work of a different writer than Genesis 1:1-2:4. The first myth of creation is ascribed to the priestly writer, who is also responsible for, among other things, the book of Leviticus. The author of Genesis 2 has been named the Yahwist because of this author's propensity to use the divine name Yahweh. For a discussion of this issue see Eissfeldt, *Old Testament*, p. 188, and Speiser, *Genesis*, pp. xxiv-xxvi, 8. The framers of the Mishnah, of course, did not ascribe the two biblical myths to separate authors. For them, both stories represented part of the Torah which God revealed to Moses.

[13] Otzen, *Myths*, pp. 27-28, 37-38. See also Mandelbaum, *Law of Agriculture*, p. 3, who argues the same point with respect to the mishnaic law dealing with the mixture of different species of animals and fabrics.

[14] See von Rad, *Genesis*, pp. 82-83, Otzen, *Myths*, p. 44, and Eichrodt, *Theology*, vol. 1., p. 40.

[15] Speiser, *Genesis*, p. 127, and Sarna, *Genesis*, p. 129.

[16] M. Sheb. 7:4, Hallah 4:1, Or. 2:6-7, Bik. 3:10, A. Z. 5:8, Zeb. 8:2.

[17] The same expression is used elsewhere in Scripture. But in these instances it refers to animal life. See, for example, Lev. 11:15, 22, Deut. 14:14.

[18] The expression "to call something a name" does appear elsewhere in the biblical writings. However, in these contexts what is being named is almost always a person or place. See, for example, Gen. 3:20, 16:15, 32:31. It is only in the Yahwist story of creation that humans name wildlife. The fact that the Mishnah adopts the same expression in referring to the classification of animals and fauna, therefore, supports the claim that this biblical myth influenced mishnaic theology.

[19] See M. Ber. 4:4, Yom. 3:8, R.H. 4:5, Sot. 7:6, San. 6:4, 7:5, 10:1, Mak. 3:6, Zeb. 4:6, Tam. 3:8, 7:2.

[20] Levinthal, "Agency," pp. 9-83, presents an excellent discussion of the issues involved in the Jewish law of agency.

[21] See M. B.M. 7:6, Ar. 1:1, Par. 12:10.

[22] In the Mishnah's view God did not give human beings any role in determining what can and cannot be a source of impurity. This is obvious from the fact that not a single rule in the Mishnah ascribes to human beings any say whatsoever in determining whether something transmits impurity. On this point, see Neusner, *Purities*, vol. 22, pp. 293-295, and *Ancient Israel*, pp. 57.

[23] Deuteronomy 14:21 explicitly states that an Israelite may give carrion to a gentile or throw it to a dog. The Deuteronomist, however, gives no indication that by giving the carrion to a gentile, an Israelite has effectively placed it into the category of food and hence made it susceptible to impurity. The Mishnah, by contrast, goes out of its way to make the point that whatever any human being eats is classified as food and hence susceptible to impurity.

[24] See note 5.

[25] Some versions of this passage list in addition to the hide of an ass the hide of an ass-driver. Presumably one refers to the saddle and the other to the hide worn by an ass-driver to keep himself clean. See Maimonides' comment to M. Kel. 26:6.

[26] The precise meaning of this stich is unclear. Maimonides explains that the leather for the child's heart is in fact a euphemism for a kind of diaper upon which a young child sits so as not to soil his clothing. Maimonides here follows T. Kel. B.B. 4:10 which says explicitly a diaper (*lwp*) for a child. Neusner (*Tosefta Tohorot*, vol. 5, pp. 69-70) interprets the word *lwp* in this passage of Tosefta in light of the Mishnah to mean a leather garment to cover the child's heart (*lyb*). It is also possible that the Mishnah is referring to a piece of leather which is used to protect the child's heart from the heat, as in T. Kel. B.B. 4:4. Bertinoro claims that the leather is meant to protect the child's heart from wild cats.

[27] Alternatively, Maimonides suggests that it is obvious from the moment that such leather goods are made that they will sometimes be used as mats for sitting. For this reason, they are by definition classified as large, useful leather goods.

[28] I here follow MA and Albeck who understand the expression *synwy m'sh* to mean a change in the object's form or appearance.

[29] The formulation of this rule is deceptive in one respect. It suggests that intention can affect the status of any object so long as it has not yet entered the category of useful things. In fact, however, the Mishnah claims elsewhere that intention also cannot affect the status of objects which clearly belong to the status of useless things. For example, an untanned hide belonging to a tanner is obviously useless. Therefore, his intention to use it cannot affect that object's status (see M. Kel. 26:8). Intention, therefore, never has the power to change an object's classification once that classification is already determined. Intention is only powerful when the status of the object is ambiguous.

[30] Maimonides understands the Mishnah's theory slightly differently. He claims that an Israelite's intention has the power to classify as food anything that most people do not use for food. In my judgment, this formulation slightly distorts the Mishnah's theory. According to my account, intention is decisive only when an substance's status is ambiguous. Therefore if a substance unequivocally belongs to the category of waste, such as a piece of rotten food (see M. Toh. 8:6), intention can no longer affect its status. Maimonides, by contrast, argues that intention can classify as food even substances which previously were in the category of waste (see Maimonides' comments to M. Toh. 8:6 and M. Hul. 4:7).

[31] The Mishnah says only that the food "requires intention." Based on the parallel case at M. Toh. 8:6, I interpret this to mean that the Israelite must intend to sell it to a gentile in order for the fowl to fall into the category of food. However, Albeck following B. Zeb. 47b interprets this statement to mean that an Israelite intends to eat the bird. According to this explanation, since he imagines swallowing it, it becomes unclean as if it had actually been swallowed.

[32] See note 5.

[33] The word *nblh* is properly translated in this context as "carcass". Although this word is often used to refer to an improperly slaughtered animal, this cannot be its meaning in the present context. Carrion refers only to the improperly slaughtered animal of a permitted species. The way an Israelite slaughters a forbidden species of animal does not matter (see Lev. 11:39-41). Furthermore, the term *tm'* must be translated in this context as "forbidden" rather than as "unclean." This is because a forbidden species of bird, according to the Mishnah, does not communicate uncleanness unless it first falls under the rubric of food and has come in contact with a source of impurity.

[34] I follow the interpretation of Maimonides and Neusner (*Purities*, vol. 2, p. 273) in my explanation of this rule. According to their account, this rule is a continuation of the preceding one, M. Kel. 26:7, which focuses on how the power of intention depends upon the stage in the leather's processing (see my discussion of this law which follows). It is also possible, however, that this law addresses the same issue as the stichs of the Mishnah which follow it. These deal with the question of whether a robber's or thief's intention can affect the status of something they have stolen. Based on this understanding, the following alternative explanation is also possible: a tanner's intentions cannot determine the status of an object because he does not in fact own the object but is merely tanning it for someone else (see, for example, M. Shab. 1:8). Like the thief or

robber who does not acquire ownership of the stolen goods, the tanner's intentions have no impact on the status of the hide. Alternatively, Bertinoro and Albeck argue that a tanner's intention has no power to alter the status of the hide because tanners normally sell their hides. Therefore, even if the tanner forms the intention of using the hide, the sages assume, until proven otherwise, that he will change his mind and decide to sell it. It seems to me, however, that these interpretations unnecessarily complicate the rule by introducing the issue of the buyer.

35 My interpretation of the phrase "a leather hide that requires no further workmanship," is based on the last stich of T. Kel. B.B. 4:10 , which understands the phrase to refer to the process of cleaning and stretching (see also TYY and MA). By contrast, Maimonides, Bertinoro and TYT explain the statement as follows: Intentions are only important if the leather is completely ready to serve the specific function which the Israelite has in mind. That is, if the householder wants to use it as a pillow, the hide must be sewn in such a way that it contains a cavity for stuffing. If it lacks this step in its processing, an Israelite cannot make it useful by intending to use it for a pillow. I disagree with this interpretation for two reasons. First, M. Kel. 16:4 says explicitly that leather goods which are ready to serve a particular purpose are considered useful whether or not a person formed the intention to use them. For example, a hide is considered useful as soon as one attaches a strap to it. Moreover, the sages provide an example of what they mean by a "hide which requires further workmanship." This is a hide that is not ready for any use except as a saddle cover. It is thus clear that by "workmanship", the Mishnah refers to the process of cleaning and stretching.

36 Neusner (*Purities*, vol. 4, pp. 103-105) following Maimonides gives a different account of why closed doors and windows allow impurity to pass outside the house. According to this account, when all the doors or windows in a house are shut, the house is treated as a sealed grave which exudes impurity in all directions. Therefore, even the doors which are shut allow impurity to pass to the other side. I follow Bertinoro and Albeck who argue that the reason all the doors allow impurity to pass beyond the house is because it is uncertain which of the doors will be used for the removal of the corpse. Due to the doubt involved, all the doors are deemed impure.

37 See Maimonides's excellent summary of this rule.

38 My understanding of this passage follows the interpretation of Sens. The Hebrew at K-L does not make sense without the addition of the language in brackets. Taken literally, the passage states, "if a minor...intends to remove the pigeon for a gentile, the pigeon remains clean. But if he [actually] removes it, the pigeon becomes susceptible to impurity." The problem with understanding this passage as it now stands, is that by watching a minor remove the pigeon from the vat, one could not possibly know whether he intends to give it to a gentile or to his dog. Since the Mishnah treats it as food, it seems that the sages are referring to a case in which the minor's action makes obvious his intention to use it as food. Following Sens, therefore, I interpret this to mean that the minor removed the pigeon from the vat and actually gave it to the gentile. An alternative view offered by Bertinoro and TYY is that one takes account of the intention a minor has in mind while performing an action (see also Rashi's comments to M. Kel. 17:5, at B. Hullin 12b). I reject this interpretation because in M. Makh. 3:8 and 6:1 the Mishnah does not take account of the intention of a minor when he leads a horse to the river or when he carries fruit to the roof of a house.

[39] Why can some items become unclean even though the owner has not moistened them? This is the case if the substance was already impure before it entered the category of food. For example, an improperly slaughtered animal is considered to be carrion and a source of impurity. Since it is impure at the outset, it need not come in contact with water in order to absorb impurity. Rather, the Mishnah treats it as impure food as soon as someone designates it for human consumption. Since it is treated as an impure foodstuff, and it now can make other food products unclean.

[40] Substances which are not impure before entering the category of food absorb impurity only if they are first moistened by water. In addition, as I explained in Chapter One, the moistening of the produce must be an intentional act.

[41] For the sake of clarity, I have translated the Hebrew words "clean" animal and "unclean" animal as meaning permitted and forbidden species of animals. This helps keep the issue of impurity distinct from the question of whether or not the animal can be consumed.

[42] For an identification of the spices mentioned in II C-E, see Albeck's commentary to this passage, Jastrow, *Dictionary*, p. 464, and Feliks, *Plant World*, pp. 214, 226.

[43] On the surface it may seem from this list that intention can classify anything as food which is not already in that category. However, this list indicates that certain items under no circumstances can be classified as food. In II A, for example, the Mishnah says that *slivers* of flesh from living animals can be classified as food. By implication, any flesh that is larger than a sliver, for example, an appendage from a living animal, cannot be classified as food under any circumstances. The reason is that, according to mishnaic law, even gentiles are forbidden to eat the flesh from a living animal if it is greater than a sliver. Since neither Israelites nor gentiles are permitted to eat such flesh, it by definition falls into the category of waste. No matter what anyone intends, it does not enter the category of food. See Maimonides, Bertinoro, and TYT.

[44] It is unclear why the Mishnah is concerned about whether the carcass of a forbidden species of animal is classified as food. An olive's bulk from such an animal has the power to make other things unclean from the moment it dies. Therefore, the fact that if falls into the classification of food does not change its status at all. Bertinoro and Albeck, following B. Ker. 21a, provide the following explanation. The Mishnah is referring to a piece of the animal which is less than an olive's bulk. According to mishnaic law, this amount of flesh does not have the power to contaminate other things. The Mishnah is saying, therefore, that if a person intends to sell a piece of flesh which is less than an olive's bulk, it falls into the category of food. Although it cannot transmit the impurity of carrion, it can now absorb the impurity since it is classified as food. This explanation, it seems to me, reads into the Mishnah an issue that is not on the sages' mind. The framers of the Mishnah were not worried about the implications of classifying this substance as food. Their interest lies elsewhere. They wish only to explain when intention is necessary to make something fall into the classification of food. Whether or not that classification has practical ramifications does not concern them.

[45] One who is familiar with rabbinic concepts in general may assume that the Mishnah conceives of destroying a useful object to be a violation of the prohibition "against destroying useful things" (*bl tshyt*). Therefore, the sages assume that an Israelite will not destroy useful objects around his home because this would be a violation of law. Closer inspection, however, shows that this

concept is foreign to the Mishnah. The Mishnah refers to "the prohibition against destroying" things only when speaking about the Scriptural injunction against shaving the corners of the face (M. Qid. 1:7). If the Mishnah did conceive of destroying objects as a transgression, it would surely impose a penalty on an Israelite who performed such an act. In fact, however, the Mishnah does not impose a penalty when an Israelite destroys something useful (see M. Kel. 26: 9).

Notes to Chapter Four

1 I have not quoted this law in its entirety because it introduces issues which are not relevant to the present discussion. Specifically, the Mishnah presents an alternative view to Meir's. Meir claims that the order in which a person articulates his or her intentions is critical. If, therefore, a person classifies the mother cow before the unborn calf, the unborn calf automatically falls into the same category as the mother, because it is part of her body. Yose, by contrast, argues that what is critical is not the order in which the person expresses his or her thoughts, but the order in which they were originally formulated. Therefore, even if a person classifies the mother cow before the unborn calf, the unborn calf does not necessarily fall into the same category. It depends upon the order in which the Israelite originally formulated those intentions in his or her mind.

2 See M. Tem. 5:3.

3 Where and when the offering can be eaten depends upon the type of offering involved. These rules are discussed in M. Zeb. chapter 5.

4 The single exception is M. B.M. 3:12, which I discuss in the conclusion to this chapter. See also Jackson, "Mere Intention," who discusses the role of mere intention in early rabbinic law.

5 M. Zeb. 2:1 specifies that impure and uncircumcised persons cannot perform any part of the sacrificial rite involving the handling of the blood. M. Zeb. 3:1, by contrast, says that "those persons who are forbidden [to perform the rite of sprinkling the blood] may nonetheless perform the ritual act of slaughter." The pericope goes on to say explicitly that an unclean person may perform the slaughter. Although this rule does not expressly say that an uncircumcised man can perform the slaughter, two facts would suggest that he can. To begin with, this rule implies that all of those persons who are not permitted to handle the blood (i.e., those listed at M. Zeb. 2:1) may perform the ritual act of slaughter. As I said above, the uncircumcised person is mentioned at M. Zeb. 2:1. Second, the Mishnah lists slaves as being able to perform the slaughter. Presumably, the Mishnah is referring to Canaanite slaves who may or may not be circumcised. Canaanite slaves, according to Scripture, only need to be circumcised before eating the Passover offering. So the mention of slaves suggests that uncircumcised men can slaughter an animal.

6 The Mishnah states explicitly that anyone is permitted to eat an offering of well-being (M. Zeb. 5:7). This presumably includes unclean and uncircumcised persons.

7 In this case, the Mishnah describes the priest as intending "to leave (*lhnyh*) the blood unsprinkled and the entrails unburned until the following day. By the use of the word "to leave," the sages indicate that it is unclear whether the priest intends to sprinkle the blood or burn the entrails at a later time. By contrast, when the priest unequivocally intends to perform these acts outside the specified place or after the designated period of time, the Mishnah states explicitly that he intends "to sprinkle the blood or burn the entrails on the following day or outside

the designated place" (see M. Zeb. 2:3-5). See Maimonides' and Albeck's comments to this rule.

[8] The following are the references to the Mishnah passages which specify the categories into which the sacrifices fall: 1) burnt offerings as most holy offerings and as voluntary offerings (M. Zeb. 5:4, M. Hul. 2:10); 2) offerings of well-being as lesser holy offerings and as voluntary offerings (M. Zeb. 5:7, M. Hul. 2:10); 3) firstlings as lesser holy offerings and as obligatory offerings (M. Zeb. 1:2, M. Hul. 2:10); 4) tithe of cattle as lesser holy offerings and as obligatory offerings (M. Zeb. 1:2, M. Hul. 2:10); 5) sin-offerings as most holy offerings and as obligatory offerings (M. Zeb. 10:6, M. Hul. 2:10); 6) Passover offerings as lesser holy offerings (M. Zeb. 5:8), and as obligatory offerings (M. Meg. 1:10, see, however, M. Hul. 2:10 which treats the passover offering as a voluntary offering).

[9] See previous note.

[10] In this rule, the Mishnah does not explicitly make a distinction between voluntary and obligatory offerings. This dichotomy, however, makes the most sense of the statements at hand, and is one which the Mishnah relies on at M. Hul. 2:10, which takes up an analogous problem.

[11] Following Rashi (B. Zeb. 2a) and Bertinoro, I interpret stichs I A-B to refer only to burnt-offerings and offerings of well-being. This interpretation makes the most sense of the Mishnah's rule. The reason that the sacrifice is only partially disqualified is because the priest only partially confused the category of offering. He was offering an animal consecrated as a voluntary offering, and he intended to offer a different type of voluntary offering. The householder who supplied the animal receives no credit, because the wrong type of offering was offered up. But God permits the priest to finish the rite, because he had the correct general category of offering in mind, namely, a voluntary offering. This interpretation also gains support from the fact that Scripture reserves the term *zbh* to refer to burnt-offerings and offerings of well-being (see TYT). Finally, this interpretation also explains why Yose (III A) declares the sacrifice completely invalid. Since he refers to a case in which the priest has totally confused the category of offering (i.e., he has mixed up obligatory and voluntary offerings), God repudiates the offering completely. Maimonides, TYY, and Albeck, however, understand stichs I A-B to be referring to all types of offerings. By their account, then, I A-B contradicts the view of Yose (III A).

[12] Maimonides argues that this rule refers to the owner of the animal. That is, according to his account, the owner of the animal is required to keep in mind the six thoughts listed here. This interpretation, however, is problematic. One of the six intentions is to think about the owner of the animal. According to Maimonides' interpretation, then, the owner would be thinking about himself!

[13] I follow Albeck who interprets F-G as a rationale appended to the entire law, and not as part of Yose's statement. Maimonides, by contrast, understands F-G as a continuation of Yose's statement. According to the latter interpretation, Yose is disagreeing with the anonymous view (A-D) which, according to Maimonides, holds that the owner of the animal needs to have in mind the six intentions listed here (see my comment in the previous note). In Maimonides' view, Yose is responding to that position by claiming that the owner's intentions are irrelevant.

[14] An alternative explanation is that since these acts are not essential parts of the sacrificial rite, it does not matter that he intends to perform them at the wrong time or place.

[15] A dispute involving a similar issue is found at M. Tem. 5:3-4.

[16] I am aware of the fact that the Talmud claims that M. Ned. 4:2 conceives of a priest as an agent of God, and not as an agent of the householder (B. Ned. 35b). In my opinion, however, the Mishnah passage in question does not rest on such an assumption. M. Ned. 4:2 says that if a man vows not to benefit from a priest, the priest nonetheless may perform certain types of sacrifices for him. According to the Talmud, this is because the priest is the agent of God and not of the householder. Consequently, the priest may perform the sacrifices for the householder, even though the householder vowed to derive no benefit from the priest.

This explanation, however, is problematic. The Mishnah does not allude to the issue of agency in this context. Moreover, in the context of the cases preceeding and following M. Ned. 4:2 a simpler explanation is available. The Mishnah is saying that when a person vows not to derive benefit from another, this vow does not override obligations which are Scriptural in origin. For example if a man vows not to derive benefit from another, the latter may still do certain things for the former. He may return a lost item to him, separate heave-offering for him, and give his wife and children food (M. Ned. 4:2-3). We see therefore that despite the Israelite's vow not to derive benefit from another, that person may still do anything for him which is commanded in Scripture. Returning lost items, feeding one's family, and giving heave-offering are all Scriptural injunctions. Hence, they by definition are excluded from the man's vow. The pericope regarding the priest may be interpreted in the same fashion. Despite a man's vow not to benefit from a priest, the priest may sacrifice animals for him because he has incurred a Scriptural obligation to offer animals to God. This extended discussion, therefore, shows that M. Ned. 4:2 does not contradict my thesis that a priest is an agent of a householder.

[17] I follow KM (see his comment to the *Mishneh Torah*, Invalidated Offerings, *pswly hmwqdsym*, 18:24) who believes Yose is merely disputing Meir on the question of whether the person who sacrifices the gentile's animal outside the Temple incurs liability. By this account, Yose *agrees* with the statement at A, namely, that the priest's intention cannot put the animal into the category of refuse. Support for this interpretation derives from the language Yose adopts. He says the priest is *liable*. Now, nowhere in the sacrificial system do we find any sage who imposes liability on a priest for merely intending to eat a holy thing outside the designated place. If we interpret Yose as disputing the claim at A, then Yose would be saying that the priest himself is guilty for merely intending to violate the law. As my discussion of M. Zeb. 2:2 indicates, this contradicts everything we have learned about the Mishnah's theory of intention. However, TYT following B. Zeb. 45a claims that Yose is disputing the position at A. In support of this view, the Talmud cites a *baraitha* which says explicitly that Yose believes a priest's intention does have the power to turn the offering into refuse. This source, however, should not have the final say, because the Tosefta (T. Zeb. 5:6) records another version of the same statement, in which Yose does not say that the intentions of the priest can make the offering refuse.

[18] See note 17.

[19] Maimonides and Bertinoro argue that Eliezer and the unnamed authority (A-B) believe that the intention of the cow's owner (i.e., the gentile) has the power to invalidate an offering, thus rejecting the view offered at M. Zeb. 4:6 which says that the intentions of the animal's owner do not have the power to invalidate the offering. In my judgment, this interpretation is incorrect because it fails to distinguish between the actual (or subjective) intention of the gentile and the

presumed intention of the gentile. (See my discussion of these types of intention in Chapter Two). According to my account, the subjective intention of the gentile does not invalidate the rite. The rite is invalidated only because gentiles are *presumed* to intend to offer their animals to their gods. This distinction is reflected in the Hebrew, which says that the "unspecified intention" (*stm mahshabah*) of a gentile is towards idolatry. Here the words "unspecified intention" mean the intention that is ascribed to any gentile who sacrifices an animal.

[20] Translated literally Yose appears to be saying that during the act of a secular slaughter, the intentions of the slaughterer do not matter. But in the two laws following this one (see my discussion of M. Hul. 2:8,10), the Mishnah says precisely the opposite: the intentions of the slaughterer do in fact have the power to invalidate the offering. Bertinoro following B. Hul. 38a offers the following forced interpretation. Yose is claiming that since the owner's intention does not invalidate the offering during a holy offering (in which the slaughterer's intention has the power to invalidate it during four parts of the rite, namely, during the slaughter of the animal, collecting, transferring and sprinkling of the blood, as in M. Zeb 1:4) then it stands to reason that during a secular slaughter (in which the intention of the slaughterer invalidates the offering only during two acts, namely, the slaughter and the sprinkling), the owner's intention certainly does not invalidate the offering. The explanation I have offered is much simpler. When Yose says that intention does not invalidate a secular act of slaughter, he is referring to the case at hand, in which the Israelite is slaughtering for a gentile. Since the Israelite householder slaughters the animal on behalf of a gentile, his intentions have no power to invalidate the offering. This is because, as I argued before, a gentile does not have the power to transfer to an Israelite powers that the gentile himself lacks.

[21] In claiming that the Mishnah equates the priest in the case at hand with a thief or robber, I mean only that the Mishnah treats the priest's intention as though it were the intention of a thief or robber. It is clear that the sages do not totally equate him with a thief or robber, for he incurs no liability for having stolen something.

[22] My interpretation follows Maimonides. Alternatively, Bertinoro and Albeck suggest that the owner gives up hope of recovering the stolen property because the man took it by force. Since the owner knows that the robber is a strong and potentially dangerous person, he despairs of recovering the stolen goods.

[23] Jaffee (*Theology of Tithing*, p. 1) and [Avery]-Peck (*Priestly Gift*, pp. 2-3) have forcefully argued this point with respect to the Mishnah's agricultural laws. In that context, when the Mishnah speaks about the offerings Israelites set aside for priests, it always takes the householder's point of view. It focuses, therefore, on when and how the householder must separate the produce. In other words, the entire discussion of these laws speaks to and for householders, not the priestly caste.

[24] It is true that Leviticus takes account of a priest doing something unintentionally. But Leviticus does not specify any legal consequences for the mere intention of doing something wrong.

[25] For a fuller discussion of this passage see Hertzberg, *Samuel*, pp. 127-129; McCarter, *Samuel*, p. 270, and Kaufman, *Religion*, p. 161.

[26] For the views of the writing prophets toward the cult and toward the importance of an inward commitment to God, see Kaufman, *Religion*, p. 160, von Rad, *Prophets*, pp. 181-182, and Bright, *Jeremiah*, p. cxv,

27 See von Rad, *Prophets*, p. 182, and von Rad, *Old Testatment*, p. 199.

28 See von Rad, *Prophets*, p. 203.

29 See Kosovsky, *Thesaurus*, Vol. 2, pp. 736-737.

30 Neusner, "Historical Hillel," pp. 45-65. See also Jackson, "Mere Intention," who provides a fuller discussion of this law from a different perspective.

31 Mere intention alone cannot put something into the category of sacred produce. The Israelite must at least verbalize his intention, and in most cases, he must perform an act of separating the produce, see [Avery-]Peck, *Priestly Gift*, p. 3.

Notes to Chapter Five

1 I am not using the term "theory" in the scientific sense of the word. In the natural or social sciences, the term generally refers to "systematically related statements including some lawlike generalization that is empirically testable" (Rudner, *Social Science*, p. 10). I am employing the term theory to capture the notion that the Mishnah presents a coherent, systematic, related set of statements on a given topic.

2 The single exception is B. M. 3:12, which I discussed in the conclusion to the previous chapter. A more extensive discussion of this law can be found in Jackson, "Mere Intention."

3 See Anscombe, *Intention*, pp. 43-44.

4 Hart, *Punishment*, p. 33.

5 I am here adopting Weber's understanding of how the priestly class systematizes a body of knowledge (Weber, *Economy and Society*, pp. 457-458, Bendix, *Max Weber*, pp. 90-91). As I will discuss below, the sages of the Mishnah do not fall into the category of priests because they neither maintain a cult nor define themselves through heredity. Nonetheless, their literary activity very much resembles Weber's understanding of priestly activity.

6 The following discussion is indebted to Neusner's excellent characterization and summary of the Mishnah's recurring concerns, *Judaism*, pp. 256-269. However, my discussion departs from Neusner's in one important respect. Neusner understands these traits of the Mishnah to be a response to the destruction of the Temple in 70 C.E.. The concern with ambiguity and sorting out conflicting legal principles expresses the sages' concern with ordering a world that is disordered and adrift (Neusner, *Judaism*, p. 271, *Ancient Israel* , p. 72-80). As I will argue, these same literary traits may simply be the result of intellectuals attempting to systematize a legal tradition. The interest in ambiguous cases and in the conflict of legal principles may represent the sages' attempt to develop a coherent and fully articulated system which takes account of all possible situations and problems. For other discussions that treat the sages primarily as an intellectual class, see Rivkin, *Hidden Revolution*, and Schürer, *Jewish People*, pp. 322-380. These accounts, however, suffer methodologically in that they rely on later rabbinic sources to testify to the character of the social group that stands behind the Mishnah.

7 Neusner, *Judaism*, pp. 257-258.

8 Neusner, *Judaism*, pp. 259-261.

[9] See, for example, M. Qin. 2:1-5 and M. Yad. 2:4. These cases both examine a single legal principle by examining various permutations of a single situation in an attempt to anticipate all eventualities.

[10] Neusner provides an alternative answer to the same question. He argues that the sages' interest in the priestly writings stems from the fact that they faced the same kind of historical situation which faced the priests. The priestly writings were formulated during and following the exile of the Jews in Babylonia and took their final form in the sixth and fifth centuries. This corresponds to the period when Israel's identity as a distinct corporate entity was threatened by the substantial influence of Greek culture in Palestine. The priestly writings, therefore, seek to maintain the distinctive identity of Israel, by prescribing laws and ideas which separate Israel from her neighbors. Neusner suggests that this problem continues unabated down to the time of the Mishnah. The sages of the Mishnah turn to the priestly conception of Judaism, therefore, because they face the same social problem as the priestly forbears. The priestly system provided a system which allowed the distinctive identity of Israel to remain intact (Neusner, *Judaism*, pp. 71-75). My account complements Neusner's. In my judgment, since the priestly writings represent the work of intellectuals they were self-evidently interesting to the sages of the Mishnah who also constituted a group of intellectuals.

[11] See Neusner, *Ancient Israel*, pp. 72-80, *Judaism*, p. 283, *Method and Meaning*, pp. 1-2, [Avery]-Peck, *Priestly Gift*, pp. 6-7, Brooks, *Support*, p. 35, Jaffee, *Theology of Tithing*, pp. 5-6, Mandelbaum, *Law of Agriculture*, pp. 3-4, Newman, *Seventh Year*, pp. 19-20.

[12] See Durkheim, *Elementary Forms*, pp. 169-170, and *Primitive Classifications*, pp. 81-88.

[13] See Hallpike, *Primitive Thought*, pp. 212-224, Needham, "Introduction," pp. vii-xlviii, and Smith, *To Take Place*, Chapter Two.

[14] See Smith, *To Take Place*, Chapter Two.

[15] For fuller accounts of the character of the priesthood, see de Vaux, *Ancient Israel*, vol. 2, pp. 345-357, 372-405 and Shürer, *Jewish People*, pp. 237-313.

[16] This is a commonplace in the study of rabbinic Judaism. See, for example, Shürer, *Jewish People*, pp. 322-336. However, as I noted earlier, most descriptions of rabbinic Judaism treat the rabbinic sources as an undifferentiated whole. Consequently, what later sources say about the character of the social group which stands behind the Mishnah is accepted as historically accurate. Neusner has recently argued, in my judgment quite conclusively, that the elaborate myth of two Torahs, one written and one oral, is not present in the earliest rabbinic sources. This myth only makes its appearance in later sources (Neusner, *Torah*). Despite this qualification, it still appears, even from the earliest sources themselves, that the status of sage depended upon one's mastery of Scripture and its interpretive tradition. For example, the Mishnah records cases in which a sage makes an argument which is rejected because it is not part of the accepted tradition of interpretation (see M. Yeb. 8:3, M. Nazir 7:4).

[17] The Mishnah states that a person cannot receive renumeration for juridical activity, M. Bekh. 4:6. Abot also expresses this view (Abot 4:5). See Shürer, *Jewish People*, pp. 328-329. In addition, Neusner basing himself on sociological description of the Mishnah's rules has argued that the Mishnah represents the interests of householders and scribes (Neusner, *Judaism*, pp. 245-255). I think Neusner is fundamentally right to see the interests of scribes and householders

standing behind the Mishnah. My account differs from Neusner's, however, in one important respect. Neusner claims that scribes constitute a profession, whereas householders are a class. Thus, according to Neusner's picture, the people who produced the Mishnah were both householders and scribes (Neusner, *Judaism*, pp. 236, 241). I find this claim problematic. It seems to me that one is either a householder, which in the context of the Mishnah means that one's profession is farming, or one is a scribe by profession. One cannot be both at once. Neusner's analysis, in my judgment, points to the fact that the sages represented a variety of class interests in Israelite society. Among them were householders and scribes.

Neusner contradicts himself when discussing whether priests actually participated in the formation of the Mishnah. At one point, Neusner claims that the Mishnah merely carries forward the priestly writings of Scripture. By this account, priests did not actually form part of the social group that produced the Mishnah (*Judaism*, pp. 72-75) Elsewhere, however, Neusner suggests that among those who produced the Mishnah was a substantial group of priests (*Judaism*, pp. 233, 236). In my judgment, the former explanation is more probable. That is, the Mishnah focuses on priestly issues, not because priests were members of the group that created the Mishnah, but because this group found the priestly tradition of Scripture to be compelling in certain respects.

18 See [Avery]-Peck, *Priestly Gift*, pp. 2-3, and Jaffee, *Theology of Tithing* , p. 1.

19 See Jaffee, *Theology of Tithing*, p. 1, and [Avery-]Peck, *Priestly Gift*, pp. 1-3.

20 Yadin, *Temple Scroll*, [Heb.], vol. 1, pp. 215-259.

21 Yadin, *Temple Scroll*, [Heb.], vol. 1, pp. 295-308.

22 Vermes, *Scrolls*, p. 90.

23 This statement is based on the Concordance compiled by Yadin, *Temple Scroll*, vol. 2, pp. 245-300.

24 Some scholars argue that the origin of the synagogue is much earlier, perhaps originating in the Babylonian exile or in the Deuteronomic reform. In my judgment, however, Gutmann's claim that the synagogue emerged in the second century B.C.E. is the most plausible reconstruction (Gutmann, "Synagogue Origins," pp. 1-4, and "Origin of the Synagogue," pp. 36-40).

25 Neusner, *Pharisees*, vol. 3, pp. 305-306.

26 Smith, *Map*, pp. 128.

Abbreviations and References

Adkins
> Arthur W. H. Adkins, *Merit and Responsibility*, Oxford: Clarendon Press, 1960

Albeck
> Hanoch Albeck, *Shishah Sidrei Mishnah*, 6 vols., Jerusalem: Bialik Institute and Dvir Co, 1957

Anscombe, *Intention*
> G.E.M. Anscombe, *Intention*, Ithaca: Cornell University Press, 1957

Ar. Arakhin

Austin
> J. L. Austin, "A Plea For Excuses," in *The Philosophy of Action*, ed. Alan R. White, Oxford: Oxford University Press, 1968

A. Z. Abodah Zarah

B. Babli, The Talmud of Babylonia

B.B. Baba Batra

BDB
> Francis Brown, S.R. Driver, C.A. Briggs, *Hebrew and English Lexicon of the Old Testament*, Oxford: Clarendon Press, 1975

Bekh. Bekhorot

Bendix, *Max Weber*
> Reinhard Bendix, *Max Weber: An Intellectual Portrait*, Berkeley: The University of California Press, 1977

Ber. Berakhot

Bernstein, *Praxis*
> Richard J. Bernstein, *Praxis and Action*, Philadelphia: University of Pennsylvania Press, 1971

Bertinoro
> Obadiah b. Abraham of Bertinoro (fifteenth century), Mishnah Commentary in Romm ed. of the Mishnah, Vilna, 1908

Bik. Bikkurim

B.M.   Baba Mesia

B.Q.   Baba Qamma

Bright, *Jeremiah*
John Bright, *Jeremiah*, The Anchor Bible Series, Garden City: Doubleday, 1965

Brooks, *Support*
Roger Brooks, *Support for the Poor in the Mishnaic Law of Agriculture: Tractate Peah*, Chico: Scholars Press, 1983

Chron. Chronicles

Danby
Herbert Danby, *The Mishnah*, a translation, Oxford: Oxford University Press, 1977

Daube
David Daube, *Aspects of Roman Law*, Edinburgh: Edinburgh University Press, 1969

Daube
David Daube, *The Sudden in Scriptures*, Leiden: E. J. Brill, 1964

de Vaux, *Ancient Israel*
Roland de Vaux, *Ancient Israel: Religious Institutions*, vol. 2, New York: McGraw-Hill Book Company, 1965

Dem.   Demai

Deut.   Deuteronomy

Dihle, *Will*
Albrecht Dihle, *The Theory of Will in Classical Antiquity*, University of California Press, 1982

Douglas, *Purity*
Mary Douglas, *Purity and Danger*, London: Routledge and Kegan Paul, 1966

Durkheim, *Elementary Forms*
Emile Durkheim, *The Elementary Forms of the Religious Life,* trans. Joseph Ward Swain, New York: The Free Press, 1965

Durkheim, *Primitive Classification*
Emile Durkheim and Marcel Mauss, *Primitive Classification*, trans. Rodney Needham, Chicago: The University of Chicago Press, 1963

Edwards, *Mens Rea*
> J. J. Edwards, *Mens Rea in Statutory Offenses,* London: Macmillan & Co. New York: St. Martin's Press, 1955

Eichrodt, *Theology*
> Walter Eichrodt, *Theology of the Old Testament,* 2 vols., trans. J. A. Baker, Philadelphia: The Westminister Press, 1961

Eilberg-Schwartz, "Language of Jewish Ritual"
> Howard Eilberg-Schwartz, "The Language of Jewish Ritual: An Anthropological Approach to the Menstrual Taboo in Judaism," in *Approaches to Ancient Judaism,* ed. William Scott Green, Scholars Press, forthcoming

Eissfeldt, *Old Testament*
> Otto Eissfeldt, *The Old Testament: An Introduction,* trans. P.R.Ackroyd, New York: Harper & Row, 1965

Enelow, "Kawwana"
> H. G. Enelow, "Kawwana: The Struggle for Inwardness in Judaism," in *Studies in Jewish Literature in Honor of Kaufman Kohler* (Berlin: 1913; repr. NY: 1980), pp. 82-107

Epstein, *Mishnah*
> Y. N. Epstein, *Mavo leNusah ha Mishnah,* Jerusalem, 1973

Erub.   Erubim

Evans-Pritchard, *Witchcraft*
> E. E. Evans-Pritchard, *Witchcraft, Oracles, and Magic Among the Azande,* (abridged ed.), Oxford: Clarendon Press, 1976

Ex.   Exodus

Ezek.   Ezekiel

Feinberg
> Joel Feinberg, "Action and Responsibility" in *Philosophy of Action,* ed. Alan White, Oxford: Oxford University Press, 1968

Feliks, *Plant World*
> J. Feliks, *Plant World of the Bible,* [Heb.] Tel Aviv: Massadah, 1957

Fitzgerald, *Criminal Law*
> P. J. Fitzgerald, *Criminal Law and Punishment,* Oxford: Clarendon Press, 1962

Gen.   Genesis

Gilath, "Intention"

Y. D. Gilath, "Intention and Action in the Teaching of the Tannaim," [Heb.], *Annual of Bar Ilan University*, IV-V, 1967, pp.104-116

Git.   Gittin

Glover

Jonathan Glover, *Responsibility*, London: Routledge & Kegan Paul, 1970

Green

William Scott Green, ed., *Approaches to Ancient Judaism,* vols. I- , Missoula: Scholars Press, 1979-

Green, *Joshua*

William Scott Green, *The Traditions of Joshua Ben Hananiah, Part One, The Early Legal Traditions*, Leiden: E. J. Brill, 1981

Greenberg, *Prayer*

Moshe Greenberg, *Biblical Prose Prayer*, Berkeley: University of California Press, 1983

Greenstein, "Biblical Law"

Edward Greenstein, "Biblical Law," in *Back to the Sources*, ed. Barry Holtz, New York: Summit, 1984

Goldenberg, "Consciousness"

Robert Goldenberg, "Commandment and Consciousness in Talmudic Thought," *Harvard Theological Review*, 68:3-4, July - October

Gutmann, "Synagogue Origins"

Joseph Gutmann, "Synagogue Origins: Theories and Facts," in *Ancient Synagogues: The State of Research*, ed. Joseph Gutmann, Chico: Scholars Press, 1981

Gutmann, "Origin of Synagogue"

Joseph Gutmann, "The Origin of the Synagogue: The Current State of Research," in *The Synagogue: Studies in Origins, Archaeology and Architecture*, ed. Harry M. Orlinsky, New York: Ktav Publishing House, 1975

Hal.   Hallah

Hallpike, *Primitive Thought*

C. R. Hallpike, *The Foundations of Primitive Thought*, Oxford: Clarendon Press, 1979

Hampshire

Stuart Hampshire, *Thought and Action*, London: Chatto and Windus, 1982

Hart, *Punishment*
>   H. L. A. Hart, *Punishment and Responsibility, Essays in the Philosophy of Law*, Oxford: Clarendon Press, 1968

Hertzberg, *Samuel*
>   Hans Wilhelm Hertzberg, *I and II Samuel*, trans. J. S. Bowden, Philadelphia: Westminister Press, 1964

Higger, *Intention*
>   Michael Higger, *Intention in Talmudic Law*, now reprinted in E. M. Gerschfield, ed., *Studies in Jewish Jurisprudence I*, New York: Hermon Press, 1971, pp. 234-293

Hoffman, *Leviticus*
>   David Hoffman, *Leviticus*, [Heb.] 2 vols., Jerusalem, 1953, trans. of *Das Buch Leviticus*, 2 vols. (1905-1906).

Hul.   Hullin

Jackson
>   Bernard Jackson, "The Concept of Religious Law in Judaism," pp. 33-52 in *Aufstieg Und Niedergang Der Römishcen Welt*, II. vol. 19.1, ed. Wolfgang Hasse, Berlin: Walter De Gruyter, 1979

Jackson, "Mere Intention"
>   Bernard S. Jackson, "Liability for Mere Intention in Early Jewish Law," pp. 202-234 in *Essays in Jewish and Comparative Legal History*, ed. Bernard Jackson, Leiden: E. J. Brill, 1975

Jackson
>   Bernard S. Jackson, ed., *Modern Research in Jewish Law*, Leiden: E. J. Brill, 1980

Jaffee, *Theology of Tithing*
>   Martin S. Jaffee, *Mishnah's Theology of Tithing: A Study of Tractate Maaserot*, Chico: Scholars Press, 1981

Jastrow
>   Marcus Jastrow, *A Dictionary of the Targumim, the Talmud Babli and Yerushalmi, and the Midrashic Literature*, 2 vols, New York, 1895-1903; repr. New York, 1975

Jer.   Jeremiah

JPS
>   *The Torah* (1962), *The Prophets* (1978), *The Writings* (1982), A New Translation, Philadelphia:The Jewish Publication Society of America

Kadushin, *Worship*
> Max Kadushin, *Worship and Ethics*, New York: Bloch Publishing
> Company, 1963

Kaufman, *Religion*
> Yehezkel Kaufman, *The Religion of Israel*, trans. and abrid. Moshe
> Greenberg, New York: Schocken,1972

Kel.   Kelim

Kenny
> Anthony Kenny, *Action Emotion and Will*, London: Routledge &
> Kegan Paul, 1963

Kenny
> Anthony Kenny, "Intention and Purpose in Law, " in *Essays in Legal
> Philosophy*, ed. Robert Summers, Berkeley: University of California
> Press, 1968

Ker.   Keritot

Ket.   Ketubot

Kil.   Kilayim

KM
> *Kesef Mishnah*, Joseph Karo, Commentary to Maimonides' *Mishnah
> Torah*. Published in Venice, 1574-5.

Kosovsky
> C. Y. Kosovsky, *Otzar Leshon HaMishnah: Concordantiae verborum
> quae in sex Mishnae Ordinibus Reperiuntur* [Heb.], Jerusalem:
> Massadah, 1956

Lev.   Leviticus

Levinthal, "Agency"
> Israel H. Levinthal, "The Jewish Law of Agency," in *Studies in Jewish
> Jurisprudence,* ed. Edward M. Gershfield, New York: Hermon Press,
> 1971

Lieberman, Torts
> B. B. Lieberman, "Torts in Jewish Law," in *Studies in Jewish
> Jurisprudence,* vol. 11, p. 231-240, ed. Edward M Gershfield, New
> York: Hermon Press, 1971

M.   Mishnah

MA
> *Mishnah Aharonah*, Ephraim Isaac of Premysla. Published in 1882.
> From reprint of Mishnah, ed. Romm.

Maimonides
    Moses b. Maimon, (1135-1204), Mishnah Commentary, in *Mishnah
    with the Commentary of R. Moses b. Maimon* , vol. I-III, trans. and
    ed. J. Qappah, Jerusalem: Mossad HaRav Kook, 1963

Mak.   Makkot

Makh.   Makhshirin

Mandelbaum, *Law of Agriculture*
    Irving Mandelbaum, *A History of the Mishnaic Law of Agriculture:
    Kilayim*, Chico: Scholars Press, 1982

McCarter, *Samuel*
    P. Kyle McCarter, *I Samuel,* The Anchor Bible Series, vol. 8, Garden
    City: Double Day & Company, 1980

Meg.   Megillah

Meiland, *Intention*
    Jack W. Meiland, *The Nature of Intention*, London: Methuen & Co.,
    1970

Men.   Menahot

Miq.   Miqvaot

Morris
    Herbert Morris, *On Guilt and Innocence: Essays in Legal Philosophy
    and Moral Psychology*, Berkeley: University of California Press, 1976

Morris
    Herbert Morris, ed., *Freedom and Responsibility: Readings in
    Philosophy and Law*, Stanford: Stanford University Press, 1961

M. Q.   Moed Qatan

M. S.   Maaser Sheni

Naz.   Nazir

Ned.   Nedarim

Needham, "Introduction"
    Rodney Needham, "Introduction," pp. vii-xlviii in *Primitive
    Classification,* by Emile Durkheim and Marcel Mauss, Chicago:
    University of Chicago Press, 1963

Neg.   Negaim

Neusner, *Ancient Israel*

> Jacob Neusner, *Ancient Israel After Catastrophe: The Religious World View of the Mishnah*, Charlottesville: University Press of Virginia, 1983

Neusner, *Form Analysis*

> Jacob Neusner, *Form Analysis and Exegesis: A Fresh Approach to the Interpretation of Mishnah*, Minneapolis: University of Minnesota Press, 1980

Neusner, "Historical Hillel"

> Jacob Neusner with Alan Avery-Peck, "The Quest for the Historical Hillel: Theory and Practise," in *Formative Judaism*, vol. 1, Chico: Scholars Press, 1982

Neusner, *Holy Things*

> Jacob Neusner, *A History of the Mishnaic Law of Holy Things*, 6 vols., Leiden: E.J. Brill, 1978-1979

Neusner, *Judaism*

> Jacob Neusner, *Judaism: The Evidence of the Mishnah*, Chicago: The University of Chicago Press, 1981

Neusner, *Method and Meaning*

> Jacob Neusner, *Method and Meaning,* vol. 1, Chico: Scholars Press, 1979

Neusner, "New Solutions"

> Jacob Neusner, "New Problems, New Solutions: Current Events in Rabbinic Studies," in *Method and Meaning in Ancient Judaism*, vol. 3, Chico: Scholars Press, 1981

Neusner, *Pharisees*

> Jacob Neusner, *The Rabbinic Traditions About the Pharisees Before 70*, vols. I-III, Leiden: E.J. Brill, 1971

Neusner, *Purities*

> Jacob Neusner, *A History of the Mishnaic Law of Purities*, 22 vols., Leiden: E.J. Brill, 1974-1977

Neusner, *Tosefta*

> Jacob Neusner, *The Tosefta: Translated from the Hebrew,* 5 vols., New York: Ktav Publishing House, 1977-81

Newman, *Seventh Year*

> Louis E. Newman, *The Sanctity of the Seventh Year: A Study of Mishnah Tractate Shebiit*, Chico: Scholars Press, 1983

Num.   Numbers

Oh.   Ohalot

Otzen, Myths
Benedikt Otzen, Hans Gottlieb, and Knud Jeppesen, *Myths in the Old Testament*, trans. by Frederick Cryer, London: SCM Press, 1980

Par.   Parah

Peck, Priestly Gift
Alan [Avery-] Peck, *The Priestly Gift in Mishnah: A Study of Tractate Terumot*, Chico: Scholars Press, 1981

Pes.   Pesahim

Porter, *Leviticus*
J. R. Porter, *Leviticus,* Cambridge: Cambridge University Press, 1976

Prov.   Proverbs

Ps.   Psalms

Qid.   Qiddushin

Qin.   Qinnim

R.   Rabbi

Rashi
Solomon b. Isaac of Troyes (1040-1105), commentary to Babylonian Talmud, Romm ed.

R.H.   Rosh Hashanah

Rist, *Stoic Philosophy*
J. M. Rist, *Stoic Philosophy*, Cambridge: Cambridge University Press, 1969

Rivkin, *Hidden Revolution*
Ellis Rivkin, *A Hidden Revolution*, Nashville: Abingdon, 1978

RSV
The New Oxford Annotated Bible, Revised Standard Version, ed. Herbert May and Bruce Metzger, New York: Oxford University Press, 1973

Rudner, *Social Science*
Richard Rudner, *Philosophy of Social Science*, Englewood Cliffs: Prentice Hall, 1966

Sam.   Samuel

San.   Sanhedrin

Sarason, "Mishnah"
>   Richard S. Sarason, "Mishnah and Scripture: Observations on the Law of Tithing in *Seder Zera^cim*," in William Scott Green, ed., *Approaches to Ancient Judaism*, vol. II, Chico: Scholars Press, 1980

Sarna, *Genesis*
>   Nahum M. Sarna, *Understanding Genesis*, New York: Schocken Books, 1966

Schürer, *Jewish People*
>   Emil Schürer, *The History of the Jewish People in the Age of Jesus Christ*, revised and edited by Geza Vermes and Fergus Millar, Edinburgh: T.&T. Clark, 1973

Searle, *Intentionality*
>   Searle, John, *Intentionality*, Cambridge: Cambridge University Press, 1983

Sens.
>   Samson ben Abraham of Sens, ca. 1150-1230, from reprint of *Mishnah Seder Tohorot* in Babylonian Talmud, Romm ed., Vilna, 1887

Shab.   Shabbat

Sheb.   Shebiit

Smith, *Map*
>   Jonathan Smith, *Map is Not Territory*, Leiden: E. J. Brill, 1978

Smith, *To Take Place*
>   Jonathan Smith, *To Take Place: Jerusalem as a Focus of Ritual*, Chicago: University of Chicago Press, forthcoming

Soler, *Dietary Prohibitions*
>   Jean Soler, "The Dietary Prohibitions of the Hebrews," *New York Review of Books*, vol. 26, no. 2 (August 1979), pp. 49-52

Sonne
>   I. Sonne, "The Schools of Shamai and Hillel Seen From Within," in *Louis Ginzberg Jubilee Volume*, New York: The American Academy for Jewish Research,1945

Sot.   Sotah

Speiser, *Genesis*
>   E. A. Speiser, *Genesis*, trans. and intro, The Anchor Bible Series, Garden City: Doubleday & Company, 1964

T.   Tosefta

Tam.   Tamid

Ter.   Terumot

Tem.   Temurah

Toh.   Tohorot

TYT

    Tosafot Yom Tov, Yom Tov Lipman Heller (1579-1694), Mishnah Commentary; in Romm ed. of Mishnah

TYY

    Tif'eret Yisra'el Yakhin, Israel b. Gedaliah Lipschütz (1782-1860), Mishnah Commentary; in Romm ed. of the Mishnah

Uqs.   Uqsin

Vermes, *Scrolls*
    Geza Vermes, *The Dead Sea Scrolls: Qumran in Perspective*, Philadelphia: Fortress Press, 1977

von Rad, *Genesis*
    Gerhard von Rad, *Genesis*, Philadelphia: The Westminister Press, 1972

von Rad, *Deuteronomy*
    Gerhard von Rad, *Deuteronomy*, Philadelphia: The Westminister Press, 1966

von Rad, *Prophets*
    Gerhard von Rad, *The Message of the Prophets*, New York: Harper & Row, 1965

Weber, *Economy and Society*
    Max Weber, *Economy and Society*, ed. Guenther Roth and Claus Wittich, Berkeley: University of California Press, 1978

Wimsatt, *Verbal Icon*
    William K. Wimsatt, *The Verbal Icon*, Lexington: University Press of Kentucky, 1954

Wright, *Explanation*
    Georg Henrick von Wright, *Explanation and Understanding*, Ithaca: Cornell University Press, 1971

Yad.   Yadayim

Yadin, *Temple Scroll*
    Yigael Yadin, *The Temple Scroll* [Heb.], vols. I-III, Jerusalem: Ahvah Press, 1977

Yeb.   Yebamot

Yom.   Yoma

Zeb.   Zebahim

Zeitlin, *Studies*

     Solomon Zeitlin, *Studies in the Early History of Judaism: History of Early Talmudic Law*, vol. IV, New York: Ktav, 1978

Index

synagogue 60-63, 199, 212, 213, 227, 232
Tabernacle 65, 146
tailors 78, 79
tanners 123, 188, 219
taxonomy 55, 140, 184, 195
Taylor 201
teleological 13, 14, 140, 182, 185, 187, 202, 203
telos 13, 14, 140, 141, 185
terms of human agency 111, 112
theological assumption 6, 7, 24, 70, 89
theological dimension 83, 91, 202
tithe 24, 35, 80, 86, 88, 156, 157, 164, 222
tort 4-6, 14-20, 22, 23, 45, 46, 204, 213, 218, 234
tort case 4, 6, 14, 16-18, 20, 22, 23, 45, 46, 213
typical Israelite 28, 68, 72, 123, 132, 134, 137, 161
typical person 28, 73, 90, 127, 132, 137

TYT 205, 209, 210, 212, 214, 219, 220, 222, 223, 239
TYY 205, 209, 210, 219, 222, 239
unintended act 14, 19
unintended result 13, 27, 28, 44
unintentional transgression 21, 22, 37
unnecessary consequence 45
Vermes 227, 238, 239
vicarious liability 110
vow 24, 68-76, 79-81, 86, 87, 91, 148, 164, 165, 188-190, 213, 223
Weber 14, 191, 225, 229, 239
Wimsatt 213, 239
Wright 201, 203, 208, 239
Yadin 227, 239
Yahwist 104, 105, 107, 149, 183, 184, 193, 216, 217
Yose 73-75, 116, 133, 155, 157, 158, 167, 168, 215, 221-224
Zeitlin 201, 202, 240